Frommer's®

Barcelona
day BY day

3rd Edition

by Neil Edward Schlecht
Updated by Patricia Harris
and David Lyon

FrommerMedia LLC

Contents

Published by:

Frommer Media LLC

Copyright © 2015 Frommer Media LLC, New York, NY. All rights reserved. No part of this publication may be reproduced, stored in a retrieval system or transmitted in any form or by any means, electronic, mechanical, photocopying, recording, scanning or otherwise, except as permitted under Sections 107 or 108 of the 1976 United States Copyright Act, without the prior written permission of the Publisher. Requests to the Publisher for permission should be addressed to support@frommermedia.com.

Frommer's is a registered trademark of Arthur Frommer. Frommer Media LLC is not associated with any product or vendor mentioned in this book.

ISBN 978-1-62887-132-6 (paper), 978-1-62887-133-3 (e-book)

Editorial Director: Pauline Frommer
Editor: Margaret Sanborn
Production Editor: Heather Wilcox
Photo Editor: Dana K. Davis
Cartographer: Roberta Stockwell
Page Compositor: Heather Pope

For information on our other products or services,
see www.frommers.com.

Frommer's also publishes its books in a variety of electronic formats. Some content that appears in print may not be available in electronic formats.

Manufactured in China

5   4   3   2   1

About This Book

Organizing your time. That's what this guide is all about.

Other guides give you long lists of things to see and do and then expect you to fit the pieces together. The Day by Day guides are different. These guides tell you the best of everything, and then they show you how to see it in the smartest, most time-efficient way. Our authors have designed detailed itineraries organized by time, neighborhood, or special interest. And each tour comes with a bulleted map that takes you from stop to stop.

Hoping to tour the best in *modernista* architecture, stroll down La Rambla, or taste your way through gourmet Barcelona? Planning a walk through *La Ribera*, or plotting a day of fun-filled activities with the kids? Whatever your interest or schedule, the Day by Days give you the smartest routes to follow. Not only do we take you to the top attractions, hotels, and restaurants, but we also help you access those special moments that locals get to experience—those "finds" that turn tourists into travelers.

The Day by Days are also your top choice if you're looking for one complete guide for all your travel needs. The best hotels and restaurants for every budget, the greatest shopping values, the wildest nightlife—it's all here.

Why should you trust our judgment? Because our authors personally visit each place they write about. They're an independent lot who say what they think and would never include places they wouldn't recommend to their best friends. They're also open to suggestions from readers. If you'd like to contact them, please send your comments our way at feedback@frommers.com, and we'll pass them on.

Enjoy your Day by Day guide—the most helpful travel companion you can buy. And have the trip of a lifetime.

About the Authors

Neil Edward Schlecht is a freelance writer based in northwestern Connecticut. His first exposure to Spain was teaching English for a summer at Collegi Sant Ignasi in Barcelona. He returned to the Catalan capital just before the 1992 Olympics and spent most of the decade there, working on social and economic development projects for the European Union and later as a contributing writer for a Spanish art and antiques magazine. He is the author of more than a dozen travel guides to spots around the world, including *Mallorca & Menorca Day by Day, Frommer's Peru,* and *Buenos Aires Day by Day.* But little motivates him like the chance to discover new restaurants, wines, and cycling routes in Spain.

Patricia Harris and **David Lyon** have journeyed the world for American, British, Swiss, and Asian publishers to write about food, culture, art, and design. They have covered subjects as diverse as elk migrations in western Canada, the street markets of Shanghai, winter hiking on the Jungfrau, and the origins of Mesoamerican civilization in the Mexican tropics. They keep returning to Barcelona for the modern and the Romanesque art, for the phantasmagoric architecture of the *modernistas,* and—of course—for the food. They are co-authors of *Frommer's Complete Spain, Frommer's Spain Day by Day,* and *Frommer's EasyGuide to Madrid and Barcelona.*

An Additional Note

Please be advised that travel information is subject to change at any time—and this is especially true of prices. We therefore suggest that you write or call ahead for confirmation when making your travel plans. The authors, editors, and publisher cannot be held responsible for the experiences of readers while traveling. Your safety is important to us, however, so we encourage you to stay alert and be aware of your surroundings.

Star Ratings, Icons & Abbreviations

Every hotel, restaurant, and attraction listing in this guide has been ranked for quality, value, service, amenities, and special features using a **star-rating system.** Hotels, restaurants, attractions, shopping, and nightlife are rated on a scale of zero stars (recommended) to three stars (exceptional). In addition to the star-rating system, we also use a **kids icon** to point out the best bets for families. Within each tour, we recommend cafes, bars, or restaurants where you can take a break. Each of these stops appears in a shaded box marked with a coffee-cup-shaped bullet ☕.

The following **abbreviations** are used for credit cards:

AE	American Express	DISC	Discover	V	Visa
DC	Diners Club	MC	MasterCard		

Frommers.com

Now that you have this guidebook to help you plan a great trip, visit our website at **www.frommers.com** for additional travel information on more than 4,000 destinations. We update features regularly to give you instant access to the most current trip-planning information available. At Frommers.com, you'll find scoops on the best airfares, lodging rates, and car rental bargains. You can even book your travel online through our reliable travel booking partners. Other popular features include:

- Online updates of our most popular guidebooks
- Vacation sweepstakes and contest giveaways
- Newsletters highlighting the hottest travel trends
- Online travel message boards with featured travel discussions

A Note on Prices

In the "Take a Break" and "Best Bets" sections of this book, we have used a system of dollar signs to show a range of costs for 1 night in a hotel (the price of a double-occupancy room) or the cost of an entree at a restaurant. Use the following table to decipher the dollar signs:

Cost	Hotels	Restaurants
$	under $100	under $10
$$	$100–$200	$10–$20
$$$	$200–$300	$20–$30
$$$$	$300–$400	$30–$40
$$$$$	over $400	over $40

An Invitation to the Reader

In researching this book, we discovered many wonderful places—hotels, restaurants, shops, and more. We're sure you'll find others. Please tell us about them, so we can share the information with your fellow travelers in upcoming editions. If you were disappointed with a recommendation, we'd love to know that, too. Please write to: Contact@FrommerMedia.com

15 Favorite Moments

1. La Rambla
2. Modernista masterpieces
3. Barri Gòtic
4. Mercat de la Boqueria
5. Palau de la Música
6. Catalan cuisine*
7. Old-school Barcelona*
8. Biking along the beach
9. Cava crawl*
10. La Ribera fashion
11. Classic Catalan culture*
12. Santa María del Mar
13. La Pedrera
14. Blue Tram to Tibidabo
15. Catalunya*

categories not mapped

Previous page: The modernista apartment building Casa Batlló.

It's not really a shock that Barcelona has become such a hot destination. What is surprising is how long it took most of the world to discover Barcelona's diverse charms, which draw architecture and design fanatics, foodies, culture hounds, history buffs, and those merely in search of an all-night party. Here are some don't-miss experiences in the thriving Catalan capital.

1 Joining the throngs on La Rambla. Barcelona's pedestrian-only boulevard is anything but commonplace; it's the epicenter of life in the capital, and joining the vibrant street parade is the best way to immerse yourself in the city. Pick up fresh flowers, kick back at a sidewalk cafe, and come face to face with outrageous human statues (but keep an eye on your belongings!). *See p 56.*

2 Marveling at *Modernista* Masterpieces. Beyond the Gaudí must-sees La Pedrera and La Sagrada Família, the L'Eixample grid teems

See outrageous performers on La Rambla.

with stunning *modernista* buildings by dozens of architects, famous and not. Start on Passeig de Gràcia's stunning Manzana de la Discórdia, and then fan out to see innumerable examples of the *modernista* craze that took over Barcelona in the late 19th and early 20th centuries. And don't miss an afternoon relaxing on the serpentine, broken-ceramic benches high above the city at Gaudí's Parc Güell. *See p 27.*

3 Wandering the Barri Gòtic. Barcelona's Gothic Quarter is a mesmerizing labyrinth of medieval buildings and narrow streets; it's a joy to take a stroll and discover a quiet square or picturesque patio. Meander down Sant Sever and slip into Plaça Sant Felip Neri or walk along Carrer Banys Nous, which is lined with antiques shops. *See p 60.*

4 Breathing in La Boquería. Barcelona's wonderfully evocative food market is a feast for the senses, with hundreds of colorful stalls overflowing with fresh seafood, wild mushrooms, meats, and vegetables. For a special treat, join locals and sample the goods at a kiosk, such as Bar Pintxo or El Quim, for breakfast or lunch at the counter. *See p 57.*

5 Tuning into El Palau de la Música. This mind-blowing 1908 *modernista* concert hall draws hordes to its architectural tours. But there's nothing quite like experiencing a performance here; the spine-tingling monument to Art Nouveau excess takes a back-

La Boquería is a food-lover's paradise.

seat to no musician, whether a chamber quartet or Pepe Habichuela. *See p 15.*

⑥ Sampling cutting-edge Catalan cuisine. Led these days by Joan Roca and Carme Ruscalleda, innovative Catalan cooking has given Barcelona the hottest dining scene in Europe. With chic tapas bars and minimalist haunts known for their celebrity chefs, the city has become a destination for gastronomic pilgrims. *See p 98.*

⑦ Dipping into old-school Barcelona. Unfazed by today's fashions and fast pace are authentic, time-stopping treasures in the old city: a 1920s *modernista* chocolate shop; a granja, or "milk bar," serving thick chocolate drinks as it has for 125 years; and a gourmet food and wine shop in the same family for four generations. All are portals to an earlier era. *See p 46.*

⑧ Biking along the beach. Just 2 decades ago, Barcelona turned its back on the Mediterranean and its polluted port; today, the revitalized waterfront is lined with leisurely bike paths and immaculate urban beaches. Take a pit stop at one of the city's most traditional seafood haunts in working-class Barceloneta. *See p 90.*

⑨ Traipsing along on a *cava* crawl. You can do a tapas crawl anywhere in Spain, but in Barcelona pre-meal snacks are washed down with glasses of cava, Catalan sparkling wine. Xampanyerías are friendly spots where good cheer bubbles over. *See p 118.*

⑩ Discovering cutting-edge fashion on medieval streets. Against a backdrop of Gothic palaces, churches, and centuries-old shops, the tangle of dark but suddenly chic alleyways of the La Ribera/Born district is also home to dozens of edgy fashion and home-design shops, a delight to discover. *See p 64.*

⑪ Experiencing classic Catalan culture. La Mercè, Barcelona's signature folklore festival, has something for everyone: castellers (human towers rising eight levels); gigants and cap grosses (massive costumed royal figures parading the streets); and devils running and chasing each other with fireworks in correfocs. It's a blast and a quintessential expression of Catalan pride. *See p 161.*

Be sure to try the cava (Catalan sparkling wine) while you're visiting the region.

⑫ **Reveling in Santa María del Mar.** This Gothic church, in the heart of bustling La Ribera, is architectural perfection, a model of graceful, soaring dimensions. A rare concert here can be thrilling, but it's also a sublime sanctuary on a quiet afternoon. You might catch guests at a society wedding spilling out onto the steps—which you can watch from a wine bar just across the plaza. *See p 15.*

⑬ **Grooving at La Pedrera.** The dreamlike rooftop of Antoni Gaudí's finest private building is topped by surreal-looking chimneys, but it really comes to life during the summertime evening program of jazz concerts. You can tap your toes, sip cava, and watch the elegant Passeig de Gràcia below turn to night. *See p 9.*

⑭ **Hopping the Blue Tram to Tibidabo.** Appreciate how Barcelona gracefully stretches from the surrounding hills out to the sea on the old trolley (Tramvía Blau) up to Tibidabo, the hilltop overlooking the city. On a clear day, you can survey the perfect grid system of L'Eixample and maybe even pick out Mallorca in the distant Mediterranean. *See p 22.*

⑮ **Getting a taste of Catalunya.** Sample even more Catalan flavor just a couple of hours outside the capital: Ride an aerial cable car to Montserrat, a monastery cleaved into a mountain; discover the idiosyncratic spots where Salvador Dalí's mad genius erupted; or lose yourself in the pristine, ancient Jewish quarter of Girona. *See p 145.* ●

Explore Dalí's stomping grounds, including the Teatre Museu Dalí in Figueres.

The Best in One Day

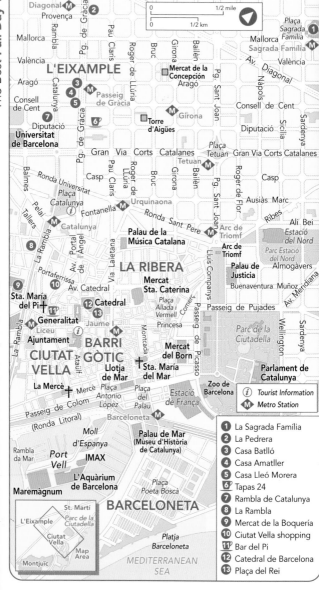

Diagonal Ⓜ
Provença ❷

Mallorca

València

L'EIXAMPLE

Aragó ❸
Consell ❹
de Cent ❺
❼
Diputació
Universitat
de Barcelona

Rambla
Pg. de Gràcia
Pau Claris
Roger de Llúria
Bruc
Girona
Bailèn

Passeig ❹Ⓜ
de Gràcia

❻

Pg. de Gràcia

Gran Via Corts Catalanes

Casp
Pau Claris
Roger de Llúria
Bruc
Girona
Bailèn

Ronda Universitat
Plaça
Catalunya ⓘ
Fontanella Ⓜ

Balmes
Pelai
Tallers
La Rambla
Ⓜ Catalunya
❽
Portal de l'Àngel
Av. de
Portaferrissa
Portal
❾
❿
Sta. María
del Pi ✝ ❶❶
Ⓜ Generalitat
Liceu ⓘ
Ajuntament
CIUTAT
VELLA
La Mercè ✝

Mercat de la
Concepción
Aragó

Torre
d'Aigües

Ⓜ Girona

Plaça
Tetuan

Tetuan
Ⓜ

Urquinaona Ⓜ
Ronda Sant Pere

Palau de la
Música Catalana

LA RIBERA

Mercat
Sta. Caterina

Plaça
Allada i
Vermell
Princesa

Av. Catedral
❶❷ Catedral
❶❸
Jaume Ⓜ

BARRI
GÒTIC

Via Laietana
Montcada

Llotja
de Mar

Plaça
Antonio
López

Mercè ✝ Mercè

Passeig de Colom
(Ronda Litoral)

Barceloneta Ⓜ

Sta. Maria
del Mar

Mercat
del Born

Estació
de França

Plaça
del
Palau

Plaça
Sagrada
Família ❶
Ⓜ
Mallorca
Sagrada Família
València

Av. Diagonal

Nàpols

Consell de Cent

Diputació

Gran Via Corts Catalanes

Ausiàs Marc

Roger de Flor

Ribes
Alí Bei
Arc de
Triomf Ⓜ
Arc de
Triomf

Palau de
Justicia

Pg. Sant Joan

Lluís Companys

Passeig de Pujades

Passeig de Picasso

Zoo de
Barcelona

Comerç

Sicília
Sardenya

Casp

Estació
del Nord
Parc Estació
del Nord
Almogàvers
Buenaventura Muñoz

Av. Meridiana

Wellington

Parc de la
Ciutadella

Parlament de
Catalunya

ⓘ Tourist Information
Ⓜ Metro Station

Rambla
da Mar
Port
Vell

Moll
d'Espanya
IMAX

Maremàgnum

L'Aquàrium
de Barcelona

Palau de Mar
(Museu d'Història
de Catalunya)

Plaça
Poeta Bosca

BARCELONETA

Platja
Barceloneta

MEDITERRANEAN
SEA

L'Eixample
Ciutat
Vella
Montjuïc

St. Martí
Parc de la
Ciutadella
Map
Area

0 ——— 1/2 mile
0 ——— 1/2 km

❶ La Sagrada Família
❷ La Pedrera
❸ Casa Batlló
❹ Casa Amatller
❺ Casa Lleó Morera
❻ Tapas 24
❼ Rambla de Catalunya
❽ La Rambla
❾ Mercat de la Boquería
❿ Ciutat Vella shopping
❶❶ Bar del Pi
❶❷ Catedral de Barcelona
❶❸ Plaça del Rei

Previous page: La Sagrada Família.

This very full day, a "greatest hits" tour, begins with the best of Barcelona's *modernista* architecture in the morning, is followed by a stroll down the epic Rambla, and ends with the highlights of the Ciutat Vella, or Old City. You'll need your walking shoes. The tour is excellent any day of the week, though La Boquería, Barcelona's famed food market, is closed on Sundays. START: **Metro to Sagrada Família.**

1 ★★★ kids **La Sagrada Família.** Antoni Gaudí's unfinished legacy, the soaring "Holy Family" church, is a testament to his singular vision: the art of the impossible. This mind-altering creation—the best-known, if not necessarily the best example, of *modernisme*—has become Barcelona's calling card. Begun in 1882, its eight bejeweled spires drip like melting candlesticks, and virtually every square inch of the surface explodes with intricate spiritual symbols. Gaudí was run over by a tram long before it could be finished, although it is now consecrated and functions as a house of worship. A private foundation works furiously to finish the building—now projected for 2026, the centennial of Gaudí's death. For the foreseeable future, the church will remain under a forest of cranes. ⏱ *1 hr. c/ Mallorca, 401.* ☎ *93-207-30-31. www.sagrada familia.org. Admission 15€ adults; 4.50€ audio or print guide. Buy tickets in advance to avoid long lines. Daily Oct–Mar 9am–6pm; Apr–Sept 9am–8pm. Metro: Sagrada Família.*

2 ★★★ kids **La Pedrera.** Thought by many to be the crowning glory of the *modernista* movement, Antoni Gaudí's avant-garde apartment building Casa Milà is better known as La Pedrera, or Stone Quarry, for its wavy mass of limestone. The exterior seems carved out of nature: It undulates like ocean waves along Passeig de Gràcia and around the corner onto Provença Street. The fascinating

roof, what most people come to see, is guarded by a set of warrior-like chimneys that look like the inspiration for Darth Vader. ⏱ *1 hr. Pg. de Gràcia, 92 (at Provença).* ☎ *90-240-09-73 or 90-210-12-12 for advance tickets. www.lapedrera.com. Admission 17€ adults, 15€ students; 8.25€ ages 7–12. Audioguide 4€. Nov–Feb daily 9am–6:30pm; Mar–Oct daily 9am–8pm. Closed Dec 25–26 & Jan 1–6. Metro: Diagonal or Provença.*

3 ★★★ **Casa Batlló.** The centerpiece of the so-called "Block of Discord," Casa Batlló owes its extraordinary facade to Antoni

Detailed carving work on La Sagrada Família.

Top Attractions: Practical Matters

ArticketBCN Discounts: One ticket (www.articketbcn.org) lets you into six top art museums without waiting in line, including **Museu Picasso, Museu Nacional d'Art de Catalunya (MNAC), Fundació Joan Miró, Fundació Antoni Tàpies, Centre de Cultura Contemporània de Barcelona (CCCB)**, and **Museu d'Art Contemporani de Barcelona (MACBA)**. Purchase the ticket (30€; good for 6 months) at museum ticket offices, the Plaça de Catalunya Tourist Information Office, the Palau de la Virreina ticket office at La Rambla, 99, or by phone or online with **Tel.Entrada** (☎ **90-210-12-12** or 34-93-326-29-46 from abroad; www.tel entrada.com). Also useful is the **Barcelona Card** (good for 2–5 consecutive days; 34€–56€ adults, 14€–29€ children), which includes free public transport and discounts at over 80 museums, tourist sites, cultural venues, restaurants, and more, and free admission to some activities and museums. Purchase online (10% discount; http://bcnshop.barcelonaturisme.com) or at the Plaça de Catalunya Tourist Information Office.

La Pedrera is considered one of Antoni Gaudí's masterpieces (p 9).

Gaudí, who completed a remodeling in 1906. Thought to represent the legend of Saint George (patron saint of Catalunya) and his dragon, the house glimmers with fragments of colorful ceramics, while the roof curves like the blue-green scales of a dragon's back, and balconies evoke Carnaval-esque masks or menacing monster jaws. The sinuous interior, full of

custom Gaudí-designed furniture, is similarly stunning (though tours are unexpectedly pricey). Circle around back to see the rear of the building, and glimpse another *modernista* masterpiece across the street on carrer Aragó, the former publishing house by Lluís Domènech i Montaner, now a museum dedicated to the contemporary painter Antoni Tàpies. ⏱ *45 min. Pg. de Gràcia, 43.* ☎ *93-488-06-66. www.casabatllo.es. Admission 22€ adults, 19€ children & students, free for children 7 & under. Daily 9am–8pm. Metro: Pg. de Gràcia.*

❹ ★★ **Casa Amatller.** Puig i Cadafalch, a Gaudí contemporary, created this brilliant house—the first building on the Manzana de la Discòrdia block of Passeig de Gràcia—in 1900. It has a medieval-looking, ceramics-covered façade, topped by a distinctive Flemish-inspired roof and beautiful carved stone and ironwork of themes

The "dragon's back" atop Casa Batlló.

related to the chocolate business and hobbies of the original owners. ① *20 min. Pg. de Gràcia, 41.* ☎ *93-487-72-17. www.amatller.org. Ground floor open to public (free admission) Mon–Sat 10am–8pm; Sun 10am–3pm. Metro: Pg. de Gràcia.*

⑤ ★ Casa Lleó Morera. The final member of the "Block of Discord" triumvirate, this gorgeously ornate corner house, built in 1905 by Domenech i Montaner, who designed El Palau de la Música Catalana, is especially appealing when illuminated at night. The building is now home to the upscale leather-goods purveyor Loewe, which lamentably destroyed a good part of the lower façade and sumptuous interior ground floor. *Pg. de Gràcia, 35. Except for the Loewe store, the house cannot be visited. Metro: Pg. de Gràcia.*

⑥ ★★ Tapas 24. The informal tapas bar of acclaimed chef Carles Abellán, who's in the kitchen at Comerç 24, is a good-looking pit stop just off Passeig de Gràcia. Grab a snack or lunch of tantalizing small bites with big flavors, and wine and cava by the glass. *c/ Diputaciò, 269.* ☎ *93-488-09-77. $$.*

⑦ ★★ Rambla de Catalunya. Passeig de Gràcia is home to some of the city's finest *modernista* architecture and a wealth of elegant fashion boutiques and high-end home-design emporiums, making it ideal for window-shopping. But an even more leisurely stroll is along Rambla de Catalunya, a delightful, pedestrian-only lane lined with trees, shops, cafes, and classic L'Eixample apartment buildings. Cross over on carrer Consell de Cent, teeming with art galleries, and follow Rambla de Catalunya down to Plaça de Catalunya. ① *30 min. Metro: Pg. de Gràcia.*

⑧ ★★★ kids La Rambla. Barcelona's monumental boulevard is the centerpiece of life in the Catalan capital. It throbs with activity, as crowds at all hours of the day file past vendors, food markets, cafes, and historic buildings, including the great Liceu opera house. Subdivided into five separate *ramblas,* each of different character and attractions, are a lively succession of newspaper kiosks, fresh-flower stands, bird sellers, and crowd-friendly human statues (mimes) in elaborately conceived costumes and face paint. About halfway down the boulevard, to the left as you

Mercat de La Boquería is a Barcelona institution.

face the port, is the Plaça Reial, a grand square with cafes, palm trees, arcades, and lampposts designed by *modernista* master Antoni Gaudí. (At night, the lower sectors of La Rambla can get a little sketchy; keep a close eye on your belongings at all times.) ⓘ *45 min. Begin at Pl. de Catalunya. Metro: Catalunya.*

⑨ ★★★ kids **Mercat de La Boquería.** One of Europe's largest and most dynamic food markets, this Catalan classic is the foundation of Barcelona's fascination with food. Wander among the more than 300 stalls and several small bar/restaurants to take in the sights and smells of an amazingly robust gastronomic scene. Keep an eye out for *bolets* and *ceps* (wild mushrooms), massive prawns, eels, and octopus. The colorful bounty is a testament to the fertile region and Catalans' desire for the freshest and tastiest foodstuffs available. True foodies will want to return one early morning when the market is at its liveliest. ⓘ *30 min. La Rambla, 91–101.* ☎ *93-318-25-84. www. boqueria.info. Mon–Sat 8am–8pm. Metro: Liceu.*

⑩ **Ciutat Vella shopping.** The old-city districts Barri Gòtic (Gothic Quarter) and La Ribera are home to dozens of fashion boutiques, bars, and souvenir shops. Check out bustling, pedestrian-only carrer de Petritxol; carrer Ferran; dark, atmospheric carrer Banys Nous, site of some of the city's best antiques shops; and carrer de la Palla. Across Vía Laetana in the El Born district are some of the chicest fashion boutiques in old Barcelona. ⓘ *1 hr. Metro: Liceu or Jaume I.*

Fresh flowers are for sale daily on La Rambla.

A snack at Tapas 24 (p 11).

⑪ ★★ Bar del Pi. One of the prettiest squares in the Old City makes a splendid spot to linger at an outdoor cafe, as Barcelonans do. Of the several cafes clustered around the square, Bar del Pi is the most traditional. People-watching opportunities abound, and on weekends artists and artisans set up booths in the plaça. *Pl. Sant Josep Orio, 1.* ☎ *93-302-21-23. $$.*

⑫ ★★ Catedral de Barcelona. The cathedral, the focal point of the Old City and a splendid example of Catalan Gothic architecture, was begun in 1298 but largely completed in the 14th and 15th centuries. Don't miss the carved choir and surprisingly lush cloister—a welcome oasis in the midst of the medieval Gothic Quarter, with its pond, magnolias, orange and palm trees, and white geese. ⏱ *45 min.*

Pl. de la Seu, s/n. ☎ *93-342-82-60. www.catedralbcn.org. Free admission to cathedral; museum, choir, rooftop terraces & towers 6€. Elevator to roof 10:30am–1:30pm & 5–6pm. Cathedral daily 8am–1pm & 4:30–7:30pm; cloister museum daily 10am–1pm & 4:30–6:30pm. Metro: Jaume I.*

⑬ ★★ kids Plaça del Rei. One of the old quarter's most beautiful and historic squares, the stately Plaça del Rei is hemmed in by a remaining section of the old Roman city walls and the Palau Reial Major, an 11th-century royal palace and residence of the kings of Catalunya and Aragón. According to legend, the Reyes Católicos, King Fernando and Queen Isabel, received Columbus here after he returned from the New World. ⏱ *1½ hr. Pl. del Rei, s/n.* ☎ *93-256-21-00. http://museu historia.bcn.cat. Admission 7€ adults, 5€ students, free for children under 16. Tues–Sat 10am–7pm; Sun 10am–8pm. Metro: Jaume I.*

The Best **in Two Days**

1 El Palau de la
   Música Catalana
2 Museu Picasso
3 Carrer de Montcada/
   Passeig del Born

4 Santa María del Mar
5 La Vinya del Senyor
6 Moll de la Fusta/
   Port Vell
7 Beaches/Port Olímpic

On day two, take in art and architecture highlights of the **Old City,** followed by leisure time at the revitalized waterfront. Begin the day in the atmospheric La Ribera district before moving on to stroll along the harbor, stop for lunch in the beachside district of Barceloneta, and hit the sands in the afternoon for sunbathing or a sunset cocktail, perhaps topped off by dinner along the waterfront. START: **Metro to Urquinaona.**

❶ ★★★ El Palau de la Música Catalana. Domènech i Montaner's magnificent 1908 music hall is over-the-top ornate but indisputably one of Barcelona's *modernista* masterpieces. The relatively sedate exterior is just a tease of what's inside: a riotous fantasy of ceramics, colored glass, and carved pumice, crowned by an enormous yellow, blue, and green stained-glass dome that looks like a swollen raindrop. It's surely the most exuberant music hall you'll ever see. A daytime guided tour addresses the architecture, but there's nothing like experiencing a concert here. ○ *1 hr. c/ Sant Francesc de Paula, 2.* ☎ *90-247-54-85 or 93-295-72-00. www.palaumusica.org. Guided tour 17€ adults. Tickets can be bought up to 1 week in advance online, by telephone, or from the gift shop (no same-day tickets by phone). Guided tours daily every half-hour 10am–3:30pm (in English on the hour 10am–3pm). Metro: Urquinaona.*

Mosaics in El Palau de la Música Catalana.

❷ ★★ Museu Picasso. Pablo Picasso was born in Málaga, but he spent part of his youth and early creative years in Barcelona. The museum is the largest collection of his works in his native country: 2,500 paintings and sculptures, many of them early works, including several from his blue period. Las Meninas, a series of 59 often-whimsical interpretations of Velázquez's masterpiece, is the highlight. The museum occupies several exquisite 15th-century palaces on a pedestrian-only street lined with medieval mansions. ○ *90 min. c/ Montcada 15–23.* ☎ *93-319-63-10. www. museupicasso.bcn.es. Admission 11€ adults (14€ with temporary exhibits), 7€/7.50€ students & ages 16–24, free for under 15 or over 65. Admission part of ArticketBCN. Free admission Sun (3–8pm) & all day 1st Sun of the month. Buy tickets In advance to avoid lines. Tues–Sun 10am–8pm. Metro: Jaume I.*

❸ ★ Carrer de Montcada/ Passeig del Born. La Ribera is at its most evocative and lively along the wonderful street lined with Renaissance palaces, including the ones that now house the Picasso Museum, and the Passeig del Born, a tree-lined promenade that's become one of the trendiest areas in old Barcelona. ○ *30 min. See p 31, ❷, and p 65, ❹.*

❹ ★★★ Santa María del Mar. A stunning 14th-century Catalan Gothic church that's neither opulent and jewel-encrusted nor home

The "Nation" of Catalunya

As the capital of Catalunya, Barcelona has an identity distinct from the rest of Spain. The fiercely independent streak of the Catalan people is forged of a unique history, language, and culture—prompting Catalan nationalists to refer to their semiautonomous region as *un país* (literally, a nation). The most prosperous region in Spain, Catalunya has often maintained a testy relationship with Madrid and the rest of the country. The long, insular Franco dictatorship outlawed the Catalan language, but the ancient tongue has experienced a dramatic resurgence and is now the principal language in public schools and on the streets (although in multilingual Barcelona, Spanish is spoken about as often). While some Catalan separatists continue to argue for full political independence from Spain, Catalunya has largely been exempt from the deadly terrorism that ETA used to wage in the Basque Country. To learn more about the Catalan people and history, visit the engaging **Museu d'Història de Catalunya** on the waterfront in the Palau de Mar (Pl. de Pau Vila, 3; ☎ **93-225-42-44;** www.mhcat.net; 4€).

to a fabulous art collection. Instead, it's a simple and solemn, but wholly inspired, space: perfectly proportioned with three soaring naves, wide-spaced columns, and gorgeous stained-glass windows. It's the kind of place architects understandably wax poetic about. ⏱ *20 min. Pl. de Santa María.* ☎ *93-215-74-11. Free admission. Mon–Sat 9am–1:30pm & 4:30–8pm; Sun 9am–2pm & 5–8:30pm. Metro: Jaume I.*

5 ★ **La Vinya del Senyor.** A hip little wine bar with much-coveted tables on a terrace at the lovely square across from Santa María del Mar, it features an excellent selection of 100 or so wines from across Spain, including two dozen by the glass, as well as Spanish ham, salami, and cheeses. *Pl. de Santa María, 5.* ☎ *93-310-33-79. $$.*

The Museu Picasso holds 2,500 paintings and sculptures (p 15).

Xavier Mariscal's crayfish at the Moll de la Fusta.

6 ★ kids Moll de la Fusta/ Port Vell/Barceloneta. The boardwalk and series of esplanades along Passeig Colom called Moll de la Fusta is a local favorite for a paseo, or stroll. It stretches from the Columbus statue at the bottom of La Rambla and past Port Vell, the old harbor, to a giant Xavier Mariscal sculpture of a playful crayfish and colorful pop-art work, *Cap de Barcelona,* by the American artist Roy Lichtenstein. The colorful old beachfront neighborhood Barceloneta received a controversial makeover for the '92 Olympics, displacing many longtime residents, but it's still renowned for its *chiringuitos,* or informal seafood restaurants—which makes it a perfect place to stop for lunch, especially on weekends. ⏱ *1 hr. Metro: Drassanes or Barceloneta.*

7 ★★ kids Beaches/Port Olímpic. It wasn't long ago that no self-respecting Barcelonan would venture down to the city's beaches, much less dream of wading into the polluted waters. The 1992 Olympics dramatically reopened the city to the Mediterranean and cleaned up the urban beaches, vastly improving water quality and transforming the long stretches of sand into a playground for city dwellers. The beaches (*platges*) are lined with palm trees, innovative public sculptures, bars, and restaurants, as well as paths for biking, in-line skating, and walking. The first major beach is Barceloneta, followed to the north by Nova Icària (the most popular, near the Port Olímpic marina and Vila Olímpica district), Bogatell, and Mar Bella (an unofficial nudist beach). Look for Frank Gehry's massive *Fish* sculpture in front of the Hotel Arts. ⏱ *2 hr. Metro: Barceloneta or Ciutadella/Vila Olímpica.*

Public sculptures can be found along Barcelona's beaches.

The Best in Three Days

1 Reials Drassanes (Museu Marítim)
2 Mirador de Colom
3 Transbordador Aeri del Port
4 Fundació Joan Miró
5 La Font del Gat
6 Estadi Olímpic
7 Museu Nacional d'Art de Catalunya (MNAC)
8 Parc Güell
9 Tibidabo/Parc d'Atraccions
10 Mirablau

ⓘ Tourist Information
Ⓜ Metro Station

El Palau de la Música Catalana

LA RIBERA

Montcada

Sta. Maria del Mar

Urquinaona

Via Laietana

Via Laietana

Plaça Catalunya

Pelai

La Rambla

Av. Catedral

Portaferrissa

Catedral

Sta. Maria

del Pi

Plaça Generalitat

St. Jaume Princesa

Plaça del Pi

BARRI GÒTIC

Antoni López

Tallers

Casa de la Caritat

Carme

Mercat de la Boqueria

Hospital

Gran Teatre del Liceu

Liceu

Ajuntament

CIUTAT VELLA

La Mercè

Paseig de Colom (Ronda Litoral)

Port Vell

Moll d'Espanya

Museu d'Art Contemporani de Barcelona

EL RAVAL

Antic Hospital de la Sta. Creu

La Rambla del Raval

St. Pau

Av. Drassanes

Reials Drassanes (Museu Marítim)

Rambla da Mar

Rambla de Mar

Ronda de St. Antoni

Villarroel

Comte d'Urgell

L'EIXAMPLE

St. Antoni

Ronda St. Pau

Riereta

Cera

Carrettes

Reina Amàlia

St. Pau del Camp

Nou de la Rambla

Av. Paral·lel

Vila i Vila

Transbordador Aeri

Sepúlveda

Floridablanca

Mercat de St. Antoni

Manso

Poble Sec

Parlament

Comte Borrell

Av. Paral·lel

POBLE SEC

Nou de la Rambla

Funicular

Cabanes

Pg. de Montjuïc

Paral·lel

Plaça Carlos Ibáñez

Av. Miramar

LA FRANÇA

Magalhaes

Rabas

França Xica

Exposició

Plaça Dante

Plaça La Sardana

Castell de Montjuïc

Plaça de Carlos Buïgas

Museu Arqueològic

Teatre Grec

Fundació Joan Miró

Av. Miramar

Plaça Dante

Jardins Mossèn Cinto Verdaguer

Passeig Migdia

Ctra. Miramar

Museu Militar

MNAC

Palau Nacional

Pavelló Albéniz

Plaça Neptú

MONTJUÏC

Av. de l'Estadi

Plaça Europa

Torre de Calatrava

Palau St. Jordi

Estadi Olímpic

Galeria Olímpica

PARC DE MONTJUÏC

Maremàgnum

Port Vell

0   1/2 mile
0   1/2 km

St. Martí

Parc de la Ciutadella

Map Area

L'Eixample   Ciutat Vella

Montjuïc

This tour begins with Barcelona's maritime roots before exploring Montjuïc hill, site of the '92 Olympics and two spectacular art museums. In the afternoon, venture uptown to a whimsical Gaudí park and finish the day with a gorgeous bird's-eye view of the city from Tibidabo. The tour includes some great stops for kids. START: **Metro to Drassanes.**

① ★★ kids **Reials Drassanes (Museu Marítim).** Barcelona's seafaring past comes to life in this rich maritime museum, located in the *Reials Drassanes*, or Royal Shipyards, which includes a glorious replica of a massive 16th-century vessel, the *Galería Reial*. Scheduled to reopen in late 2014 after extensive restoration, the medieval shipyard's evocative arches, columns, and vaults remain magnificently intact. Here the kingdom's ships were constructed, repaired, and dry-docked. The *Santa Eulàlia* schooner (included in admission) is docked at Port Vell. This is a winner for both kids and parents. ⏲ *1 hr. Av. de les Drassanes, s/n.* ☎ *93-342-99-20. www.mmb.cat. Admission 5€ adults, 4€ seniors & children 7–16. Daily 10am–8pm. Metro: Drassanes.*

See relics from Barcelona's seafaring past at the Museu Marítim.

Mirador de Colom.

② kids **Mirador de Colom.** Although this monument to Christopher Columbus, built in 1888, has him pointing the wrong direction to the New World, it's a focal and meeting point, dividing the lower end of the Rambla from the waterfront. An elevator takes visitors inside to a mirador for panoramic harbor views. ⏲ *30 min. Portal de la Pau, s/n.* ☎ *93-302-52-24. Admission 4€ adults, 3€ children 4–12. June–Sept daily 9am–1:30pm & 4–8:30pm; Oct–May daily 9am–2pm & 3:30–7:30pm. Metro: Drassanes.*

③ ★ kids **Transbordador Aeri del Port.** Traveling 70m (230 ft.) above the old port and across lower Barcelona up to Montjuïc hill, this aerial cable car (also called the Telefèric de Montjuïc), inaugurated in 1931, is the most memorable way to travel the city. The views of the

Mediterranean, La Rambla, and the grid of Barcelona rising up to the hills are unforgettable. ① 30 min. Pg. Joan de Borbó, s/n, Barceloneta. ☎ 93-328-90-03. www.teleferic demontjuic.cat. Admission round-trip 11€ adults, 7.80€ children; one-way 7.50€ adults, 5.80€ children. Daily every 15 min. from 10:15am–7pm (until 9pm in summer). Metro: Barceloneta.

④ ★★ **Fundació Joan Miró.** A resolutely Catalan surrealist painter and sculptor, Miró (1893–1983) created a unique, whimsical artistic language—which to the uninitiated may look like colorful doodles—on his way to becoming one of the 20th century's most celebrated artists. In minimalist galleries bathed with natural light are several hundred of Miró's canvases, as well as a wealth of his drawings, graphics, and sculptures. A rooftop terrace and sculpture garden provides lovely views of Barcelona below. ① 1½ hr. Parc de Montjuïc, s/n. ☎ 93-443-94-70. www.fundaciomiro-bcn.org. Admission 11€ adults, 7€ students, free for children under 15. Also part of ArticketBCN joint admission. July–Sept Tues–Wed & Fri–Sat 10am–8pm, Thurs 10am–9:30pm, Sun

Visit the rooftop terrace and sculpture garden at the Fundació Joan Miró.

10am–2:30pm; Oct–June Tues–Wed & Fri–Sat 10am–7pm, Thurs 10am–9:30pm, Sun 10am–2:30pm. Bus no. 50 at Pl. d'Espanya, or Funicular de Montjuïc.

⑤ **La Font del Gat.** This resurrected modernista cafe and restaurant, built by the acclaimed architect Puig i Cadafalch, is ensconced in gardens of the Montjuïc hillside and makes for a relaxing spot for a coffee or beer, or even an inexpensive fixed-priced lunch. Pg. Sta. Madrona, 28. ☎ 93-289-04-04. $.

⑥ **Estadi Olímpic/Museu Olímpic i de L'Esport.** The setting for the majority of events during Barcelona's hosting of the 1992 Summer Olympics was Montjuïc, including the Olympic Stadium, originally built in 1929 for the World's Fair, and Arata Isozaki's sleek Palau d'Esports Sant Jordi, the indoor stadium that hosted gymnastics and volleyball events (and now also hosts concerts). Nearby are a new sports museum (Av. de l'Estadi, 60), Galería Olímpica, and the outdoor pool and diving pavilion, which overlooks the city below. ① 1 hr. Av. de L'Estadi, s/n (Parc de Montjuïc). ☎ 93-292-53-79. www.museuolimpicbcn.cat. Museum admission 5.10€ adults, 3.20€ students, free for seniors & children 7 and under. Oct–Mar Tues–Sat 10am–6pm, Sun 10am–2:30pm; Apr–Sept Tues–Sat 10am–8pm. Metro: Pl. de Espanya (then take the escalator from Palau Nacional), bus no. 50 at Pl. d'Espanya, or Funicular de Montjuïc.

⑦ ★★★ **Museu Nacional d'Art de Catalunya (MNAC).** At the base of Montjuïc, within the domed Palau Nacional, this museum is anything but a stale repository of religious art. Its

A piece from the Museo Nacional de Catalunya (Taula of Esqulus, 12th c.).

medieval collection, which includes Romanesque works salvaged from churches all over Catalunya, is unequaled; many of the superb altarpieces, polychromatic icons, and treasured frescoes are displayed in apses, just as they were in the country churches where they were found. Other highlights are paintings by some of Spain's most celebrated Old Masters, including Velázquez, Ribera, and Zurbarán, as well as eight Picassos on indefinite loan from the family. If it's gotten late in the day and you don't have the energy for the last two stops, you might stick around for the light-and-sound show of the Font Màgica, at the base of the steps up to the Palau Nacional. ⏱ 1½ hr. *Palau Nacional (Parc de Montjuïc). ☎ 93-622-03-60. www.mnac.cat. Admission 12€ adults, 8.40€ ages 15–20, free under 16 & over 65; free to all Sat after 3pm, first Sun of month; part of ArticketBCN joint admission. Tues–Sat 10am–7pm; Sun 10am–2:30pm. Metro: Pl. de Espanya.*

❽ ★★★ kids **Parc Güell.** Yet another of Gaudí's signature creations, this open-air park on the outskirts of the Eixample district is pure whimsy. Resembling an idiosyncratic theme park, it features a mosaic-covered lizard fountain, Hansel and Gretel pagodas, and undulating park benches swathed in broken pieces of ceramics, called *trencadis.* Gaudí carved part of the park out of a hillside, fashioning a forest of columns like tree trunks. A

Casa-Museu Gaudí in the Parc Güell.

planned housing development that was never fully realized, the park is home to but a single house, now the Casa Museu Gaudí, a small museum about Gaudí's life and work (where the ascetic architect lived while working on the project). On clear days, you can see much of Barcelona laid out beneath your feet, including the spires of La Sagrada Família and the twin towers on the beach. ① *1 hr. Ctra. del Carmel, 28.* ☎ *93-213-04-88. www. bcn.cat/parcsijardins. Free admission to park; Casa Museu Gaudí 4€. Daily Dec–Feb 10am–6pm, Mar & Nov 10am–7pm, Apr & Oct 10am–8pm, May–Sept 10am–9pm. Metro: Lesseps (then a 15-min. walk uphill). Bus: 24 or 28.*

⑨ ★ kids Tibidabo/Parc d'Atraccions. High above Barcelona is Tibidabo Mountain, which has been a getaway destination for Barcelonans since the early 1800s for its cooler temperatures and panoramic views of the city and the ocean. The historic Tramvía Blau, or Blue Tram, carries visitors to an overlook with bars and restaurants. Crowning Tibidabo is the odd juxtaposition of a neo-Gothic church

and a 1950s-style amusement park, Parc d'Atraccions (the gentle swing ride is spectacular; it seems to suspend riders over the city). ① *1–2 hr. Pl. Tibidabo, 3.* ☎ *93-211-79-42. www.tibidabo.es. Parc d'Atraccions 29€ adults, 10€ children under 1.2m (4 ft.), free for children under 90cm (35 in.); 10€ over 60.. Summer Tues–Thurs noon–10pm, Fri–Sat noon–11pm; off-season hours vary (check website); closed most of Jan–Feb. From Pl. Kennedy (Metro: Tibidabo), the Blue Tram connects with the Funicular Tibidabo, a cable car that completes the trek to the top of the mountain (mid-Sept to the end of Apr, weekends only); round-trip 4.10€ (funicular cost refunded with park admission). A T2 Tibibus also travels from Pl. de Catalunya (2.95€) and is refunded with park admission.*

⑩ ★ Mirablau. This bar perched on Tibidabo Mountain is sedate in the late afternoon and early evening, when it's perfect to relax and contemplate all of Barcelona, stretching out to the sea beneath you. *Pl. Doctor Andreu, 2.* ☎ *93-418-58-79. $$.* ●

A ride at Tibidabo amusement park.

Modernista Barcelona

1. Parc Güell
2. La Sagrada Família
3. Hospital de Santa Creu i Sant Pau
4. La Pedrera (Casa Milà)
5. Passeig de Gràcia
6. El Palau de la Música Catalana
7. Els Quatre Gats
8. Palau Güell
9. Casa Calvet

M Metro Station

Previous Page: The chimneys of La Pedrera.

arcelona is renowned for the wildly original *modernisme*, or Catalan Art Nouveau, style of architecture that flourished in the late 19th and early 20th centuries. Best known are the stunning works of Antoni Gaudí, but so many talented architects left their mark on Barcelona that it's a big task even to do a greatest hits tour in a single day. START: **Metro to Lessep, then a taxi or 15-min. walk uphill to Parc Güell, the first stop on the itinerary.**

1 ★★★ kids Parc Güell. In 1900 Gaudí's lifelong patron, the Catalan industrialist Eusebi Güell, envisioned a real-estate development in a garden setting. Although never completed, the project bears Gaudí's visionary stamp and reflects the naturalism beginning to flower in his work. The architect set out to design every detail in the park, but much of the work was in fact completed by a disciple, Josep María Jujol, best known for the park's colorful splashes of *trencadís* (designs of broken shards of ceramics). Yet the unique man-made landscape is all Gaudí. At the main entrance are fairy-tale-like gatehouses topped with chimneys resembling wild mushrooms. The covered marketplace, with an extraordinary tiled lizard fountain at the entrance, is supported by 86 Doric columns (not the 100 planned). But most famous are those sinuous, mosaic-covered benches that trace the perimeter of the plaza above. ⏱ *45 min. See p 54,* **9**.

Mosaic benches in Parc Güell.

2 ★★★ kids La Sagrada Família. Gaudí's most famous building is a work of unbridled ambition. He dedicated 4 decades of his life to it, and though the architect left behind no detailed plans, he expected that the basilica—the world's largest if completed—would take several generations to finish. Gaudí envisioned 12 spires (one for each of the Apostles), a massive dome over the apse, and four additional, higher spires, as well as one central bell tower, representing the Virgin Mary. Portals in the dramatic Nativity facade represent Faith, Hope, and Charity, and biblical elements, such as the Tree of Calgary, pack the dense surface. ⏱ *45 min. See p 9,* **1**.

3 ★★ Hospital de la Santa Creu i Sant Pau. Just a few blocks' walk from La Sagrada Família, this hospital campus—undergoing a massive restoration and visited only by guided tour—reveals that Domènech i Montaner

(1850–1923), like Gaudí, also thought in grand terms. Hospital Sant Pau, begun in 1902, was also left unfinished at the time of its architect's death, with just 18 of a planned 48 pavilions completed (12 of those are by Domènech i Montaner, and all are classified as World Heritage monuments). The fanciful brick-and-tile pavilions feature vaulted ceilings and decorative mosaics and sculpture, techniques that reach their apex in El Palau de la Música Catalana (p 15, ❶). ⏱ 45 min. c/ Sant Antoni María Claret, 167–171. ☎ 93-488-20-78. www. santpau.es. Tour 10€ adults, 5€ students & seniors. Guided tours daily at 10am, 11am, noon & 1pm in English. Metro: Hospital de Sant Pau or Sagrada Família (& 10-min. walk along Av. de Gaudí).

❹ ★★★ kids **La Pedrera.** Gaudí's most inspired civic work, is formally named Casa Milà for the patron who dreamed of creating a showstopper on elegant Passeig de Gràcia. This sinuous landmark apartment block is for many the pinnacle of *modernisme*. The rooftop

The modernista rooftops of Sant Pau.

El Pis apartment building is refurbished to its early-20th-century look.

chimneys (which some claim represent Christians and Moors battling for Spanish turf) are spectacular, but those with an interest in architecture will be fascinated by the museum (Espai Gaudí), which exposes the splendid arches of the attic and delves into the life, times, and techniques of the architect, while the restored original apartment (El Pis) shows off its peculiar shapes, handcrafted doorknobs, and period furniture, all of Gaudí's design. ⏱ 1 hr. See p 9, ❷.

❺ ★★★ **Passeig de Gràcia.** This elegant shopping boulevard is ground zero for *modernisme*, the one place to see an amazing collection of *modernista* architecture without covering much distance. In fact, on a single block are pivotal buildings by Gaudí and the other two architects that make up the movement's great troika, Domènech i Montaner and Puig i Cadafalch. The competing proximity of these landmarks earned the block the nickname "Manzana de la Discórdia" (Block of Discord). *See mini-tour on following page.*

At the foot of La Pedrera are some *modernista* surprises: **5A** **The street tiles** on the sidewalk (trumpeting nature and ocean themes) are by Gaudí, while the white **mosaic-covered benches** that flow into ornate, **wrought-iron lampposts** are by Pere Falqués. On the same block is the design shop **5B** **Vinçon** (p 78), which occupies an elegant house built for the *modernista* painter Ramón Casas. Three blocks down is the famed **Manzana de la Discórdia.** First take a peek at **5C** ★ **Fundació Tàpies** (p 37, **2**), just off the boulevard at c/ Aragó, 225, a museum dedicated to the Catalan artist Antoni Tàpies. Domènech i Montaner designed the erstwhile publishing headquarters in 1884. Gaudí's spectacular

5D ★★★ **Casa Batlló** (p 9, **3**), open to the public since 2004, is as stunning inside as out; it features flowing staircases, a mushroom-shaped fireplace, and a gallery with bonelike columns. **5E** ★★ **Casa Amatller** (p 10, **4**), Puig i Cadafalch's most famous building, was the first *modernista* building on the block. The exterior of carved stone is the work of a celebrated artisan, Eusebi Arnau. Domènech i Montaner's **5F** ★ **Casa Lleó Morera** (p 11, **5**) is ornate but less groundbreaking than its *modernista* companions on the block; it suffers even more in comparison because commercial tenants altered the ground floor and destroyed several magnificent sculptures.

The spectacular Palau de la Música Catalana.

⑥ ★★★ El Palau de la Música Catalana. Domènech i Montaner designed this audacious concert hall as a home for the Orfeó Catalán (Catalan Choral Society). The interior is hallucinatory: from colored-glass canisters on staircases and a ceiling dominated by a colossal teardrop of stained glass to a stage framed by pumice busts of the composers Bach, Beethoven, and Wagner by the sculptor Pau Gargallo. Long surrounded by apartment buildings, the Palau was given some breathing space when the noted Barcelona architect Oscar Tusquets completed a tasteful extension in 2003. ⏱ *45 min.* See p 15, **①**.

⑦ ★★ Els Quatre Gats. A favorite hangout of Pablo Picasso, Ramón Casas, and other turn-of-the-century *modernista* bohemian intellectuals, this restaurant and cafe—one of the first commissions for the architect Puig i Cadafalch and site of Picasso's first exhibition—is the perfect stop on a *modernisme* tour of Barcelona, either for a late lunch or coffee and a pastry. *c/ Montsió, 3.* ☎ *93-302-41-40.* $–$$.

⑧ ★★ Palau Güell. Undergoing a large-scale renovation and with limited visits and hours (10am–2:30pm), this 1888 mansion, not in

Ruta del *Modernisme*

You could easily spend days visiting *modernista* landmarks in Barcelona. If your appetite has been whetted, check out the **Ruta del Modernisme de Barcelona** (*modernisme* route) promoted by the city (☎ **902-07-66-21;** www.rutadelmodernisme.com; 12€–18€). A map and book of a self-guided tour of 115 sites, it offers discounts up to 50% at major and lesser-known buildings—everything from palaces to pharmacies. Information and discount vouchers are available at a desk in the entry of the main tourist information office on Plaça de Catalunya. Besides the highlights listed in this chapter, several other of the Route's Top 30 sites are also included in the Eixample walking tour; see p 68.

The Curious Life & Work of Gaudí

"Play the violin," the visionary architect Antoni Gaudí i Cornet (1852–1926) once told a client who was distressed to find no place for his piano in the unorthodox form of his La Pedrera apartment. Gaudí remains best known for his unfinished magnum opus, La Sagrada Família, which continues to baffle and amaze visitors more than 125 years later. Yet few fans realize that the architect's life was as eccentric as his signature works. A pious Catholic and ardent Catalan nationalist who became a religious zealot in his later years, Gaudí had a devil of an imagination but lived an ascetic life. After 1910, he devoted himself entirely to the Sagrada Família, abandoning almost all secular works, and he lived the last years of his life in the workshop of the temple to which he dedicated 44 years. He died ignominiously, run over by a street trolley; taxis refused to take him—destitute, dressed like a pauper, and unrecognizable—to a hospital.

the Eixample but in the much less fashionable district of El Raval, was Gaudí's first big commission from Eusebi Güell, the textile magnate who would become a lifelong confidante and patron. It's heavier and less whimsical than Gaudí's later works—on the outside it looks like a fortress—but the architect's early genius is evident in the underground stables, interconnected floors, and Moorish-style decorative skylights. On the roof is the building's crowd-pleasing surprise, a preview of what would later come with La Pedrera: a small contingent of colorful, *trencadí*-covered chimneys. ⏱ 1 hr. *c/ Nou de la Rambla, 3–5.*

☎ 93-317-39-74. Admission 12€, 8€ *students & seniors. Apr–Oct Tues–Sun 10am–7pm, Nov–Mar Tues–Sun 10am–5:30pm. Metro: Liceu.*

9 ★★ **Casa Calvet.** The best way to cap a day of touring *modernista* landmarks is dinner at this upscale restaurant, in one of Gaudí's earliest (and best preserved) apartment buildings. The 1899 house features one of Barcelona's first elevators and elegant *modernista* details throughout, making for a unique dining experience. *c/ Caspe, 48.* ☎ 93-412-40-12. $$$.

Picasso was a regular at Els Quatre Gats.

Ciutat Vella: Ancient Barcelona

1. Santa Maria del Mar
2. Carrer de Montcada
3. Mercat Princesa
4. Catedral de Barcelona
5. Conjunt Monumental de la Plaça del Rei
6. Roman walls
7. Temple d'Augustus
8. Museu Frederic Marès
9. Plaça de Sant Jaume
10. Caelum
11. Sant Pau del Camp

i Tourist Information
Ⓜ Metro Station

Barcelona is one of Spain's most historic cities. Founded as Barcino by the Romans in A.D. 15, it expanded outside the ancient walls—sections of which still remain—in the 11th century. Much of medieval Barcelona lives on gloriously in the Ciutat Vella (old city) quarters of Barri Gòtic and La Ribera. See the Barri Gòtic walking tour (p 60) for additional details of the Roman and medieval city, including El Call, the old Jewish Quarter. START: **Metro to Jaume I.**

① ★★ **Santa María del Mar.** Designed by the architect Berenguer de Montagut in the mid–14th century and completed in just 5 decades, Santa María del Mar is a soaring Catalan Gothic church that once faced the Barcelona waterfront; its name ("St. Mary of the Sea") refers to its history as a place of worship for ship owners, merchants, and sailors (and wives left behind) who came to pray for safe returns. ⏱ 30 min. See p. 15, **④**.

② **Carrer de Montcada.** At the back entrance to Santa María del Mar, this narrow, pedestrian-only lane through the La Ribera quarter is one of the most handsome medieval streets in Barcelona. From its origins in 1148, the street became an epicenter of commercial life. From the 14th to 17th centuries, Montcada's *palaus*, or mansions, were home to wealthy and noble families, many of whom were patrons of Santa María del Mar. While many *palaus* are private, a few are occupied by museums and galleries, giving visitors a chance to see their gorgeous courtyards and massive central stone staircases. ⏱ 45 min. Metro: Jaume I. See mini-tour on following page.

③ **Mercat Princesa.** Fifteen small vendors offer great food at bargain prices in this medieval courtyard that's been glassed over to create a dining room. Snack on pastry and coffee or lunch on charcuterie, tapas, noodles or rice plates. c/ del Flassaders, 21. ☎ 93-268-15-18. $–$$.

Santa María del Mar is one of Barcelona's purest examples of Catalan Gothic architecture.

④ ★★★ **Catedral de Barcelona.** A Roman temple and later a mosque once stood on this site in the heart of the Gothic Quarter. The lush cloister, built between 1350 and 1448, continues to be home to white geese, which in the Middle Ages functioned as guard dogs, their squawks alerting priests to intruders. Beneath the ancient slabs of the stone floor lie the remains of members of the Barri Gòtic's ancient guilds. ⏱ 30 min. See p 13, **⑫**.

⑤ ★★★ **kids Conjunt Monumental de la Plaça del Rei.** Plaça del Rei abuts a remaining section of the old Roman walls, and in the 1930s archaeologists unearthed ruins of Barcino, the old Roman city. The subterranean ruins (1st c. B.C.–7th c. A.D.) can be visited as part of the fine **Museu d'Història de Barcelona.** The five-story tower Mirador del Rei Martí, which rises above the square, dates to 1555, when it was built as a

lookout for foreign invasions and peasant uprisings. 🕐 *45 min. Pl. del Rei, s/n.* ☎ *93-256-21-00. Admission 7€ adults, 5€ students & seniors. Oct–Mar Tues–Sat 10am–2pm & 4–9pm; Apr–Sept Tues–Sat 10am–8pm; Sun year-round 10am–8pm. Metro: Jaume I.*

Tiny **2A** **Carrer de les Mosques** ("street of the flies") is reputed to be the narrowest street in Barcelona; residents are able to reach out and touch the building across the street from their windows. The 15th-century **2B** **Palau dels Cervelló (no. 25),** today home to a famous contemporary art gallery (Galería Maeght), maintains its original Gothic facade, while the 17th-century **2C** **Palau Dalmases (no. 20)** retains a Gothic chapel and richly carved Renaissance staircase and elegant arches. **2D** **Palau**

Nadal (no. 12–14) was constructed in the 15th and 16th centuries. Next door, the 13th- to 15th-century **2E** **Palau dels Marquesos de Lió (no. 12)** is perhaps the oldest Gothic palace on the street. The tower dates from the 1200s. The 15th-century **2F** **Palau Aguilar (no. 15–23)** is today the site of the **Museu Picasso.** Even if the art weren't inside, the museum would be worth visiting to see the extraordinary Gothic patios and staircases. *See p 15, ②.*

Exploring Barcelona's Hidden History

Visitors to Mercat Santa Caterina in the La Ribera district can enjoy more than a dazzling array of food stalls displaying local fruits, vegetables, flowers, and meats. On one side of the market is an archaeological site, another in the collection of the Museu d'Història de la Ciutat. The excavations trace Barcelona culture from the Bronze Age to the present, including a tomb dating to 1800 B.C. Chief among the ruins are the Dominican monastery of Santa Caterina. The original market was built on the site of the 13th-century church and convent. The complex included a Gothic church, a 14th-century cloister, and a 40m-high bell tower. Both convent and church were burned during anti-clerical riots on July 25, 1835. The city's second enclosed market was erected on the site 10 years later, after the land was ceded to the city by royal decree. Originally named for the then-reigning queen of Spain, Isabel II, it is traditionally known by the name of the destroyed convent and church. Mercat Santa Caterina is located at 16, Av Francesc Cambó; admission to the glass-enclosed interpretive site is free.

Another archaeological site can be found at the Mercat del Born in the nearby Born district. This long-abandoned open-air market reopened in late 2013 to display the remains of structures demolished in the early 1714 following the defeat of Catalunya in the War of Succession, fought to determine who had the right to succeed Charles II as king of Spain. This portion of Barcelona was ordered destroyed by the new King Philip V to make way for the construction of a military installation. El Born Centre Cultural, as it is now known, features the restored 19th-century cast-iron structure, roof, and facade of the market. Inside are thousands of artifacts found during excavations along with interpretive models and videos showcasing everyday life in 18th-century Barcelona. Mercat del Born is located at Plaça Comercial and is open daily from 10am to 6:45pm; admission is free.

6 ★ **kids Roman walls.** Barcino was a small settlement, comprising just 10 hectares (25 acres) enclosed by walls 2m (6½ ft.) thick. Several sections of the Roman walls, enlarged in the 3rd and 4th centuries A.D., remain; some of the best examples are on Plaça Ramon Berenguer, parallel to Via Laietana. To the right of the front entrance to the Catedral de Barcelona, the Portal de l'Angel's twin semicircular towers frame the entrance to carrer del Bisbe. ⏱ *15 min. Metro: Jaume I.*

7 ★ **Temple d'Augustus.** Three massive Corinthian columns, the best-preserved relics of the Roman city, are all that remain of the Temple d'Augustus, the principal temple built in the 1st century B.C. Hidden from view and lower than Barcelona's modern street

The (Hairy) Birth of a Nation

Although the Moors invaded Spain in 711 and would rule over much of its territory for 8 centuries, Catalunya only briefly succumbed to the invaders from North Africa. The Moors retreated after a defeat near the Pyrenees in 732, never establishing a lasting foothold in Catalunya. A 9th-century count with a descriptive name, Guifré el Pilós—Wilfred the Hairy—became a feudal lord and the founding father of Catalunya, unifying and then forging the region's independence. He founded a dynasty in 878 that ruled for nearly 500 years. Much of Spain remained under Moorish domination, but Barcelona and Catalunya were linked instead to northern Europe, a geopolitical wrinkle that formed the basis for the fiercely independent and northward-looking Catalan character. The hero of Catalunya has been mythologized in the region's flag, which features four horizontal red stripes on a yellow field (and is said to be the oldest still in use in Europe today). According to legend, the red bars were first etched in Wilfred's own blood on his golden shield (perhaps as he lay dying in battle). Scholars cast doubt on the veracity of the tale, but most Catalans believe it to be true.

level, they are one of the Barri Gòtic's great secrets. The temple once formed part of the Roman Forum dedicated to the emperor Caesar Augustus. *c/ del Paradis, 10 (inside Centre Excursionista de Catalunya).* ☎ 93-315-23-11. *Free admission. June–Sept Mon–Sat 10am–8pm, Sun 10am–2pm; Oct–May daily 10am–2pm & 4–8pm. Metro: Jaume I.*

❽ ★★ **Museu Frederic Marès.** Marès, a 20th-century sculptor and obsessive collector, amassed one of Spain's finest private collections of medieval sculpture, from the pre-Roman to the Romanesque, Gothic, Baroque, and Renaissance eras. The vast majority of the collection is polychrome Gothic religious sculpture. The collection is housed in a palace—itself worthy of study, with its handsome interior courtyards, carved stone, and expansive ceilings—just behind the Catedral. ⏱ *45 min. Pl. de Sant Lú,*

5–6. ☎ *93-310-58-00. www.museu mares.bcn.es. Admission 4.20€ adults, 2.40€ seniors & students. Mon & Wed–Sat 10am–7pm; Sun 11am–8pm. Free Sun 3–8pm. Metro: Jaume I.*

The Temple d'Augustus columns date to the 1st century B.C. (p 33).

Barcelona's Roman walls (p 33).

⑨ ★ Plaça de Sant Jaume.
The site of the city and regional governments, this stately plaza is also a popular gathering place for Barcelonans during holiday celebrations and political demonstrations. The **Palau de la Generalitat,** home to the autonomous Catalunian government, dates to the 15th century, while across the square the 14th-century **Casa de la Ciutat,** built around a central courtyard, houses the municipal government. The **Saló de Cent** (Room of 100 Jurors) features immense arches, typical of the Catalan Gothic style. ⏱ *30 min. Casa de la Ciutat: Pl. de Sant Jaume, s/n.* ☎ *93-402-70-00. Free admission. Sun 11am–3:30pm. Metro: Jaume I.*

🔟 ★ Caelum. On the surface this appears to be simply an appealing shop selling teas, jams, olive oil, sweets, and other products made by nuns and religious orders in Spain and Europe. But downstairs in the cafe (where you can have tea, coffee, pastries, and sandwiches), in a space referred to as "the crypt," is another treat altogether: the exposed foundations of 14th-century Jewish baths (mikves or mikva'ot). *c/ de la Palla, 8.* ☎ *93-302-69-93. $.*

⑪ ★★ Sant Pau del Camp.
The oldest church in Barcelona, dating back to the 9th century, "Saint Paul of the Countryside" was once a rural church and part of a monastery, far beyond the city walls. It remains remarkably intact, with original Romanesque capitals and bases of the portal complementing sections from a rebuilding in the 11th and 12th centuries. The chapter house holds the tomb—which reads A.D. 912—of Count Guífre Borrell, son of Wilfred the Hairy (above). ⏱ *30 min. c/ de Sant Pau, 99 (El Raval).* ☎ *93-441-00-01. Admission to cloister 3€. Mon–Sat 10am–12:30pm & 4–6:30pm. Metro: Paral.lel.*

Barcelona for Modern-Art Lovers

Map labels:

Casa Milà (La Pedrera)
Casa de les Punxes
Rosselló
Provença
Provença
Casa Thomas
Av. Diagonal
Verdaguer
Mallorca
Av. Diagonal
Rambla
Pg. de Gràcia
Pau Claris
Roger de Llúria
Bruc
Girona
Bailèn
Mallorca
Balmes
Aribau
València
L'EIXAMPLE
Passeig de Gràcia
Mercat de la Concepció
Aragó
Pg. Sant Joan
Nàpols
Plaça Dr. Letamendi
Aragó
Consell de Cent
Consell de Cer
Manzana de la Disconcordia
Pg. de Gràcia
Diputació
Girona
Diputació
Universitat de Barcelona
Torre d'Aigües
Plaça Tetuan
Roger de Flor
Universitat
Gran Via Corts Catalanes
Tetuan
Casp
Rda. de St. Antoni
Ronda Universitat
Plaça Universitat
Casp
Pau Claris
Roger de Llúria
Bruc
Girona
Bailèn
Pg. Sant Joan
Casa de la Caritat
Plaça Catalunya
Urquinaona
Ausiàs Marc
Alí Bei
Ribes
Museu d'Art Contemporani de Barcelona
Fontanella
Ronda Sant Pere
Arc de Triomf
Estació del Norc
Catalunya
Antic Hospital de la Sta. Creu
Palau de la Música Catalana
Portal de l'Àngel
Via Laietana
LA RIBERA
Arc de Triomf
Lluís Companys
Palau de Justicia
Portaferrissa
Av. Catedral
Mercat Sta. Caterina
Robador
Mercat de la Boqueria
Sta. María del Pi
Catedral
Plaça Allada Vermell
Comerç
Passeig de Pujade
Museu Zoologia
Parc de la Ciutadella
Generalitat
Jaume I
Princesa
Montcada
Museu Geologia
Gran Teatre del Liceu
Liceu
Ajuntament
BARRI GÒTIC
Mercat del Born
Passeig de Picasso
Parlament de Catalunya
Nou de la Rambla
CIUTAT VELLA
Arauí
Llotja de Mar
Sta. María del Mar
La Mercè
Mercè
Plaça Antonio López
Plaça del Palau
Estació de França
Zoo de Barcelona
Av. Drassanes
Drassanes
Passeig de Colom (Ronda Litoral)
Barceloneta
Reials Drassanes (Museu Maritim)
Palau de Mar (Museu d'Història de Catalunya)
Moll de Barcelona
Rambla da Mar
Port Vell
IMAX
Maremàgnum
L'Aquàrium de Barcelona
BARCELONETA
MEDITERRANEAN SEA

Scale: 0 — 1/4 mile / 0 — 1/4 km

Inset map: St. Martí / L'Eixample / Parc de la Ciutadella / Ciutat Vella / Map Area / Montjuïc

i Tourist Information
Ⓜ Metro Station

1 Fundació Joan Miró
2 Fundació Antoni Tàpies
3 Carrer Consell de Cent galleries
4' Bar Lobo
5 Museu d'Art Contemporani de Barcelona (MACBA)
6 Museu Picasso
7' El Xampanyet
8 Ciutat Vella galleries

Barcelona has a long tradition of embracing adventurous art and eccentric artists. Picasso began his career here, and the Catalans Miró, Dalí, and Tàpies all made their marks in Barcelona before becoming international superstars. Barcelona's lively art scene of museums and galleries is especially strong in contemporary and modern art, though this is a tour for those who have the stamina to take in several museums back to back. For a superb collection of Gothic art, don't miss **MNAC** (p 20, ⑦). START: **Metro to Espanya (or funicular to Montjuïc).**

❶ ★★★ **Fundació Joan Miró.** Miró, born in rural Catalunya in 1893, became one of the 20th century's most important artists. His whimsical and enigmatic abstract forms expressed complex themes, including sexuality, Catalan national identity, and opposition to the Spanish Civil War. Miró himself donated 11,000 works to the museum. Pivotal works include the 1970s tapestry *Tapis de la Fundació; L'Estel Matinal,* part of the Constellation Series; and mid-century sculptures, including *Sun Bird* and *Moon Bird.* The museum's audioguide is especially insightful. ⓘ *1 hr. See p 20,* ❹.

❷ ★★ **Fundació Antoni Tàpies.** One of Spain's great artists of the 20th century is the abstract expressionist Antoni Tàpies, born in Barcelona in 1923. Tàpies is known for his collage and mixed-media "matter" paintings that incorporate earth, sand, and even pedestrian items such as socks into large canvasses. His work is replete with politically charged and religious imagery, as well as graffiti-like words and insignias. Few artists before or since have done so much with an X. The giant tangle of steel on the roof of this emblematic *modernista* building, designed by Domènech i Montaner, is the artist's once-controversial sculpture (now accepted by most Barcelonans) called *Cloud and Chair.* ⓘ *45 min. c/ Aragó, 255.*

The sculpture Cloud and Chair *sits atop the Fundacío Antoni Tàpies.*

☎ *93-487-03-15. www.fundacio tapies.org. Admission 7€ adults, 5.60€ students. Tues–Sun 10am–7pm. Closed Mon, Dec 25–26 & Jan 1–6.*

❸ **Carrer Consell de Cent.** This leafy Eixample street, between Passeig de Gràcia and Muntaner, is one of the most frequented in Barcelona for its contemporary art galleries. Among the galleries to keep an eye out for: **Sala Dalmau** (no. 349; ☎ 93-215-45-92); **Jordi Barnadas** (no. 347; ☎ 93-215-63-65); **Senda** (no. 337; ☎ 93-487-67-59); **Galería René Metras** (no. 331; ☎ 93-487-58-74); **Galería Llucià Homs** (no. 315; ☎ 93-467-71-62); **Galería Carles Tache** (no. 290; ☎ 93-487-88-36); **Ambit** (no. 282;

☎ 93-488-18-00); and **Galería Eude** (no. 278; ☎ 93-487-93-86). ⏱ *1 hr. Metro: Pg. de Gràcia.*

④ **Bar Lobo.** This cool tapas bar is decorated with graffiti murals and the kind of concert posters and ads that usually litter city walls. It's great for lunchtime snacks or late-night drinks. *c/ Pintor Fortuny, 3.* ☎ 93-481-53-46. $–$$.

⑤ ★ **Museu d'Art Contemporani de Barcelona (MACBA).** This gleaming white 1995 Richard Meier design remains a stark contrast in the emerging Raval quarter, but the Museum of Contemporary Art is continually expanding its permanent collection of works by Calder, Basquiat, and Klee, as well as major Catalan artists such as Tàpies and Miquel Barceló. ⏱ *45 min. Pl. dels Angels, 1.* ☎ *93-412-08-10. www.macba.es. Admission 10€ adults, 8€ students, free for seniors & children 14 & under (also part of ArticketBCN joint admission). Mon & Wed–Fri 11am–7:30pm; Sat 10am–8pm; Sun 10am–3pm. Free guided tours in English Mon 4 & 6pm, Wed–Sat 4pm. Metro: Catalunya or Universitat.*

⑥ ★★★ **Museu Picasso.** Picasso (1881–1973) donated 2,500

Sunlight provides brilliant, natural interior lighting at Museo d'Art Contemporani.

paintings and sculptures to this museum, the largest representation of his work in Spain, in 1970. While especially strong on the artist's early development, including his Blue and Rose periods (Picasso's early talents for traditional portraiture and figurative painting are a revelation), the highlight is his playful series of 59 paintings based on Velázquez's seminal work *Las Meninas.* Also of note are *The Harlequin* and the young artist's sketch notebooks of Barcelona street scenes. Picasso fans should not miss the new gallery of eight works, including *Woman in Hat and Fur Collar,* at the superb **MNAC** (p 20, ⑦) on Montjuïc hill. ⏱ *1 hr. See p 15,* ②.

⑦ **El Xampanyet.** A wonderful throwback, this classic and gregarious cava bar serves its sparkling wine (here, more a fizzy white wine than cava) in '50s-style glasses. An excellent selection of Catalan cheeses, salamis, and more is on offer. *c/ de Montcada, 22.* ☎ 93-319-70-03. $.

The Carles Tache gallery.

Barcelona's Outdoor Sculpture

Not all of Barcelona's great art is behind museum doors; the city is full of outdoor sculpture. If you arrive by air, you may first see Joan Miró's giant **mosaic mural** (1970) outside Terminal B at the Barcelona Airport. Look also for the great Basque sculptor Eduardo Chillida's **Topos V** in Plaça del Rei; Roy Lichtenstein's **Cap de Barcelona** (1992) at the intersection of Moll de la Fusta and Vía Laietana; Antoni Tàpies's glass-enclosed **Homage to Picasso** (1983) on Passeig Picasso, at the entrance to Parc de la Ciutadella; Miró's **Woman and Bird** (1982) in Parc Joan Miró, near Estació de Sants; **Pla de l'Ós,** the Miró mosaic underfoot on La Rambla (across from the Teatre Liceu opera house); and a couple for the kids, Xavier Mariscal's **giant crayfish** on Moll de la Fusta and Frank Gehry's monumental **Fish** sculpture on the beach at Vila Olímpica in front of Hotel Arts.

Antoni Tápies's Homage to Picasso.

⑧ Ciutat Vella galleries.

Although the bulk of contemporary and modern art galleries are in L'Eixample, those in the old city pose a dramatic contrast to the ancient surroundings. The Barri Gòtic streets Petritxol and Palla mix art galleries in with boutiques and antiques dealers. Galleries worth seeking out are **Galería Maeght** (c/ de Montcada, 25; ☎ 93-310-42-45); **Artur Ramón Espai Contemporani** (c/ de la Palla, 10; ☎ 93-301-16-48); **Trama** (Petritxol, 8; ☎ 93-317-48-77); and the city's oldest gallery, **Sala Parés** (Petritxol, 5; ☎ 93-318-70-08). ⏱ *1 hr. Metro: Jaume I.*

Inside the Museu Picasso.

Barcelona for Design & Architecture Fans

1. CaixaForum
2. Pavelló Mies van der Rohe
3. Palau d'Esports Sant Jordi
4. Transbordador Aeri del Port
5. Vila Olímpica
6. Cuines de Santa Caterina
7. Mercat de Santa Caterina
8. Museu d'Art Contemporani de Barcelona (MACBA)
9. Casa de la Caritat
10. L'Eixample shopping
11. Suites Avenue
12. Roca Bar

LES CORTS

Plaça Francesc Macià

Av. Buenos Aires

Av. Diagonal

Av. Josep Tarradellas

Av. Sarrià

Londres

Paris

Ecola Industriel

Còrsega

Rosselló

Viladomat

Comte d'Urgell

Hospital Clinic

Provença

Mallorca

Av. Roma

València

Aragó

L'EIXAMPLE

Villarroel

Casanova

Muntaner

Aribau

Parc de Joan Miró

Consell de Cent

Creu Coberta

Ctra. de la Bordeta

Diputació

Plaça Toros Las Arenas

Gran Via Corts Catalanes

Plaça Espanya

Gran Via Corts Catalanes

Sepúlveda

Plaça Univers

Av. Paral·lel

Mistral

Floridablanca

Ronda de St. Antoni

MACBA

Poble Espanyol

Pavelló

Plaça de Carlos Buigas

Tamarit

Mercat de St. Antoni

EL RAVAL

MNAC

LA FRANÇA

Manso

Ronda St. Pau

Palau Nacional

Museu Arqueológic

Parlament

Av. Paral·lel

La Rambla del Raval

Palau St. Jordi

Estadi Olímpic

Plaça Neptú

Fundació Joan Miró

POBLE SEC

Exposició

Nou de la Rambla

Av. Drassanes

MONTJUÏC

PARC DE MONTJUÏC

Av. Miramar

Plaça Carlos Ibáñez

Reials Drassanes (Museu Marítim)

Transbordador Aeri

Castell de Montjuïc

Museu Militar

Ronda Litoral

World Trade Center

Moll de la Costa

Moll de Ponent

0   1/2 mile

0   1/2 km

Although visitors flock to Barcelona for its *modernista* architecture and picturesque Gothic Quarter, the forward-looking Catalan capital is also a favorite with fans of contemporary architecture and design. The 1992 Olympic Games provided a huge impetus for adventurous urban planning projects. As the dean of Harvard's Graduate School of Design proclaimed, "Unlike many other cities, Barcelona seems to have chosen architecture and urbanism as its most conspicuous, long-lasting, and crowning glory." From the new Ricardo Bofill terminal at El Prat airport to the emerging El Raval neighborhood, cutting-edge design is everywhere in Barcelona. START: **Metro to Plaça Espanya.**

① ★ CaixaForum. The 2002 conversion of a 1911 red-brick *modernista* textile factory (by Puig i Cadafalch), by the Japanese architect Arata Isozaki and three others, transformed it into a brilliant new art exhibition space. It's a terrific synthesis of Barcelona's dominant design motifs—*modernista* and cutting-edge contemporary—and a terrace on the roof provides great views of the Palau Nacional, home to the Museu Nacional d'Art de Catalunya, and Montjuïc hill (p 20, **⑦**). ① *30 min. Av. Marquès de Comillas, 6–8.* ☎ *93-476-86-00. www.fundacio.lacaixa.es. Free admission. Tues–Sun 10am–8pm (Sat until 10pm). Metro: Pl. Espanya.*

② ★★ Pavelló Mies van der Rohe. The famous minimalist German architect created this steel, glass, and marble structure as the German Pavilion for the 1929 World's Fair. Considered a classic of 20th-century design, it is recognized for its pure, precise lines. The interior holds little save van der Rohe's original Barcelona Chair, today a much-reproduced icon of modern design. The pavilion, unceremoniously banished from the city after the Fair, was returned to its original location in 1985 after prominent architects petitioned the city. ① *30 min. Av. Marquès de Comillas, s/n.* ☎ *93-423-40-16. www.miesbcn.com. Admission 5€ adults, 2.60€ students, free for children 15 & under. Daily 10am–8pm. Metro: Pl. Espanya.*

③ Palau d'Esports Sant Jordi. Arata Isozaki's sleek indoor sports stadium held gymnastic, volleyball, and basketball events during the '92 Olympics. When it was first

The Pavelló Mies van der Rohe is considered a classic of 20th-century design.

Frank Gehry's Fish *sculpture at the Vila Olímpica.*

opened to the public, some 50,000 Barcelonans turned out to see the new addition to Montjuïc's Olympic Ring. Today it hosts both sporting events and concerts. Lording over it is the once-despised **Telefónica communications tower,** also built for the '92 Olympics, by the famed architect from Valencia, Santiago Calatrava. The tower's base is decorated with broken ceramic tiles, an homage to Gaudí. ⓘ *30 min. Av. del Estadi, s/n (Parc de Montjuïc). Metro: Pl. Espanya (then take the escalator from Palau Nacional); alternatively, take bus no. 50.*

④ ★ kids **Transbordador Aeri del Port.** A great way to appreciate the layout of Barcelona, especially L'Eixample's grid designed by Ildefons Cerdà in 1859, is to take the aerial cable car from Montjuïc down to the port area and Barceloneta. *See p 19,* ③.

⑤ ★ **Vila Olímpica.** The award-winning urban-design project that revamped the waterfront created an entirely new neighborhood of apartment buildings, gardens, and large public sculptures, by a host of both celebrated and young architects, designers, and artists. The apartment blocks first housed Olympic athletes before being turned over to private buyers, and in the years since, Vila Olímpica has

become a fashionable neighborhood. The waterfront's twin towers, among Barcelona's only skyscrapers (one is Hotel Arts, the other an office complex), were initially polemical, but their presence is now widely accepted. In front of Hotel Arts is Frank Gehry's massive, metal-lattice *Fish* sculpture, which appears to glow in the afternoon sun. ⓘ *45 min. Metro: Ciutadella–Vila Olímpica.*

The Antoni Llena sculpture David and Goliath *in front of the Hotel Arts.*

Architecture Superstars

For design-crazy sorts who can't get enough, a number of relatively recent contributions to Barcelona's urban landscape are by celebrated architects in the zone north of Vila Olímpica, near Plaça de les Glòries. Pritzker prizewinner Rafael Moneo built the sleek white concert hall **L'Auditori** (c/ Lepant, 150), while nearby the glass-fronted **Teatre Nacional de Catalunya** (Pl. de les Arts, 1) is by Barcelona native Ricardo Bofill. Fast becoming a symbol of the city is Jean Nouvel's **Torre Agbar** (Av. Diagonal, 209–211), a tall (142m/465 ft.), phallic skyscraper that's illuminated at night with the blue and red of Barça, the local *fútbol* (soccer) team. Several blocks west (along Ronda St. Martí at Felip II) is Santiago Calatrava's *Pont Bac de Roda*, a white, arching bridge and work of stellar engineering by the man who has quickly become Spain's most famous architect, with projects in place across the globe.

6 ★★ **Cuines de Santa Caterina.** This cool tapas bar and restaurant makes the best of its privileged location inside the market and offers the freshest of seafood and vegetables, and inexpensive wines by the glass or carafe. It's a great spot for an array of small plates. *Av. Francesc Cambó, 16.* ☎ 93-268-99-18. $–$$.

7 ★★ **Mercat Santa Caterina.** The 21st-century remodeling of this 1848 food market—the first covered market in Barcelona—is famed for its colorful and undulating mosaic-tile roof. The project was the work of the celebrated firm of Enric Miralles and Benedetta Tagliabue. ⏲ *30 min. Av. Francesc Cambó, 16. www.mercatsantacaterina.net. Mon 7:30am–2pm; Tues–Wed and Sat 7:30am–3:30pm; Thurs–Fri 7:30am–8:30pm.*

8 ★ **Museu d'Art Contemporani de Barcelona (MACBA).** Much as Frank Gehry's Guggenheim Bilbao stimulated the arts and urban development in that Basque city, Richard Meier's MACBA has been the impetus for updating and

The colorful, wavelike roof of Mercat Santa Caterina.

The Richard Meier–designed Museu d'Art Contemporani de Barcelona (MACBA).

integrating the district of El Raval. Art galleries, boutiques, bars, and restaurants, as well as new hotels and apartment buildings, have followed, displacing many longtime residents but overall making the northern section of the neighborhood safer and more attractive. ⏱ *45 min. See p 38,* ❺.

❾ ★ **Casa de la Caritat.** One of the first projects undertaken in the revamping of the formerly marginal Raval district was the conversion of this 13th-century convent and charity hospital into an art and culture space. Two avant-garde Catalan architects, Albert Viaplana and Helio Piñón, gave the Centre de Cultura Contemporània de Barcelona (CCCB) an angled wall of glass that reflects neighborhood rooftops and the Mediterranean Sea. ⏱ *45 min. c/ de Montalegre, 5–9.* ☎ *93-306-41-00. www.cccb.org. Tues–Sun 11am–8pm. Admission 6€, seniors & students 4€. Metro: Catalunya or Universitat.*

❿ ★ **L'Eixample Shopping.** A day of design for the fashion-conscious would be senseless without at least a couple of stops at Barcelona's renowned design emporiums. **Vinçon** (Passeig de Gràcia, 96) is a local institution for housewares, lamps, and furniture, all selected

for their innovative design. Also visit the shops of Catalan fashion designers **Antonio Miró** (La Rambla Catalunya, 125) and **Armand Basi** (Pg. de Gràcia, 49), two of the hippest clothiers in town. ⏱ *45 min. Metro: Pg. de Gràcia or Provença. See p 78.*

⓫ ★ **Suites Avenue.** It seems there's always a new building by an important international architect creating a buzz in Barcelona. One of the newest talked-about entries is this hotel facade by famed contemporary Japanese architect Toyo Ito. The undulating stainless-steel facade mimics the waves of Gaudí's La Pedrera, which is right across the street, and is a fascinating addition to the *modernista* structures lining elegant Passeig de Gràcia. Architecture buffs will dig the expansive views of La Pedrera from the apartments here. ⏱ *15 min. Pg. de Gràcia, 83. Metro: Pg. de Gràcia or Provença.*

⓬ **Roca Bar.** In the lobby of the high-design Hotel Omm, a hot spot with fashionable types, is the informal and less pricey cousin to Moo, the ultra-hip restaurant of the Roca brothers. Serving street food and great drink, it won't break the bank. *c/ Roselló, 265– 269.* ☎ *93-445-40-00. $$.*

The Best Special-Interest Tours

Gourmet Barcelona

1 Crustó	**9** La Pineda
2 Colmado Quílez	**10** Mesón del Café
3 Cacao Sampaka	**11** Formatgeria La Seu
4 La Cuina d'en Garriga	**12** E & A Gispert
5 Granja Viader	**13** Vila Viniteca/La Teca
6 Mercat de la Boqueria	**14** Mercat de la
7 El Quim de	Barceloneta
la Boqueria	**15** L'Electricitat
8 Carrer Petritxol	

With its rise as a foodie capital, Barcelona now rivals San Sebastián and even Paris. Barcelona's innovative dining scene, the new boites by the Adrià brothers, and the exploits of the Roca brothers are prompting food pilgrims to discover the coolest culinary stops in the Catalan capital. Besides haute-cuisine restaurants and chef-driven tapas bars, you'll find scores of old-school colmados (grocery stores), inventive chocolatiers, and gourmet food and wine shops. Strap on your feed bag, but note that on Mondays several shops are closed (and on Sundays La Bouquería market is), and some places (like Granja Viader) have odd hours, closing for long stretches of the afternoon. START: **Metro to Liceu.**

❶ ★ Crustó. Start your day off with some incredible baked goods and artisanal breads from this rustic yet modern bakery/cafe, prized by chefs and gourmands as one of the finest in the city. It's low-key but always swarmed with locals, leaving the buzz to competitors like (admittedly very cool-looking) Barcelona-Reykjavik (Doctor Dou, 12; Raval). ⏱ *20 min. c/ València, 246.* ☎ *93-487-05-51. www.crusto.es. Metro: Pg. de Gràcia.*

Gourmet Tip

For more suggestions on where to buy and eat your favorite gourmet items, see also "The Best Shopping," p 71, and "The Best Dining," p 93.

❷ ★★ Colmado Quílez. This 1908 grocery store and wine shop, the most famous *colmado* in Barcelona, is a charming throwback. Floor-to-ceiling shelves are stocked with gourmet packaged goods, while back rooms stock wines from across Spain and even 300 types of beer. You have to select your item, pay for it, and get a ticket before picking up the goods. ⏱ *20 min. Rambla de Catalunya, 63.* ☎ *93-215-23-56. www.lafuente.es. Metro: Pg. de Gràcia.*

❸ ★★ Cacao Sampaka. Best described as designer chocolate, with items categorized into "collections," such as "flowers and herbs," and so on. Repair to the bar/cafe for delicious hot chocolate, pastries, and sandwiches. ⏱ *30 min. c/ Consell de Cent, 292.* ☎ *93-272-08-33. Metro: Pg. de Gràcia.*

❹ ★★ La Cuina d'en Garriga. Helen Garriga's gourmet temple dedicated to all things culinary stocks carefully selected Catalan foodstuffs from the city's finest independent purveyors, such as artisanal bread, and sought-after appliances and items for the kitchen. Sample the goods at the tasting room in back. ⏱ *20 min. c/ Consell de Cent, 308.* ☎ *93-215-72-15. Metro: Pg. de Gràcia.*

Colmado Quílez is an old-school Barcelona grocery store.

5 ★ **Granja Viader.** Although the old neighborhood of El Raval has seen a huge amount of upheaval, this place with marble-topped tables has resisted change. A gloriously authentic granja, or "milkbar," (the oldest in Barcelona, since 1870), it's known for thick chocolate drinks, such as xocolata desfeta and the original cacaolat, a bottled chocolate drink famous throughout Spain. c/ Xuclà, 4–6. ☎ 93-318-34-86. www.granjaviader.cat. $.

6 ★★★ **Mercat de la Boquería.** Barcelona's largest food market is a gastronomic paradise. The market, just off La Rambla, dates to 1840; today it has more than 300 stalls stocked with eye-popping displays of salted fish, exotic fruits, wild mushrooms (ceps and bolets), and more. You can eat, too, at the gourmet kiosks El Quim and Bar Pintxo as well as a couple of restaurants in the back. ⏱ 1 hr. See p 12, **9**.

7 ★★ **El Quim de la Boquería.** Quim has been at the helm of this bustling kiosk bar (taburete) within La Boquería food market nearly a quarter-century. Prized by fellow chefs and foodies-in-the-know, it's a place for fresh grilled seafood and tapas of the highest order. La Rambla, 91 (parada no. 584/585). ☎ 93-301-98-20. $$. See p 102.

8 **Carrer Petritxol.** One of the Gothic Quarter's most atmospheric streets is lined with granjas, or milk bars, xocolaterias, and pastisserias, all tempting the taste buds. ⏱ 25 min. Metro: Liceu.

9 ★ **La Pineda.** This tiny char-cuterie storefront, in business since 1930, is where many visitors first tasted real Spanish ham. It is jam-packed with jamón Serrano, chorizos, cheeses, wines, olive oils, canned goods, and other gourmet products. If you're lucky enough to score one of the few marble-topped tables and not too full from previous stops, dive into a selection of tapas. ⏱ 15 min. c/ del Pi, 16. [tel 93-302-43-93. Metro: Liceu.

10 **Mesón del Café.** This tiny, century-old place is just ineffably cool. Locals drop in at all hours for superb cortado, but after several gourmet stops, go for a mean picardía (coffee with layers of condensed milk and whiskey). c/ Llibretería, 16. ☎ 93-315-07-54. $.

11 ★ **Formatgeria La Seu.** A Scotswoman passionate about artisanal Spanish farmhouse cheese runs this cool cheese shop, which stocks a couple dozen mostly unpasteurized cheeses from across Catalunya and Spain (formal tastings, breakfast, and lunch are offered). ⏱ 30 min. c/ d'Augeria, 16. ☎ 93-412-65-48. www.formatgeriala-seu.com. Metro: Jaume I. Closed Aug.

The old-fashioned milk bar Granja Viader.

A few of the bountiful offerings at La Boquería.

⑫ ★★ **E&A Gispert.** One of the oldest continuously running shops in Barcelona (since 1851) sells coffee and teas, dried fruits and nuts, honey and jams, and traditional Catalan *torrón* desserts, as well as gift baskets and other artisanal and organic products. Possibly the most redolent place you'll ever poke your nose into, the shop retains the original one-piece counter and wood shelves and still uses a spectacular 150-year-old, wood-burning nut roaster—the only one of its kind in Europe. ⏱ *30 min. c/ dels Sombrerers, 23.* ☎ *93-319-73-35. www.casagispert.com. Metro: Jaume I.*

⑬ ★★ **Vila Viniteca/La Teca.** From cult wines like Pingus to small-yield Priorats, including plenty of bottles you can't get outside Spain, this is Barcelona's wine temple, with more than 6,000 choices. Check out scheduled *catas* (wine tastings) at www.vilaviniteca. es. Don't miss the little gourmet shop, La Teca, next door. ⏱ *30 min. c/ Agullers, 7.* ☎ *93-268-32-27. Metro: Jaume I.*

⑭ **Mercat de la Barceloneta.** Redesigned, just like much of the formerly blue-collar and fishermen's neighborhood that surrounds it, this covered food market has a new spring in its step, and like Mercat

de Santa Caterina and La Boquería, is also a great place to sit down for lunch or dinner once you've checked out all the fresh fish, meats, and produce inside. ⏱ *30 min. Pl. de la Font, 1.* ☎ *93-221-64-71. Metro: Barceloneta.*

⑮ ★ **L'Electricitat.** Just a block from the market, this popular old-time tapas bar justifies its name—the atmosphere is positively electric. Among the best bets are steamed mussels, fried fish, anchovies, and crab salad. Along with wine and beer, there's house vermouth on tap from big barrels. *c/ Sant Carles, 15.* ☎ *93-221-50-17. Metro: Barceloneta. $.*

Mercat de la Barceloneta.

Barcelona with Kids

1. La Rambla
2. Reials Drassanes
   (Museu Marítim)
3. Mirador de Colom
4. Waterfront
5. Parc Zoològic/
   La Ciutadella
6. Agua
7. El Transbordador
   Aeri del Port
8. El Poble Espanyol
9. Parc Güell
10. CosmoCaixa
    (Museu de la Ciència)

Sophisticated Barcelona might seem like a city just for grown-ups, but it has plenty to offer children of all ages. Much of the fun is outdoors, from La Rambla's amusing, costumed mimes and Gaudí's whimsical park to the family-oriented waterfront and zoo in the city's largest green space. Kids are sure to love the aerial cable car from the port to Montjuïc and the antique Blue Tram that climbs the hill to Tibidabo, but you might want to tackle this tour over 2 days, leaving Parc Güell and Poble Espanyol for tomorrow.
START: **Metro to Plaça de Catalunya.**

① ★★★ **La Rambla.** You'll need to watch your kids closely amid the throngs, but La Rambla's human theater is enhanced by creative human statues—from Roman soldiers to mummies—that spring to life for a coin or two. ⏱ *45 min. See p 11,* **⑧.**

② ★★ **Reials Drassanes (Museu Marítim).** Older kids will love the magnificent ships at this seafaring museum, housed in stunning medieval shipyards. ⏱ *1 hr. See p 19,* **①.**

③ **Mirador de Colom.** Take the elevator to the top of this Christopher Columbus monument overlooking the old port for fantastic views. ⏱ *30 min. See p 19,* **②.**

④ ★★ **Waterfront.** On the other side of the cool, pedestrian-only Rambla del Mar drawbridge are excellent options for families:

A performer on La Rambla.

L'Aquàrium, a huge, well-designed aquarium with a glass-enclosed tunnel that produces the effect of fish, eels, and sharks swimming around and over wide-eyed visitors; a traditional **carousel** for younger children; and **Maremàgnum** shopping mall, with lots of shops geared

View marine life galore at L'Aquàrium.

Evening Entertainment for Families

If kids and parents are both raring to go at night, consider these options:

The nostalgic amusement park **Parc d'Atraccions Tibidabo,** with a magnificent chair ride that appears to dangle high above the city below. *See p 22,* ⑨.

Font Màgica, the colorful, dancing fountains set to pop tunes at the base of Montjuïc (Pl. Carles Buïgas, 1; May–Oct Thurs–Sun every half-hour between 9:30 and 11:30pm, Oct–Sept Fri–Sat every half-hour between 7 and 8:30pm; free admission; Metro: Pl. Espanya).

IMAX Port Vell theatre (Moll de Espanya; ☎ 93-225-11-11; www.imaxportvell.com; admission 8.75€–13€; Metro: Drassanes).

A match of Barcelona's hugely popular **fútbol,** or soccer, team, "Barça," at **FC Barcelona/Camp Nou,** c/ Aristides Maillol, s/n (☎ **93-496-36-00;** www.fcbarcelona.com). Tickets (available online) start at 26€. Visits to the Camp Nou stadium and museum are also available, 19€ children, 25€ adults. Metro: Collblanc.

---

toward kids. You can also board double-decker swallow boats, **Las Golondrinas,** to cruise the harbor, or stroll along the **Moll de la Fusta** boardwalk; there's a sculpture of a giant, cartoon-like crayfish waiting for kids at the end. ⏰ *2 hr. L'Aquàrium:* ☎ 93-221-74-74. www. aquariumbcn.com. *Admission 20€ adults, 15€ children 5–10 & seniors, 5€ 0.9m–1.1m tall, free under 0.9m. July–Aug Mon–Fri 9:30am–9pm, Sat–Sun 9:30am–11pm; June & Sept Mon–Fri 9:30am–9pm, Sat–Sun 9:30am–9:30pm; Oct–May daily 9:30am–9pm. Metro: Drassanes.*

⑤ ★★ **Parc Zoològic/La Ciutadella.** Barcelona's largest city park is a great place for kids to unwind, with a large pond and rowboats, a massive Gaudí-designed fountain, and a vintage greenhouse. But the zoo is probably the main draw. Although its star attraction, an albino gorilla, passed on a few years ago, several of his (non-albino) off-spring are here, as well as llamas, lions, bears, hippos, and a large primate community—most are not behind bars, but kept in their "enclosures" by a slightly more humane moat. ⏰ *1 hr. Parc de la Ciutadella.* ☎ 902-45-75-45. www. zoobarcelona.cat. *Admission 20€ adults, 12€ students & children 3–12, 10€ seniors. Summer daily 10am–7pm; off season daily 10am–5:30pm. Metro: Ciutadella or Arc de Triomf.*

⑥ **Agua.** Near Port Olímpic and the beach is this informal and good-value restaurant with outdoor tables overlooking the water. The Mediterranean menu features seafood and risottos, with plenty of items for the kids, and you can just get some small plates and drinks and feast your eyes on the beach. *Pg. Marítim de la Barceloneta, 30.* ☎ 93-225-12-72. $–$$.

Parc de la Ciutadella is one of Barcelona's most popular green spaces.

❼ ★★ El Transbordador Aeri del Port. Taking the aerial cable car from Barceloneta high above the port and city on the way up to Montjuïc is like a theme-park ride for kids. *See p 19,* ❸.

❽ ★ El Poble Espanyol. Created for the 1929 Barcelona International Exhibition, this re-creation of a Spanish village contains 100-plus styles of architecture from across Spain, with emblematic mansions, churches, streets, and squares reduced to scale. Though purists may find it well-meaning kitsch, it's a fun and instructive place for families and a great introduction to the country's architectural diversity—a taste of Spain's whitewashed Andalusian alleyways, small-town plazas, and Renaissance palaces. ⏱ *1 hr. Av. Marqués de Comillas, s/n (Parc de Montjuïc).* ☎ *93-508-63-00. www.poble-espanyol.com. Admission 11€ adults, 7.40€ seniors & students, 6.25€ children 4–12, free for children 3 & under; 30€ family ticket, 6.50€ night ticket; joint admission to MNAC 18€. Mon 9am–8pm; Tues–Thurs 9am–2am; Fri 9am–4am; Sat 9am–5am; Sun 9am–midnight. Metro: Espanya, then 10-min. walk uphill, or bus no. 13 or 50 from Pl. de Espanya.*

❾ ★★★ Parc Güell. Gaudí's wildly imaginative park is mostly playground, and kids love it. Stone columns look like trees, gatehouses look transported from Hansel and Gretel, and the gurgling, mosaic-covered lizard fountain simply looks adorable. It's a great place for hide-and-seek. On a clear day, you can see past the spires of La Sagrada Família all the way to the beach. ⏱ *1 hr. See p 25,* ❶.

❿ ★★★ CosmoCaixa (Museu de la Ciència). One of the biggest and best science museums anywhere, this learning center is high-tech, hands-on, and a blast for kids. In an original *modernista* building with a daring underground extension, the huge museum features thrilling exhibitions like *The Flooded Forest,* a living Amazonian rainforest with over 100 species of animal and plant life (kids are encouraged to pick up and touch frogs, spiders, and other fauna). The 3-D planetarium and cool Geological Wall are also big draws. ⏱ *1½ hr. c/ Teodor Roviralta, 55.* ☎ *93-212-60-50. http://obrasocial.lacaixa.es. 4€ planetarium & other activities, 2€ supplement; 2€ children 8–16; free for children 16 & under. 1st Sun every month free admission. Tues–Sun 10am–8pm. FGC: Av. Tibidabo (then 10-min. walk). Bus: 17, 22, 58, or 73.* ●

CosmoCaixa.

La Rambla

Map Area
L'Eixample
Parc de la Ciutadella
St. Martí
Ciutat Vella
Montjuïc

(i) Tourist Information
(M) Metro Station

1 Café Zurich
2 Rambla de Canaletes
3 Rambla dels Estudis
4 Rambla de les Flors
5 Mercat de la Boqueria
6 Gran Teatre del Liceu
7 Café de la Ópera
8 Rambla dels Caputxins
9 Plaça Reial
10 Rambla de Santa Mònica
11 Mirador de Colom

Previous page: Take a stroll through the historic Barri Gòtic.

Is there a finer boulevard for strolling in the world? Victor Hugo proclaimed La Rambla "the most beautiful street in the world," while the Spanish poet Federico García Lorca said it was the "only street he wished would never end." The tree-shaded, pedestrian-only promenade stretches nearly 2km (1.2 miles) down a gentle slope from the city's hub, Plaça de Catalunya, to the waterfront. To the left (as you walk down it) is the Barri Gòtic; to the right is El Raval, an emerging artsy neighborhood. START: **Metro to Plaça de Catalunya.**

1 **Café Zurich.** At the very top of La Rambla, to the west of Plaça de Catalunya (and at the base of El Triangle shopping mall), is this terrace cafe, the best spot in the city for people-watching and a jolt of coffee before you start your stroll. The cafe was much more atmospheric before it was rebuilt and sanitized a few years back (the mall's to blame), but it remains a pivotal reference point in Barcelona. *Pl. Catalunya, 1.* ☎ *93-317-91-53. $.*

2 **Rambla de Canaletes.** The beginning of La Rambla usually swarms with people, particularly on game days of Barça, the local football (soccer) club. Kiosks sell foreign newspapers and magazines, and the first of La Rambla's celebrated mimes, or "human statues," begin to appear. The rotating cast of flamboyant characters includes opera singers, bearded nuns, and Roman soldiers, all vying for a few coins. The 19th-century Font (fountain) de Canaletes is said to convert anyone who drinks from it into a lifelong resident of Barcelona.

3 ★★ kids **Rambla dels Estudis.** Hear that squawking? Popularly called *Rambla dels Ocells* ("of the birds"), this section becomes an outdoor aviary, with parakeets, parrots, and other winged creatures in cages for sale. At the end of the day, vendors simply board up the stalls, and the birds remain overnight.

4 ★★ kids **La Rambla de les Flors.** Birds are replaced by flowers in this section, officially La Rambla de Sant Josep. Keep an eye out, to your right, for the *modernista* chocolate shop, **Escribà** (Antiga Casa Figueres, La Rambla, 83), one of the oldest chocolatiers in Barcelona. Another notable *modernista* building to look for is the **Farmacia Genové** (no. 77). **Palau de la Virreina** (no. 99), a grand, late-18th-century palace built for the widow of the viceroy of colonial Peru and today a museum hosting rotating contemporary art exhibits, is also worth a look.

5 ★★★ **Mercat de La Boquería.** Set back from La Rambla, on the right side, is a constant in the life of Barcelonans: Mercat de Sant Josep, better known as La

The Font de Canaletes.

A throng of people strolling popular La Rambla Boulevard.

Boquería. This bustling 19th-century covered market overflows with gastronomic delights. Longtime shoppers and merchants greet each other by name and shout across the aisles. The market opens before dawn, and the best shoppers know to arrive early (note that it's closed Sun, though). *La Rambla, 91–101.* ☎ *93-318-25-84.*

⑥ ★★ Gran Teatre del Liceu. The midpoint and heart of the Ramblas is the bustling intersection Pla de la Boquería, with a **Joan Miró** mosaic underfoot. One of Europe's great opera houses, the

Beautiful flowers at La Rambla de les Flors.

Liceu (lee-say-oo), is to the right. Since 1874 it has been home to all the Catalan greats, including Montserrat Caballé and Josep Carreras. Gutted by fire in 1994 (its third), it reopened after a restoration added high-tech improvements but preserved its soul. *La Rambla, 51–59.* ☎ *93-485-99-13.* www.liceu barcelona.com. *Guided tours (80 min.), including the private Cercle del Liceu, daily at 10am. Admission 12€, nonguided tours daily 11:30am–1pm every 30 min., 5.50€; stage & service area tours selected weekdays at 9:15am, 13€.*

⑦ ★ Café de la Ópera. This Belle Epoque cafe is a longtime gathering spot for operagoers and literary types and now a hangout for young people, tourists, gays, and old-timers. A good spot for coffee, beers, and snacks during the day, it gets more animated at night. *La Rambla, 74.* ☎ *93-317-75-85. $.*

⑧ ★ Rambla dels Caputxins. As the Rambla descends down a slight incline, so does its reputation. But you'll also find some of the Rambla's best entertainment—jugglers, tarot-card readers, more mimes, and street artists whipping out portraits and caricatures. On the right is **Hotel Oriente;** it was

Les Rambles? Las Ramblas?

The name La Rambla is derived from Arabic, signifying a dry riverbed—which is what this spot was until the 14th century, when Barcelonans began to populate the area. The stream was soon paved over, and it developed into a pedestrian-only boulevard. Some call it by the plural name, Les Rambles (*Las Ramblas* in Spanish), since in fact it comprises five distinct sections with individual names. However, they all blend together so seamlessly that most Barcelonans call the whole stretch by the singular, *La Rambla*. It's most crowded just before the lunch hour and in the early evening, but it's never deserted. In the wee hours it's the haunt of a sometimes motley mix of early morning newspaper sellers, street sweepers, and party animals stumbling back to their apartments and hotels.

Hemingway's favorite place to stay in Barcelona. Nearby is **Palau Güell,** a Gaudí-designed mansion built in 1885. The high-Gothic palace can and should be visited; make sure to see the impressive tiled chimneys on the rooftop.

9 ★ **Plaça Reial.** Across La Rambla and down a short passage is a pretty, arcaded square with a central fountain and soaring palm trees. Once home to a convent and later the haunt of junkies and thieves, today it is greatly cleaned up, and full of bars, cafes, and restaurants pushing legal stimulants.

10 ★ **Rambla de Santa Mònica.** The final section leads down to the harbor. Though the sleek **Centre d'Art Santa Mònica** hosts contemporary art exhibits, this zone is the least savory part of La Rambla (the maze of small and still-scruffy streets to the right, or west, comprise Barcelona's once-notorious Barri Xino, or Chinatown). The **Drassanes Reials,** beautifully vaulted medieval shipyards and home to the excellent **Museu Marítim,** are the highlight of La Rambla before you arrive at the waterfront. *See p 19,* **1**.

The Hotel Oriente was Hemingway's favorite Barcelona hotel.

11 **Mirador de Colom.** Marking the end of the Rambla and the start of the waterfront is a statue honoring Christopher Columbus. Though he is ostensibly indicating the way to the New World, snarky observers like to point out that Columbus is actually looking towards Mallorca rather than the Americas. Columbus is reputed to have come to Barcelona after his maiden journey to the Americas to meet with the Catholic monarchs Isabel and Fernando. *See p 19,* **2**.

Barri Gòtic

1 Catedral de Barcelona
2 Plaça de Ramon
Berenguer el Gran
3 Mesón del Café
4 Plaça del Rei
5 Temple d'Augustus
6 Plaça de Sant Just

7 Plaça de Sant Jaume
8 Carrer del Bisbe
9 Plaça de Sant Felip Neri
10 El Call
11 La Vinateria del Call
12 Carrer dels Banys Nous
13 Plaça del Pi

The Barri Gòtic, or Gothic Quarter, is where Barcelona was born, and it remains the heart of the city. It includes remnants of Barcelona's 2,000-year-old Roman past, as well as the medieval Jewish district, El Call, and is a joy to wander. Its labyrinth of narrow, cobblestone streets is lined with palaces, convents, and churches and a thriving collection of bars, restaurants, and chic shops. START: **Metro to Jaume I.**

❶ ★★ Catedral de Barcelona. The Barri Gòtic has long been known as the "Cathedral Quarter," so this is the logical place to start. Locals gather at the **Plaça Nova** ("new square," dating from 1358!) in front of the cathedral to perform the *sardana*, a Catalan folk dance (Sun mornings and national holidays). To the right of the main entrance to the cathedral is the **Portal de Bisbe,** semicircular twin towers and one of three gateways to the walled settlement of Roman Barcino (4th c. A.D.). *See p 13,* **⓬**.

❷ ★★ Plaça de Ramon Berenguer el Gran. In this square is one of the largest surviving sections of the second Roman wall, dating to the 4th century A.D. The equestrian statue is of the 12th-century hero who extended the reign of independent Catalunya. Rising above the wall are the

Plaça Ramon Berenguer.

Mirador del Rei Martí (King Martin's Watchtower) rises above the Plaça del Rei.

14th-century *Palau Reial Major* (Royal Palace), Santa Àgata chapel, and a Gothic tower. These are all best seen from Plaça del Rei, which you'll visit shortly. *Vía Laietana, s/n.*

❸ ★★ Mesón del Café. A tiny, charming cafe that dates back to 1909, this is the kind of good-vibes spot where some neighborhood folks stop by every day for some of the city's best coffee. Belly up to the bar or see if you can score a table in back. *c/ Llibretería, 16.* ☎ 93-315-07-54. $.

❹ ★★★ Plaça del Rei. This noble and austere square is the most beautiful part of the Barri Gòtic. Here you'll find subterranean Roman ruins and the medieval Royal Palace where *Los Reyes Católicos* (Catholic Monarchs) are said to have

El Caganer in a Manger

Barcelona's annual nativity crafts fair and Christmas market in the square in front of the cathedral features one traditional folkloric figure that in recent years has taken on all kinds of modern permutations. It is **el caganer.** Placed in nativity scenes, the small figure, traditionally donning a red peasant's cap, is depicted squatting and defecating. **El caganer** symbolizes Catalans' ties to the land and the hope for continued fertility. With an eye toward young consumers and tourists, today **el caganer** is not limited to peasant figures. You'll also see figurines of priests, nuns, Bart Simpson, local and international politicians, and more—all squatting and fertilizing the earth.

The Plaça de Sant Jaume.

received Columbus on his return from the New World in 1493. The sculpture in the square, *Topos V,* is by the Basque sculptor Eduardo Chillida, one of Spain's great 20th-century artists. *See p 13,* ⑬.

⑤ ★★ **Temple d'Augustus.** *See p 33,* ⑦.

⑥ ★★ **Plaça de Sant Just.** This quiet, diminutive square is one of the most representative and unadulterated of medieval Barcelona. The **Església dels Sants Just**

i Pastor, a church begun in 1342, features a single nave in the Catalan Gothic style. It's usually open only for Sunday Mass. The Gothic fountain in the square dates to 1367. **Palau Moxó,** a seigniorial mansion across the square, was added in 1700.

⑦ ★ **Plaça de Sant Jaume.** An important crossroads during the Roman era, this broad square has been the political epicenter of Barcelona for more than 5 centuries. On one side is the **Palau de la Generalitat.** Across from it is the 14th-century **Ajuntament,** Barcelona's Town Hall. *See p 35,* ⑨.

⑧ ★★ **Carrer del Bisbe.** One of the loveliest streets in the Gothic Quarter, the former principal artery of the Roman city connects the cathedral to Plaça Sant Jaume. On one side are the **Cases dels Canonges,** a series of 14th-century Gothic palaces. On the other is the **Palau de la Generalitat,** home to the Regional Government of Catalunya. Notice the rooftop gargoyles watching over the street action below. Arching over the lane is a bridge of carved stone, which only looks to be Gothic; it was added in 1928.

The walkway above carrer del Bisbe was added in 1928.

❾ ★★★ Plaça de Sant Felip Neri. Down a tiny passageway off carrer Sant Sever (home to an extraordinary, if rarely open Baroque chapel) is one of the most tranquil and poetic spots in the Ciutat Vella. It was once the site of a parish cemetery and the specter of the dead lingers. Behind the gurgling fountain is a reminder of Spain's not-too-distant violence: The walls of the 17th-century church are scarred by Civil War bombs that killed 42 people in 1938.

❿ ★ El Call. Carrer del Call leads into the warren of small streets that once made up the Call, or Jewish Quarter, in medieval Barcelona (until the Jews were expelled from Spain in 1492). Only a few important vestiges of the community remain. The **Sinagoga Medieval de Barcelona** claims to be the oldest synagogue in Spain (based on a royal document from 1267). A nearby medieval Hebrew inscription marking a death in A.D. 692 reads, "Rabbi Samuel Hassareri, may his life never cease." ⏱ 30 min. c/ Marlet, 5. ☎ 93-317-07-90. www.calldebarcelona.org. Admission 2.50€. Mon–Fri 10:30am–6pm, Sat–Sun 10:30am–3pm.

⓫ La Vinateria del Call. This romantic little spot in the heart of the ancient Jewish Quarter is the perfect nook to duck into for local wines and Catalan tapas, such as cured meats and cheeses. c/ Sant Domènec del Call, 9. ☎ 93-302-60-92.

⓬ ★ Carrer dels Banys Nous. This atmospheric street (named for the location of the "new baths," dating from the 12th century) follows the line of the old Roman wall and today is known as el carrer dels antiquaris—the street of antiques dealers. No. 10, now S'Oliver, a furniture store, was the site of Jewish baths for men.

⓭ ★★ Plaça del Pi. A trio of pretty, contiguous plazas surrounds the 15th-century church **Santa María del Pi,** known for its rose window. **Plaça de Sant Josep Oriol** adjoins Plaça del Pi and, behind the church, tiny **Placeta del Pi.** The squares are recognized for the unusual sgraffito decorative technique on the plaster facades of several buildings, an 18th-century style imported from Italy. But the leafy squares are most popular for the weekend artisans' market and open-air cafe-bars, making this an excellent place to while away the hours and finish a walking tour.

A relic from Barcelona's El Call (Jewish Quarter).

The Best Neighborhood Walks

La Ribera

1. Carrer de l'Argenteria
2. Santa María del Mar
3. Fossar de les Moreres
4. Passeig del Born
5. Antic Mercat del Born
6. Passeig de Picasso
7. Carrer del Comerç
8. Montiel Espai Gastronòmic
9. Carrer de Montcada
10. Carrer dels Sombrerers
11. La Ribera fashion boutiques
12. Capella del Marcús
13. Mercat Santa Caterina
14. Sant Pere de les Puel.les
15. El Palau de la Música Catalana

As maritime commerce grew in the 13th and 14th centuries, Barri de la Ribera ("neighborhood of the waterfront," reflecting a time when the shoreline reached this far), became a populous residential neighborhood for the merchant class. Until recently the quarter was known principally for its great church, Santa María del Mar, and the much-frequented Museu Picasso. But in the last decade, La Ribera (and particularly the zone within it called "El Born") has become the city's most fashionable district, exploding with bars, restaurants, and boutiques. Though it can get rowdy late at night, it still retains its medieval character. START: **Metro to Jaume I.**

❶ Carrer de l'Argenteria.
Leave behind the congestion of Vía Laeitana, a thoroughfare cut through the Ciutat Vella in the 1930s, for the foot traffic of the "street of silversmiths," a name dating to the 16th century. Fashion boutiques, bars, tapas restaurants, and hotels have taken over, but take a detour onto carrer Grunyí or carrer Rosic, for example, and you'll glimpse the old Ribera district.

❷ ★★★ Santa María del Mar.
It's hard pass by without taking at least a quick, always-inspiring spin through this extraordinarily graceful 14th-century Catalan Gothic church built by the merchant class. It's the kind of contemplative place that should clear your head before you continue through this bustling neighborhood. *See p 15,* ❹.

❸ Fossar de les Moreres. An eternal flame burns on a small square around the right side of the main entrance to Santa María del Mar. It commemorates the royal sacking of Barcelona on September 11, 1714, which marked the end to the Spanish War of Succession. King Felipe V then outlawed Catalan culture and its institutions, including the Catalan language. The date, 9/11 (or 11/9 in Spain), is now celebrated as the National Day of Catalunya. From here, duck into the tiny passageway carrer de Malcuinat (literally, "poorly cooked")

and walk out to **Plaça de les Olles** and back to Passeig del Born, along carrer de la Vidreria, just to get a feel for this part of the quarter that leads to the waterfront.

❹ ★★ Passeig del Born. This wide and elegant tree-lined promenade, with its stone benches, is a good place for a breather. Once the site of medieval jousting tournaments, it became the main square and heart of the city during Barcelona's seafaring heyday (13th–18th c.). Today apartment dwellers in its Gothic mansions are more commonly up in arms against the busy outdoor cafes and late-night bars that populate the ground

Santa María del Mar.

A bustling scene on Passeig del Born (p 65).

floors and every side street leading off the *passeig*.

5 Antic Mercat del Born. At the end of Passeig del Born is the old Ribera covered market, with its distinctive wrought-iron roof. Constructed in 1876, it is now El Born Centre Cultural, with a subterranean exhibit of the excavated medieval village — "the city within the market." Ground level is open daily 10am to 10pm to connect El Born and the Parc de la Ciutadella.

6 Passeig de Picasso. This avenue borders the western edge of Parc de la Ciutadella, the largest green space in downtown Barcelona. Here you'll find Antoni

Tàpies's 1981 sculpture, *Homenatge a Picasso*, a glass cube containing a cubist-like assemblage of running water and furniture. A bit farther up are remnants of the 1888 Universal Exhibition: the Castell dels Tres Dragons, originally a restaurant designed by Domènech i Montaner, and the winter greenhouse, L'Hivernacle.

7 Carrer del Comerç. This street, bending around the edges of La Ribera, is one of many that have been inundated with shops and restaurants—not surprisingly, given its name, Commerce Street. The **Museu de la Xocolata** is found at Comerç, 36. The street parallel to Comerç, carrer del Rec, is flush with designer clothing and furniture boutiques.

8 ★ Montiel Espai Gastronòmic. This attractive little gourmet food store–cum–informal restaurant serves Catalan and Spanish standards, including jamón de Jabugo (Iberian ham), pa amb tomàquet (peasant bread with rubbed tomatoes and olive oil), Catalan sausages, and local wines. Have a selection of tapas or the good-value fixed-price lunch. *c/ Flassaders, 19.* ☎ *93-268-37-29. $.*

Archaeological remains in the Mercat del Born.

The carrer de les Mosques.

9 ★★★ Carrer de Montcada.

Famous for its collection of stately Gothic mansions and Museu Picasso, this elegant avenue is a joy to stroll. Don't miss the incredibly narrow and poetically named *carrer de les Mosques* ("street of the flies"). *See p 31,* 2.

10 Carrer dels Sombrerers.

Just off carrer de Montcada, and flanking Santa María del Mar, is this small and atmospheric street, formally named "St. Anthony of the Hat Makers." **E&A Gispert** (p 49, 12), at no. 23, is a wonderful old epicurean shop with a 150-year-old roasting oven.

11 ★ La Ribera fashion boutiques.

Off carrer de la Princesa is a series of alleyways that have given over to a handful of chic designer boutiques, typifying the neighborhood's stunning transformation. Make a brief detour along carrers Carassa and Vigatans before returning to Princesa.

12 ★ Capella del Marcús.

Worth a look is this small Romanesque chapel, built in 1166 next to what was once the main thoroughfare in and out of the Roman city (today c/ dels Carders). *Pl. Marcús, s/n.*

13 ★★ Mercat de Santa Caterina.

This colorfully reimagined covered market has become a hit with foodies and architecture fans. *See p 44,* 7.

14 Sant Pere de les Puel.les.

Little remains of the original (A.D. 945) church and Benedictine monastery, although you can still see a section of the 10th-century Greek-cross floor plan, lone surviving bell tower, and a few Corinthian capitals beneath the 12th-century dome of the heavily restored Romanesque church. *c/ Lluís el Piadós, 1.* ☎ *93-268-07-42. Free admission. Mon–Fri 8:30am–1pm & 5–7:30pm, Sat 8:30am–1pm & 4:30–7pm, Sun 11am–2pm.*

15 ★★★ El Palau de la Música Catalana.

If you haven't already had a chance to tour this extraordinary concert hall, Domènch i Montaner's masterpiece, this would be the time to do it. *See p 15,* 1.

El Palau de la Música Catalana

L'Eixample

0 .... 1/4 mile
0 .... 1/4 km

Map Area Parc de la Ciutadella
L'Eixample
Ciutat Vella
Montjuïc

Perill

Plaça Rei Joan Carles I

Còrsega

Còrsega

Diagonal

Av. Diagonal

8

Rosselló

Rosselló

Casa de les Punxes

7

Passatge de la Concepción

Provença

Casa Milà (La Pedrera)

Pau Claris

Provença

Av. Diagonal

Bruc

Provença

Verdaguer

Passeig de Gràcia

6

5 Casa Thomas

Mallorca

Rambla Catalunya

Mallorca

Passatge de Domingo

Passatge dels Camps Elisis

Girona

Bailèn

València

València

Roger de Llúria

4

L'EIXAMPLE

Mercat de la Concepción

Fundació Antoni Tàpies

Aragó

Passatge de Méndez Vigo

Aragó

Bruc

Casa Batlló

Casa Amatller

Casa Lleó Morera

Passeig de Gràcia

Consell de Cent

Consell de Cent

Girona

3

Diputació

Rambla Catalunya

2

Torre d'Aigües

Girona

Diputació

Bailèn

Passeig de Gràcia

Gran Via Corts Catalanes

Roger de Llúria

Gran Via Corts Catalanes

Ronda Universitat

Casp

Pau Claris

1

Casp

Plaça Catalunya

Ronda Sant Pere

Plaça Urquinaona

Urquinaona

Catalunya

Fontanella

1 Casa Calvet
2 Passatge de Permanyer
3 Pati de les Aigües
4 Queviures J. Murrià
5 Casa Thomas
6 Cor Caliu
7 Casa de les Punxes
8 Palau del Baró de Quadras

ⓘ Tourist Information
Ⓜ Metro Station

L'Eixample is an area best known for its extraordinary collection of late-19th- and early-20th-century *modernista* (Catalan Art Nouveau) buildings, which earned it the nickname El Quadrat d'Or (the Golden Square). This tour takes you off the Eixample's well-trodden path. If you have time and energy at the end of this tour, you should tack on a stroll down Passeig de Gràcia or pedestrian-only Rambla de Catalunya, both of which lead back to Plaça de Catalunya. START: **Metro to Urquinaona.**

① Casa Calvet. Antoni Gaudí's 1899 apartment building, one of his first commissions, is an understated work, best appreciated for its wrought-iron and sculptural details. The building saw the installation of Barcelona's first elevator, which has an impressively embellished cupola. A top-flight restaurant, Casa Calvet, inhabits the first floor——originally a textile shop designed by Gaudí—allowing architectural and gastronomic enthusiasts an enticing look up-close at an important early work of Gaudí. **c/ Caspe, 48. See p 29, ⑨.**

Dinner at Casa Calvet allows for a sneak peek inside the remarkable building.

② ★ Passatge de Permanyer. This inner courtyard, with a brick water tower in the center, is now open to the public. You'll find this lovely side street off Roger de Llúria, between Diputació and Consell de Cent. It is home to a small community of impeccable town houses and English-style gardens, tucked behind an engraved iron gate. It is perhaps the finest example of what Ildefons Cerdà, who

designed L'Eixample, had in mind for the district.

③ Pati de les Aigües. In the next block along Diputació, between Roger de Llúria and Bruc, this inner courtyard with a brick water tower in the center has been reclaimed and opened to the public. It's one of the few opportunities to view the central courtyards of the original Eixample apartment buildings as Cerdà intended—as

The charming Passatge de Permanyer.

The castlelike Casa de les Punxes is hard to miss.

open, green public spaces. Most have been built over or otherwise appropriated by private interests. *c/ Roger de Llúria, 56.* ☎ *93-424-38-09.*

④ ★★ **Queviures J. Murrià.** This wonderful, old-school *colmado* (grocery or packaged-goods store) has remained in the same family for 150 years. *See p 81.*

⑤ ★★ **Casa Thomas.** Just down carrer Mallorca is this spectacular house (1895–98) by Domènech i Montaner. Originally just two floors, it was expanded in 1912. It now houses a furniture store, Cubiñá, so feel free to enter and wander among the two floors of this seminal building. *c/ Mallorca, 291–293.* ☎ *93-476-57-21.*

⑥ **Cor Caliu.** An attractive corner restaurant-bar, this surprisingly elegant spot is perfect for coffee, a beer, or tapas in the front bar or a full meal in the restaurant at back. It's a longtime neighborhood favorite. *c/ Roger de Llúria, 102.* ☎ *93-208-20-29. $$.*

⑦ **Casa de les Punxes.** Also called Casa Terrades, or "House of Spikes," for its sharp turrets, this massive and eccentric 1905 house is one of Josep Puig i Cadafalch's and *modernisme*'s most prized buildings. It's a neo-Gothic fairy tale and castle-like mansion with distinctive features, such as three separate entrances (built for each of the family's daughters), outer walls facing all four points of the compass, and patriotic ceramic motifs. *Av. Diagonal, 416–420.*

⑧ **Palau del Baró de Quadras.** This 1904–06 mansion, by Puig i Cadafalch, is a great example of the architect's creativity. The interior's Moorish-style ceiling, carved wood, and leaded glass are not accessible at the moment. Casa Asia, the previous occupant of the building, had welcomed visitors to tour the interior. The façade alone is worth the visit. It is carved in an intricate style that nods to Castilla's Plateresque tradition, while employing imagery and iconography of French and German medieval stone carving. The long, ornate balcony is covered with busts of eminent medieval and Renaissance figures, floral motifs, and heraldic shields. *Av. Diagonal, 373.* ●

Palau del Baró de Quadras was designed by Puig i Cadafalch.

Shopping Best Bets

Best **Dreamy Antiques**
★★ L'Arca, c/ Banys Nous, 20 (p 76)

Best **Hip Designer Clothing (Men's)**
★★ Antonio Miró, La Rambla de Catalunya, 125 (p 78)

Best **Drop-Dead-Gorgeous Designer Clothing (Women's)**
★★ Nunita, c/ del Rec, 6 (p 79)

Best **Creative Leather Goods**
★★★ Lupo Barcelona, c/ Mallorca, 257, bajos (p 81); and ★★ Iriarte Iriarte, c/Cotoners, 12 (p 80)

Best **Shop for Slaves to Design**
★★★ Vinçón, Pg. de Gràcia, 96 (p 78)

The treats at Caelum in Barri Gòtic. Previous page: The Camper store in El Triangle Plaça de Catalunya.

Best **Barcelona Souvenirs**
★★ Vaho Gallery Barcelona, Pl. del Pi, 1 (p 80); and ★ BCN Original Shops, c/ Citutat, 23 (p 80)

Best-**Smelling Gourmet Food**
★★★ E&A Gispert, c/ dels Sombrerers, 23 (p 49, ⑫)

Best **Wine Cellar Fantasy Shop**
★★★ Vila Viniteca, c/ Agullers, 7 (p 49, ⑬)

Best **Dip into Old-World Barcelona**
★★ Herbolisteria del Rei, c/ del Vidre, 1 (p 82)

Best **Vintage Finds**
★ Le Swing, c/ del Rec, 16 (p 79)

Best **Old-City Spot for an Antiques Stroll**
★★ Carrer de la Palla; and ★★ Carrer Banys Nous

Best **Mall for Kids**
Maremàgnum, Moll d'Espanya, 5 (p 78)

Most **Theatrical Clothing Boutique**
★★★ Natalie Capell Atelier de Moda, c/ Carassa, 2 (p 79)

Best **Products by Nuns & Priests (or Best Archaeological Surprise in a Store)**
★★ Caelum, c/ de la Palla, 8 (p 80)

Best **Catalan Goodies for Foodies**
★★ Colmado Quílez, Rambla de Catalunya, 63 (p 47, ❷); and ★★ La Cuina d'en Garriga, c/ Consell de Cent, 308 (p 47, ❹)

Best **Unpronounceable T-Shirt Shop**
★★ Kukuxumusu, c/ L'Argenteria, 69 (p 80)

'Eixample

Agatha Ruiz de la Prada **9**
Antonio Miró **7**
Arenas de Barcelona **11**
Bulevard dels Antiquaris **3**
Camper **13**
Casa del Llibre **4**
El Corte Inglés **14**
El Triangle **16**
FNAC **15**
Jamonísimo **10**
LAIE **12**
Loewe **8**
Lupo Barcelona **2**
Queviures J. Murrià **5**
Regia **6**
Vinçón **1**

Av. Diagonal

Còrsega

Plaça Rei
Joan Carles I

Còrsega

Av. Diagonal

Balmes

Diagonal **M**

Rosselló

Rosselló

Passatje de
la Concepció

Passeig de Gràcia

1 Casa Milà
(La Pedrera)

Provença

Passatje de
Mercader

Rambla Catalunya

Passeig de Gràcia

Provença

Mallorca

Passatje de
Domingo

2

Passatje dels
Camps Elisis

Mallorca

València

10
11

L'EIXAMPLE

3

Pau Claris

5 →

València

Plaça
Dr. Letamendi

Aragó

Fundació
Antoni Tàpies

4

Aragó

Aribau

Balmes

Casa Batlló
Casa Amatller

6
7 **8**

M
Passeig
de Gràcia

Passatje de
Mendez Vigo

Consell de Cent

9

Consell de Cent

Diputació

Rambla Catalunya

Diputació

Passeig de Gràcia

Passatge de
Permanyer

Universitat
de Barcelona

Plaça
Universitat

Gran Via Corts Catalanes

Gran Via Corts Catalane

Rda. de St. Antoni

M Universitat

Ronda Universitat

Casp

12

Pau Claris

Plaça
Castella

Tallers

Pelai

Balmes

Bergara

13

Ronda St. Pere

Plaça
Urquinaona

Plaça
Catalunya

16 **15**

Pelai

Passeig de Gràcia

14

Urquinaona **M**

Fontanella

Map
Area
L'Eixample

Parc de la
Ciutadella

Ciutat
Vella

Montjuïc

Tallers

La Rambla

M Catalunya

i Tourist Information
M Metro Station

0 — 1/4 mile
0 — 1/4 km

Ciutat Vella & Waterfront

Barcelona **Shopping A to Z**

Art & Antiques
Bulevard dels Antiquaris
L'EIXAMPLE An indoor mall containing some 70 small shops of art and antiques. Stall owners set their own hours, which can be wildly inconsistent. *Pg. de Gràcia, 55.* ☎ *93-215-44-99. www.bulevard delsantiquaris.com. Metro: Pg. de Gràcia. Map p 73.*

★ **Heritage** BARRI GÒTIC A theatrical-looking shop, stuffed with old costumes, jewelry, and Spanish shawls. It's worth a snoop under the proprietor's watchful eye. *c/ Banys Nous, 14.* ☎ *93-317-85-15. MC, V. Metro: Jaume I. Map p 74.*

★★ **Iguapop** LA RIBERA From the works of modern and pop artists to fashion and art books, this place (also an indie concert promoter) is one-stop shopping for downtown *au courant* artheads. *c/ Comerç, 15.* ☎ *93-310-07-35. MC, V. Metro: Arc de Triomf. Map p 74.*

★ **Krappa** LA RIBERA This graphic design store makes engravings based on historic woodcuts, some

Theatrical treasures abound at Heritage.

from medieval books. Many of the maps, cards, bookplates, and larger prints are colored by hand. *c/ Freneria, 1.* ☎ *93-442-51-00. AE, MC, V. Metro: Jaume I. Map p 74.*

★★ **L'Arca** BARRI GÒTIC Antique lace, linens, and curtains, as well as handkerchiefs and other textiles from the 18th to early 20th centuries are found at this uniquely lovely shop, where some of the period clothing for the movie *Titanic* was purchased. *c/ Banys Nous, 20.* ☎ *93-302-15-98. www.larca.es. MC, V. Metro: Liceu. Map p 74.*

★★ **Sala d'Art Artur Ramón** BARRI GÒTIC A top antiques and art dealer and longtime family gallery known for its 19th- and 20th-century paintings, sculptures, engravings, and decorative arts. *c/ de la Palla, 23.* ☎ *93-302-59-70. AE, DC, MC, V. Metro: Jaume I. Map p 74.*

Books
Casa del Llibre L'EIXAMPLE A large bookshop covering the gamut of titles, including English and foreign-language books. *Pg. de Gràcia, 62.* ☎ *90-202-64-07. MC, V. Metro: Pg. de Gràcia. Map p 73.*

★★ **LAIE** L'EIXAMPLE With a cafe and nice stock of English-language books, including literature, travel maps, and guides, LAIE's a favorite with foreigners resident in Barcelona. *c/ Pau Claris, 85.* ☎ *93-318-17-39. MC, V. Metro: Urquinaona. Map p 73.*

Ceramics & Pottery
1748 Artesana i Coses EL BORN Near Museu Picasso, this crowded ceramics shop stocks largely inexpensive pottery and porcelain from all over Spain (and

Prime Shopping Zones

Barcelona's elegant Passeig de Gràcia is home to some of the most fashionable and expensive retail space in Spain. Pedestrian-only **Rambla de Catalunya,** which runs parallel to Passeig de Gràcia, is like an open mall of stores, perfect for strolling, and the cross streets between the two are loaded with interesting shops of all kinds—particularly València, Provença, and Consell de Cent, the last known for its art galleries. The long boulevard **Avenida Diagonal** is the site of many high-end furnishings and fashion boutiques. In the **Ciutat Vella,** the main streets Portal d'Angel, Portaferrisa, and Ferrán are packed with clothing stores and young shoppers. Small boutiques and one-of-a-kind retailers are tucked in the neighborhoods of **El Born** and **Barri Gòtic,** and increasingly hip clothing stores are located in **El Raval.** Antiques dealers, meanwhile, are largely clustered around the labyrinth of streets near carrer de la Palla, Banys Nous, and Plaça del Pi in the **Barri Gòtic.**

Portugal). *Pl. de Montcada, 2.* ☎ *93-319-54-13. AE, MC, V. Metro: Jaume I. Map p 74.*

★ **Itaca** BARRI GÒTIC On hand is handmade pottery from Spain, Portugal, Mexico, and Morocco. Pieces are simple but well conceived, and there are a number of Gaudí-esque objects fashioned with *trencadís* (broken ceramic tiles). *c/ Ferran, 26.* ☎ *93-301-30-44. MC, V. Metro: Liceu. Map p 74.*

Cosmetics

★★ **La Galería de Santa María Novella** LA RIBERA This is the Barcelona outlet of a famed Florence apothecary, the oldest in the world. The perfumes and soaps are extraordinary, and the packaging delightfully antiquated. *c/ Espasería, 4–8.* ☎ *93-268-02-37. MC, V. Metro: Jaume I. Map p 74.*

★ **Regia** L'EIXAMPLE This high-end cosmetics shop has a treat: a museum (free admission) with 5,000 examples of perfume bottles and flasks dating back as far as ancient

Greece, including a cool bottle by Salvador Dalí. *Pg. de Gràcia, 39.* ☎ *93-216-01-21. AE, MC, V. Metro: Pg. de Gràcia. Map p 73.*

Department Stores/Shopping Centers

Arenas de Barcelona PLAÇA D'ESPANYA The structure was originally Barcelona's bullring, built 1889–1900, but closed in 1977. British architect Richard Rogers transformed it into a 21st-century shopping center with six floors of shops, a movie theater, and a good food court. *Gran Via, 373–385.* ☎ *93-289-02-44. Metro: Plaça d'Espanya. Map p 73.*

Ceramics, like these at 1748 Artesana i Coses, make great souvenirs and gifts.

El Corte Inglés PLAÇA DE CATALUNYA Spain's largest department store chain sells everything from wine and music to furnishings and fashion. You'll also find a restaurant, travel agent, and excellent supermarket (Plaça de Catalunya branch only). *Pl. de Catalunya, 14.* ☎ *93-306-38-00. AE, DC, MC, V. www.elcorteingles.es. Metro: Catalunya. Map p 73.*

El Triangle PLAÇA DE CATALUNYA This large white elephant occupies a good chunk of Plaça de Catalunya across from La Rambla. It may stick out, but it's convenient for hitting shops like Sephora, FNAC, Camper, and Habitat. *c/ Pelai, 39.* ☎ *93-318-01-08. Metro: Catalunya. Map p 73.*

Maremàgnum WATERFRONT This mall, perched out in the old harbor near L'Aquarium, has plenty for the whole family, from toy stores to high-end fashion. *Moll d'Espanya, 5.* ☎ *93-225-81-00. Metro: Drassanes. Map p 74.*

Designer Home Goods & Furnishings
★★★ **Vinçón** L'EIXAMPLE Fernando Amat's temple of good design, Vinçón features more than 10,000 products—everything from household items to the finest Catalan and Spanish contemporary furnishings—housed in the former home of *modernista* painter Ramón Casas. The singular window displays alone are always a conversation piece. *Pg. de Gràcia, 96.* ☎ *93-215-60-50. AE, MC, V. Metro: Pg. de Gràcia. Map p 73.*

Fashion & Accessories
★★ **Agatha Ruiz de la Prada** L'EIXAMPLE The playful, brightly colored, almost childlike fashions of this Madrid designer have hit the big time, and she now has shops in

The Maremàgnum mall at the waterfront.

Paris, Milan, and New York. *c/ Consell de Cent, 314–316.* ☎ *93-215-52-88. AE, MC, V. Metro: Pg. de Gràcia. Map p 73.*

★★ **Antonio Miró** L'EIXAMPLE Pieces by the Catalan designer Antonio Miró are chic and sleek, with a retro edge; in addition to sophisticated, high-end men's and women's items, you'll find a less expensive Miró Jeans line. *La Rambla de Catalunya, 125.* ☎ *93-238-99-42. AE, MC, V. Metro: Catalunya. Map p 73.*

★★ **b huno** RAVAL An adorable shop with stylish, contemporary dresses, tops, earrings, and bags by a coterie of young Catalan and Spanish designers, some of whose designs are coveted by Spain's fashionable Princess Letizia. *c/ Elisabets, 18.* ☎ *93-412-63-05. MC, V. Metro: Liceu. Map p 74.*

★ **Desigual** LA RAMBLA This casual fashion firm started in Barcelona in 1984 and has spread virally around the globe with its playful clothes that rely on a flippant style and flamboyant colors. This shop and the one next door are home base. *La Rambla, 136.* ☎ *93-343-77-67. AE, MC, V. Metro: Catalunya. Map p 74.*

★ **Le Swing** LA RIBERA Attitude-heavy vintage finds, from sunglasses and bags to boots (including brands like Chanel and Dior) and some provocative fare, too. Hipsters, this is ground zero. More in sister shop Blow at c/ Bonaire, 6. *c/ del Rec, 16.* ☎ *93-310-14-49. MC, V. Metro: Jaume I. Map p 74.*

Custo-Barcelona LA RIBERA Custo's emblematic tops and tees, skirts, and pants are emblazoned with wildly colored retro-cool motifs. Seen on Hollywood starlets and in the fashion pages, these now-international pieces aren't cheap, but they are distinctive. There's another location at c/ Ferran, 36. *Pl. de les Olles, 7.* ☎ *93-268-78-93. MC, V. Metro: Jaume I. Map p 74.*

★★ **Etxart & Panno** EL BORN Unabashedly sexy fashions for women with style and money to burn, in a cool little shop in the heart of the chic Born district.

Antonio Miró designs chic clothes for men and women.

Custo-Barcelona.

Pg. del Born, 14. ☎ *93-310-37-24. MC, V. Metro: Jaume I. Map p 74.*

★★ **Jocomomola de Sybilla** EL BORN The brightly colored, informal women's fashions from this Madrileña designer have a retro bent and look as though they might have dressed Amelie, the heroine of the style-conscious French film of a decade or so ago. *c/ Vigatans, 6 (off Princesa).* ☎ *93-310-36-66. AE, MC, V. Metro: Jaume I. Map p 74.*

★★★ **Natalie Capell Atelier de Moda** EL BORN Timeless, handmade, oh-so-delicate high fashion designs for chic and slender women, dramatically lit in an atmospheric boutique that looks like a theater set. *c/ Carassa, 2 (off Princesa).* ☎ *93-319-92-19. MC, V. Metro: Jaume I. Map p 74.*

★★ **Nunita** EL BORN Some of the chicest modern women's fashions in the old quarter are found at this pricey, elegant boutique, with a handful of carefully selected designers, most of them Danish. *c/ del Rec, 61.* ☎ *93-315-07-70. AE, MC, V. Metro: Arc de Triomf. Map p 74.*

★ **Minu Madhu** EL BORN Terrific, colorful scarves and shawls from India, Asia, and Spain, as well as embroidered jackets and sumptuous fabrics. c/ Santa María, 18. ☎ 93-310-27-85. MC, V. Metro: Jaume I. Map p 74.

Gifts & Souvenirs

★ **BCN Original Shops** BARRI GÒTIC If you're after particularly Barcelona-themed gifts and souvenirs, this is your place. Art and architecture books, mugs, ceramics, jewelry, T-shirts, notebooks, and more. c/ Citutat, 2. ☎ 93-270-24-29. AE, MC, V. Metro: Jaume I. Map p 74.

★ **Beardsley** BARRI GÒTIC This classic Barcelona shop is seductive-looking, featuring home goods, candles, great glassware, chandeliers and lighting, paper products, and much more. c/ Petritxol, 12. ☎ 93-412-26-55. AE, MC, V. Metro: Liceu. Map p 74.

★ **The Cha Cha Original Shop** LA RIBERA A funky little pop-art shop, with retro-cool placemats, barware, T-shirts, and more, all with a fun, hipster sensibility. c/ Sant Antoni dels Sombrerers, 7. ☎ 93-19-37-79. MC, V. Metro: Jaume I. Map p 74.

★ **FC Botiga** LA RIBERA This official shop of FC Barcelona, or Barça to its real fans, has all the official red, blue, and gold gear to make your teammates (or your kids' teammates) envious. c/ Jaume 1, 18. ☎ 93-269-15-32. AE, MC, V. Metro: Jaume I. Map p 74.

★ **Ivo & Co.** EL BORN Snag cool kitchen utensils, housewares, journals, candles, and books in this invitingly retro-looking shop. c/ del Rec, 20 baixos. ☎ 93-268-33-31. MC, V. Metro: Arc de Triomf. Map p 74.

★★ **Kukuxumusu** LA RIBERA Don't even try to pronounce the name of this shop, originally from Navarra but now all over Spain. Do pop by for witty, hip T-shirts and accessories. With a fun take on Spanish cultural traditions, they make great souvenirs. c/ L'Argenteria, 69. ☎ 93-310-36-47. AE, MC, V. Metro: Jaume I. Map p 74.

★★ **Vaho Gallery Barcelona** BARRI GÒTIC This funky bag maker uses recycled heavy-duty PVC culture posters (used as cultural advertising by the city and regional governments) to create unique messenger bags and purses (which they call "trashion"). A unique souvenir from Barcelona for eco- and fashion-conscious sorts. There's another location at Bonsuccés, 13. Pl. del Pi, 1. ☎ 93-412-78-94. AE, MC, V. Metro: Liceu. Map p 74.

Gourmet Shopping Tip

For more information on where to buy and eat your favorite gourmet items, check "Gourmet Barcelona," p 46.

Gourmet Food Shops

★★ **Caelum** BARRI GÒTIC Cloistered nuns and religious orders produce everything in this shop, including jams and preserved fruit, biscuits, marzipan, and liquors, all handsomely packaged. In the cafe downstairs are the remains of ancient Jewish baths. c/ de la Palla, 8. ☎ 93-302-69-93. MC, V. Metro: Jaume I. Map p 74.

Demasié LA RIBERA A gourmet cookie shop with all kinds of treats both sweet and savory, including expected and very unusual cookies

A mosaic at Escribà.

(black tea, Roquefort and nuts, mustard, curry). c/ Princesa, 28. ☎ 93-269-11-80. MC, V. Metro: Jaume I. Map p 74.

★★ **Jamonísimo**. L'EIXAMPLE This is the place in town to see what the Spanish fascination with fine, cured (and pricey) ham is all about, and you'll be in the company of some of the world's greatest chefs who buy their acorn-fed Bellota, Ibérico, and Serrano jamones here. You can sample some thin slices, croquetas, or canelloni, or do a full-on tasting with a glass of wine. c/ Provença, 85. ☎ 93-324-81-54. www.jamonisimo.com. MC, V. Metro: Hospital Clínic. Map p 73.

★ **Pastisseria Escribà**. LA RAMBLA Talk about eye candy. One of Barcelona's oldest and best-known chocolatiers is this little shop on La Rambla with a shimmering modernista exterior (of colorful broken glazed tiles, à la Gaudí) and tea salon within. La Rambla, 83. ☎ 93-301-60-27. www.escriba.es. MC, V. Metro: Liceu. Map p 74.

★★★ **Queviures J. Murrià** L'EIXAMPLE This food-and-wine emporium has been in the same family since the late 19th century. Its handsome exterior, the work of the modernista artist Ramón Casas, is only a prelude to the 200 types of cheese, 300 wines, Iberian jamón (ham), and canned goods inside. c/ Roger de Llúria, 85. ☎ 93-215-57-89. MC, V. Metro: Pg. de Gràcia. Map p 73.

Jewelry
★★ **BCN Art Design** LA RIBERA Catalan modern artists like Dalí, Gaudí, and Picasso inspire the motifs for rings, bracelets, necklaces, and earrings created by these designers. c/ Princesa, 24. ☎ 93-268-13-08. MV, V. Metro: Jaume I. Map p 74.

★★ **Diana Cristó** LA RIBERA Contemporary jewelry executed in sterling silver and leather tends to hug the lines of the body and intricacies of the wrist. c/ Princesa, 12. ☎ 667-04-84-19. MC. V. Metro: Jaume I Map p 74.

★★ **Helena Rohner** LA RIBERA A very elegant but still edgy collection of silver, porcelain, wood, and leather necklaces and big, funky rings for women, men, and even kids, as well as stylish enameled earthenware and lamps for the home. c/ L'Espaseria, 13. ☎ 93-319-88-79. MC, V. Metro: Barceloneta. Map p 74.

Leather Goods
★★ **Iriarte Iriarte** LA RIBERA Crafters and purveyors of some of the hippest, sexiest handmade leather goods for both men and women, this chic little shop is above all a great spot for men to pick up elegant European-style briefcases that can't be derided as "man purses." c/ Cotoners, 12. ☎ 93-269-00-74. AE, DC, MC, V. Metro: Jaume I. Map p 74.

★★ **Loewe** L'EIXAMPLE This prestigious Spanish leather-goods and luxury fashion chain occupies the ground floor of a splendid modernista building on Passeig de Gràcia. Chic and expensive, this is where the elite shop. Pg. de Gràcia, 35. ☎ 93-216-04-00. AE, DC, MC, V. Metro: Pg. de Gràcia. Map p 73.

★★★ **Lupo Barcelona** L'EIXAMPLE Hipper and skewing younger than Loewe, Lupo is the hottest name in stylish leather goods. Bags and belts mold and fold leather into unexpected shapes and feature vivid colors. c/ Mallorca, 257 baixos. ☎ 93-487-80-50. AE, DC, MC, V. Metro: Pg. de Gràcia. Map p 73.

The old-fashioned hat shop Sombrerería Obach.

Music

★★ Discos Castelló RAVAL This independent music shop has three locations on one street alone, a corridor replete with music and vinyl outlets. The flagship store at no. 7 is mainly pop rock. Next door, you'll find jazz, Spanish, and world music. *c/ Tallers.* ☎ *93-301-59-46. MC, V. Metro: Catalunya. Map p 74.*

FNAC PLAÇA DE CATALUNYA The FNAC megastore is full of mainstream choices, with a nice selection of Spanish music and flamenco. *Pl. de Catalunya, 4.* ☎ *93-344-18-00. AE, DC, MC, V. Metro: Catalunya. Map p 73.*

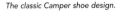

The classic Camper shoe design.

Old World Emporiums
★★ Cereria Subira BARRI GÒTIC The oldest continuous shop in Barcelona, this iconic store specializes in candles, from those used at Mass to more creative

and colorful numbers. *c/ Baixada de Llibreteria, 7.* ☎ *93-315-26-06. MC, V. Metro: Jaume I. Map p 74.*

★ Ganiveteria Roca BARRI GÒTIC An old-school specialty shop dealing exclusively in sharp objects: knives, blades, scissors, and other cutting instruments. *Pl. del Pi, 3.* ☎ *93-302-12-41. AE, MC, V. Metro: Jaume I. Map p 74.*

★★ Herbolisteria del Rei RAVAL A purveyor of herbs, natural remedies, cosmetics, and teas since 1823, this atmospheric shop looks the part. *c/ del Vidre, 1.* ☎ *93-318-05-12. MC, V. Metro: Catalunya or Liceu. Map p 74.*

★ Sombrerería Obach BARRI GÒTIC Proudly old-fashioned, this shop in the old Jewish quarter sells nothing but hats, including classic Spanish berets (boinas). *c/ del Call, 2.* ☎ *93-318-40-94. MC, V. Metro: Jaume I. Map p 74.*

Shoes
★★ Camper L'EIXAMPLE Camper shoes, which originated in Mallorca, are now famous across the globe. You can get the latest models of this hipster shoemaker, in unusual colors and shapes, in Barcelona. Shop interiors are even quirkier than the shoes. *Pg. de Gràcia, 2.* ☎ *93-521-62-50. AE, DISC, MC, V. Metro: Universitat. Map p 73.*

★ Casas BARRI GÒTIC Stocking the top Spanish brands of footwear as well as Italian and other imports, this is as close to one-stop shoe shopping as you'll find. *Portal de l'Angel, 40.* ☎ *93-302-11-12. AE, MC, V. Metro: Catalunya. Map p 74.* ●

5 The Best of the Outdoors

Montjuïc

1. Transbordador Aèri
2. Castell de Montjuïc/ Mirador de l'Alcalde
3. Jardí Botànic
4. La Font del Gat
5. Jardins del Claustre
6. Teatre Grec
7. Font Màgica

The largest green space in Barcelona, this gentle hill over-looking the city and out to the Mediterranean is treasured by families for its serene parkland as well as its museums and cultural attractions. First settled by Iberian Celtic peoples and then used by the Romans for ceremonies, Montjuïc has continued to play a central role in modern celebrations, including the 1929 International Exhibition and the 1992 Olympic Games. For other attractions in Montjuïc, see "The Best in Three Days," p 18, and "Barcelona with Kids," p 50. START: Aerial cable car or funicular to Montjuïc.

1 ★★ kids **Transbordador Aèri del Port.** The best way to get to the green expanse of Montjuïc is to soar over the city in this aerial cable car that travels from the harbor up to the hill—and

Previous page: Bicycles lined up in Parc de la Ciutadella.

drops you off near the spectacular cactus gardens of **Mossèn Costa i Llobera** (Ctra. Miramar, 1), the largest of their kind in Europe. See p 89, **5**.

2 Castell de Montjuïc. Pass the Plaça de la Sardana (marked by a sculpture of the folkloric Catalan

The fortress (castell) at Montjuïc.

group dance) and continue through the Miramar and Mirador gardens in Parc de Montjuïc. Then head up Carretera Montjuïc to **Mirador de l'Alcalde,** a viewpoint overlooking the sea. Just beyond is a castell (fortress) built in the 18th century to defend Barcelona. The courtyard is open to the public, and inside the castle is a modest military museum. The views of the sea, though, are the star attraction. *Ctra. de Montjuïc, 66.* ☎ *93-256-44-45.*

❸ ★★ **kids Jardí Botànic.** The Botanic Gardens of Barcelona, originally inaugurated in 1930, reopened as a new and improved, and beautifully landscaped, green space in the late '90s. The gardens show off Mediterranean-climate plants from all over the globe, including Africa, Australia, California, the Canary Islands, and Chile. The 71 zones have a cool modern aesthetic. They are connected by paths and feature walkways over ponds. *Dr. Font i Quer, 2 (Parc de Montjuïc).* ☎ *93-256-41-60. www. jardibotanic.bcn.es. Nov–Jan, Apr– May & Sept daily 10am–5pm; Feb– Mar & Oct daily 10am–6pm; June–Aug daily 10am–8pm. Admission 3.50€ adults, 1.70€ seniors, free under age 16. Free admission the last Sun of every month.*

❹ **La Font del Gat.** Down a path from the Fundació Joan Miró (see p 20) is this historic *modernista* cafe, now revived as a cafe and restaurant surrounded by gardens. It's a nice, open-air spot for a breather and refreshments, which might even be a fixed-price lunch. *Pg. de Santa Madrona, 28.* ☎ *93-289-04-04. $.*

❺ **Jardins del Claustre.** The Cloister Garden is one of the prettiest spots on Montjuïc, with a tree-lined pond, pergola, and sculpture by the Catalan artist Antoni Alsina for the 1929 International Exposition. *Av. Miramar/Pg. de Santa Madrona.*

❻ **Teatre Grec.** This replica of a bowl-shaped Greek theater, built for the 1929 World's Fair, continues to host open-air concerts and dance performances. Surrounded by gardens, it's a focal point of the **Festival Grec** music and arts festival held every summer. *Pg. de Santa Madrona, 36.* ☎ *93-301-77-75. http://grec.bcn.cat.*

❼ ★ **kids Font Màgica.** The wondrous waters of the "Magic Fountain" dance to a light and pop-music show at the center of a plaza in front of the Palau Nacional. *See p 21.*

Font Màgica.

Parc de la **Ciutadella**

1 Arc de Triomf
2 Castell dels Tres Dragons
3 L'Hivernacle/L'Umbracle
4 Passeig dels Til.lers
5 Cascada Fountain
6 El Llac
7 Parlament de Catalunya
8 Parc Zoològic

In a dense city with few green spaces, Barcelona's largest urban oasis is this 30-hectare (74-acre) park between the old city and waterfront. The park makes for an ideal respite from the city, with the Barcelona Zoo, a massive waterfall fountain, lake, sculptures, and monuments, and wide promenades and tree-lined trails for strolling or cycling. The park has a peculiar history: After the end of the Spanish War of Succession in 1714, King Felipe V ordered the neighborhood "of traitors" razed, and he built a citadel, which later functioned as a prison for political opponents, in its place. Local authorities demolished the citadel and in 1872 built a large park, which hosted the 1888 World's Fair. START: **Arc de Triomf.**

1 ★ **Arc de Triomf.** The formal gate to Parc de la Ciutadella is this massive red-brick triumphal arch, built in 1888. The wide avenue Passeig de Lluís Campanys, lined with large palm trees and ornate pale-blue iron lampposts, leads into the park. *Pg. de Lluís Campanys, s/n.*

2 **Castell dels Tres Dragons.** You can't miss this Moorish-influenced brick and sheet iron building that was the former home of the Museu de Zoologia. It was originally designed by Domènech i Montaner in 1888 as a restaurant and cafe for the Exposición Universal de Barcelona. *Pg. Picasso, 5.*

The Arc de Triomf marks the entrance to Parc de la Ciutadella.

③ kids L'Hivernacle/ L'Umbracle. The Hivernacle, located just beyond the Castell dels Tres Dragons, is an iron-and-glass greenhouse designed in 1884. Today it occasionally hosts concerts. Slightly farther down Passeig de Picasso is the Umbracle, a peaceful spot full of tropical plants and palm trees under its tall nave.

④ Passeig dels Til.lers. The wide "Avenue of Lime Trees" is marked at the southern end by an equestrian statue of General Prim, who ordered the old fortress demolished. Although the original statue was melted down during the Civil War, a replacement was commissioned from the sculptor Frederic Marès in 1940.

⑤ ★ kids Cascada Fountain. This massive ornamental fountain, featuring Aurora's chariot, is the work of Josep Fontserè, although much of its recognition is due to the contributions of his young apprentice, Antoni Gaudí, who was just a student at the time. Gaudí added the decorative lampposts and other details.

⑥ kids El Llac. In the center of the park is this tree-ringed lake,

with rowboats for rent, just as they were at the end of the 19th century.

⑦ Parlament de Catalunya. Home to the regional parliament since 1932, this grand building, once the arsenal of the citadel, faces a pond and the 1903 *modernista* sculpture, *El Desconsol* (Grief), by Josep Llimona.

⑧ ★★ kids Parc Zoològic. The Barcelona Zoo, which has been in Ciutadella Park since 1892, features a gardenlike setting that occupies nearly half the park's expanse, with 4,000 animals kept not in cages, but behind moats. *See p 53,* ⑤.

A bear in the Parc Zoològic.

The **Waterfront**

Tourist Information
Metro Station

Ronda Litoral

Balboa

Ginebra

Plaça del Llagut

Plaça Maquinista

Plaça Pompeu Gener

La Maquinista

Plaça Andrea Dòria

BARCELONETA ❸

Plaça Poeta Boscà

Sant Carles

Plaça Pau Vila

Barceloneta Ⓜ

Palau de Mar
(Museu d'Història
de Catalunya)

❹

Clara

Almirall Cervera

Santa

Passeig Marítim
de la Barceloneta

Platja
Barceloneta

Cap de
Barcelona

Moll de
Dipòsit

Moll de la
Barceloneta

Passeig Joan de Borbó

Almirall Aixada

Comte

MEDITERRANEAN SEA

Moll
d'Espanya

IMAX

**L'Aquàrium
de Barcelona**

Dàrsena
del Comerç

Drassana

Plaça
del Mar

Judici

Platja
St. Sebastià

Plaça Duc
de Medinaceli

Passeig de Colom

Moll de
la Fusta ❷

CLUB
NÀUTIC

**Port
Vell**

Moll dels
Pescadors

Escar

Pg. de l'Escullera

Plaça
Palmeres

Drassanes Ⓜ

**Reials
Drassanes**
(Museu Marítim)

La Rambla

**Mirador
de Colom**

Plaça
Portal de
la Pau

Moll de
les Drassanes

❶

(Ronda Litoral)

Rambla
de Mar

REIAL
CLUB
MARÍTIM

Maremàgnum

Dàrsena
Nacional

Moll de
Balears

Transbordador Aeri

❺

Plaça
Drassanes

To Montjuïc ←

Moll de
Barcelona

**World
Trade
Center**

Dàrsena de
Sant Bertran

Moll de
Sant Bertran

Ronda Litoral

0 1/4 mile
0 1/4 km

St. Martí

Parc de la
Ciutadella

L'Eixample

Map
Area

Ciutat
Vella

Montjuïc

❶ Las Golondrinas
❷ Moll de la Fusta
❸ Barceloneta
❹ La Bombeta
❺ Transbordador Aeri
❻ Platges/Port Olímpic

For much of the 20th century, Barcelona's Mediterranean waterfront was a polluted, industrial, and marginalized sector. But Barcelona took advantage of the 1992 Olympic Games to completely revamp the old port and beaches and create new areas for leisure. Today it's Barcelona's outdoor playground, an essential part of the city. START: **Metro to Drassanes.**

1 [kids] **Las Golondrinas.** You'll see these double-decker "swallow boats" lined up across from the Mirador de Colom, boarding passengers for 35- to 90-minute cruises around the old harbor and coast. *Pl. Portal de la Pau, s/n.* ☎ *93-442-31-06. www.lasgolondrinas.com. Daily 10am–8pm summer, 10am–5pm winter. 7€–15€ adults, 3€–5€ ages 4–10.*

2 ★ **Moll de la Fusta.** The tree-lined boardwalk in front of Port Vell (the old port) extends to the Barceloneta district and is extremely popular with locals on weekend strolls. At the eastern end of the promenade are massive pop-art sculptures of a giant crayfish by Xavier Mariscal and a head by Roy Lichtenstein.

3 ★ **Barceloneta.** Barcelona's fishermen and their families inhabited this picturesque beachfront neighborhood for decades before it received a stylistic makeover starting in 1992 (its ongoing renovation continues apace). Although it's gone upscale, a few traditional low-key seafood restaurants called *chiringuitos* have survived.

4 ★ **La Bombeta.** This authentic tapas joint serves great seafood snacks like mussels and fried calamari. The bombas are the house take on patatas bravas (fried potatoes with a spicy sauce). *c/ Maquinsta, 3.* ☎ *93-319-94-45. $–$$.*

5 ★ [kids] **Transbordador Aèri.** The aerial cable car that climbs from the port to Montjuïc starts out in Barceloneta and stops at the World Trade Center before soaring above the harbor. *See p 84,* **1**.

6 ★★ **Platges/Port Olímpic.** Barcelona's urban beaches (*platges*) have been wholly transformed, and the water quality is now excellent. Popular with families, topless sunbathers, and surfers, the beaches are lined with public sculptures, bars and restaurants, and paths for biking, in-line skating, and walking. Moving east, they are, in order: Barceloneta, Nova Icària, Bogatell, and Mar Bella (unofficially a nudist beach). Nova Icària is the most popular, the best spot for people-watching and with the most bars and restaurants within easy reach; Bogatell and Mar Bella are even prettier and less populated. The Port Olímpic marina between the first two beaches is full of chic sailboats and trendy restaurants and bars.

The beach at Barceloneta.

Barcelona **by Bike**

2 Tibidabo

El Coll   Horta
El Puget   Parc Güell
El Guinardó   St. Andreu
Gràcia   El Clot
L'Eixample   Map   Poble Nou
Area   St. Martí
Parc de la
Ciutadella
Ciutat   Barceloneta
Vella
Sarrià   Ciutat
Les   Vella
Corts
Parc de
Montjuïc

1/2 mile
1/2 km
0

GRÀCIA

Sagrada
Família

La Pedrera

Av. Diagonal

Gran Via Corts Catalanes

Estació
del Nord

Arc de
Triomf

Plaça
Glòries
Catalanes

Torre
Agbar

Av. Meridiana

Pere IV

Pujades

SANT
MARTÍ

Parc de
Diagonal-Mar

Diagonal
Mar
Forum

POBLE NOU

Av. Diagonal

Pere IV

Av. d'Icària

Marítim

Passeig

Port
Olímpic

Parc de la
Ciutadella

Parlament de
Catalunya

Parc
Zoològic

Estació
de França

Start

Finish **1**

BARCELONETA

Museu
Picasso

LA
RIBERA

Catedral

BARRI
GÒTIC

CIUTAT
VELLA

Mirador
de Colom

Passeig de Gràcia

Rambla Catalunya

Start

Finish

Plaça
Catalunya

3

Rambla

La Rambla

Gran Teatre
del Liceu

EL RAVAL

Rda. St. Antoni

Univ. de
Barcelona

L'EIXAMPLE

Av. Roma

Gran Via Corts Catalanes

Av. Paral·lel

POBLE
SEC

Fundació
Joan Miró

Parc de
Montjuïc

LA
FRANÇA

Plaça
Països
Catalans

Parc de
Joan Miró

Av. Josep Tarradelles

Tarragona

Av. Diagonal

1 Waterfront
2 Mont Tibidabo
3 L'Eixample

Barcelona has gone wild for bicycling and you'll see people everywhere using the city's popular community "bicing" red-and-white bikes, picking them up in one spot and dropping them off in another. On two wheels you can navigate the narrow streets of the old city and the broad avenues of L'Eixample, but the most relaxed areas for cycling are the designated bike paths of the Waterfront and Tibidabo.

① ★★ **Waterfront.** Starting out at Barceloneta, take Passeig Marítim and head northeast along the beach, to Port Olímpic and Vila Olímpica, where you can ride around the wide avenues of the former Olympic Village. Cycle along the paths lining the beaches; you can continue as far north as Parc del Fòrum. For an easy ride, return to Barceloneta along the same path. Or opt for a more ambitious ride: Travel west along Avinguda

Carretera de les Aigües, on Mont Tibidabo, is a scenic bike path.

L'Estel Ferit sculpture on the beach at Barceloneta.

Diagonal to Plaça de les Glòries and then head south along Avinguda Meridiana, which leads right to Parc de la Ciutadella. Within the park, you can bike around wide, unpaved avenues. From here, it's a short distance back to Barceloneta.

② ★ **Mont Tibidabo.** Winding across the hillside of Mt. Tibidabo is the Carretera de les Aigües, a

Modernisme by Bike

From the late 19th century until the 1930s, a school of *modernista* architects thrived in Barcelona, building hundreds of private houses and public works, most concentrated in the L'Eixample quarter, a geometric grid that enlarged the city northward from its medieval core. By bike, you'll be able to roam the streets and see dozens more examples of the movement so identified with Barcelona than you could on foot.

Practical Matters: Barcelona by Bike

City bike lanes are indicated on the CicloBus Barcelona map, available at the Tourist Information Office (Pl. de Catalunya, 17; underground) or at most bike-rental shops. Bike-rental rates are about 5€ per hour or 15€ to 18€ per day. The ubiquitous red-and-white **bicing** bikes (www.bicing.cat) of the city's massively popular community bicycling program are intended only as alternative transportation for city residents who pay a low annual fee, and are not available to rent for leisure activities.

Barcelona by Bike (c/ Esparteria, 3; ☎ 93-268-21-05; www.bicicletabarcelona.com): Rentals and guided bike tours of the old city and harbor.

Biking in Barcelona (Pg. Marítim de la Barceloneta, 33; ☎ 93-221-97-78; www.bikinginbarcelona.net): Cruiser, adult tricycle, and tandem bike rentals, as well as organized and self-guided bike tours along nature and cultural routes.

Classic Bikes Barcelona (c/ Tallers, 45; ☎ 93-317-19-70; www.barcelonarentbikes.com): Guided cyclotours and rentals of folding and Dutch bikes.

Barcelonabiking.com (c/ Baixada de Sant Miquel, 6; ☎ 656-356-300; http://barcelonabiking.com): Organized bike tours of the city, including routes (and machines) for experienced road cyclists and mountain bikers, as well as rentals for touring on your own.

Terra Diversions (☎ 93-416-08-05; www.terradiversions.com): Organized bike tours that are particularly appealing if you don't want to bike in the city—a half-day guided mountain bike tour of Parc de Collserola on the hillside of Mount Tibidabo or a self-guided 6-day tour of the Penèdes wine region.

Cooltra scooter touring (Pg. Juan de Borbó, 80–84; ☎ 93-221-40-70; www.cooltra.com): The Cooltra scooter company offers several guided tour options, including a city tour, *modernisme* tour, and a "beach and fun" tour. Must be 21 and have a driver's license.

cycling and jogging path that's a favorite of locals on weekends. Part of the Parc de la Collserola, the 8km (5-mile) unpaved path has drinking fountains at regular intervals and splendid views of Barcelona spread out below. The beginning of the route is about 1km (.6 miles) from Avenida del Tibidabo; take the Tramvia Blau (see p 22) there and walk. You might want a mountain bike for this ride.

❸ **L'Eixample.** Although much of the city is clogged with traffic, there are several major thoroughfares with safe biking lanes. Avinguda Diagonal, Gran Via de les Corts Catalanes, and Rambla de Catalunya all provide clearly marked lanes on medians. A ride in this neighborhood is a great way to take in the Eixample's dense collection of *modernista* architecture (see p 40 and p 68). ●

Dining Best Bets

Best **Traditional Catalan Dining**
★ Agut d'Avignon $$$ c/ Trinitat, 3 (p 98)

Best **Upstart Gourmet**
★★★ Cinc Sentits $$$ c/ Aribau, 58 (p 101); and ★★★ Dos Palillos $$$ c/ Elisabets, 9 (p 101)

Best **Worth the Wait**
★★ Cal Pep $$ Pl. des les Olles, 8 (p 100); and ★★ Quimet i Quimet $ c/ Poeta Cabanyes, 25 (p 105)

Best **Desserts (for All Courses)**
★★ Espai Sucre $$ c/ de la Princesa, 53 (p 102)

Best **for Foodies, Wine & Design Freaks**
★★★ ABaC $$$$ Av. Tibidabo, 1 (p 98); and ★★★ Roca Moo $$$$ c/ Rosselló, 265 (p 105)

Best **Comfort Food**
★ Senyor Parellada $$ c/ L'Argenteria, 37 (p 105)

Best **Classic Tapas**
★★ Alta Taberna Paco Meralgo $$ c/ Muntaner, 117 (p 98); and ★★ Lolita Tapería $ c/ Tamarit, 104 (p 103)

Best **Designer Tapas**
★★ Comerç 24 $$$ c/ Comerç, 24 (p 101)

Best **Mammoth Portions (The Antithesis of Tapas)**
★★ 7 Portes $$ Pg. d'Isabel II, 14 (p 105)

Best **Seaside Dining**
★★ Can Majó $$$ c/ Almirall Aixada, 23 (p 100)

Best **Seafood**
★★ Big Fish $$ Comercial, 9 (p 99); and ★★★ Els Pescadors $$$ Plaça Prim, 1 (p 102)

Best for a **Fancy Family Meal**
★★ 7 Portes $$ Pg. d'Isabel II, 14 (p 105)

Best **for Impatient Kids**
★ La Paradeta $$ c/ Comercial, 7 (p 103)

Best **Modernista Digs**
★★ Casa Calvet $$$ c/ Casp, 48 (p 100); and ★ Els Quatre Gats $$ c/ Montsió, 3 (p 102)

Best **Relaxed Beachfront Dining**
★ Agua $$ Ps. Marítim de la Barceloneta, 30 (p 98)

Best **Dining within a Food Market**
★★ El Quim de la Boquería $$ La Rambla, 91 (p 102)

Best **Lunch Deal**
★ Dolso $ c/ Valencia, 227 (p 101); and ★★ Restaurant Embat $$ c/ Mallorca, 304 (p 105)

Best **Value Foodie Restaurant**
★★ Hisop $$ Pge. Marimón, 9 (p 102)

Previous page: A menu board at Tapas 24.

L'Eixample

0 _____ 1/4 mile
0 _____ 1/4 km

ZONA ALTA

Plaça Lesseps
Lesseps
Galdos
Torrent de l'Olla
Robi

Av. Príncep d'Astúries
Gran de Gràcia

GRÀCIA

Madrazo

Fontana M

Plaça Diamant
Verdi

Casa Calvet
Amigó
Santaló
Muntaner
Aribau
Avenir
Alfons XII
Balmes

Plaça Gal.la Placídia

Parc Güell

Plaça rancesc Macià

Travessera de Gràcia

Map Area
Gràcia
L'Eixample
Montjuïc
Ciutat Vella

Buenos Aires

Av. Diagonal
Tuset
Balmes
Via Augusta
Riera St. Miquel

ⓘ Tourist Information
Ⓜ Metro Station

Londres
Villarroel
Casanova
Muntaner

Paris

Plaça Rei Joan Carles I

Torrent de l'Olla

Còrsega
Aribau
Enric Granados

Diagonal M
Rosselló

Av. Diagonal

Casa de les Punxes

Casa Milà (La Pedrera)
Provença

Hospital Clínic

Provença

Rambla Catalunya
Passeig de Gràcia
Claris

Casa Thomas

Mallorca

8 →
9 →

Mallorca

L'EIXAMPLE

València

Balmes

Fundació Antoni Tàpies

Pau Claris
Roger de Llúria
Bruc

Av. Roma
Villarroel
Casanova
Muntaner
Aribau

Aragó
Plaça Dr. Letamendi

Consell de Cent

Casa Batlló
Casa Amatller
Casa Lleó Morera

Passeig de Gràcia

Aragó

Consell de Cent

Diputació
Universitat de Barcelona

Rambla Catalunya
Passeig de Gràcia

Diputació

ran Via Corts Catalanes
Urgell

Plaça Universitat
Universitat Ⓜ

Gran Via Corts Catalanes

Casp
Pau Claris
Roger de Llúria
Bruc

Villarroel

Plaça Castella
Ronda de St. Antoni

Pelai
Tallers
Balmes

Ronda Universitat
Bergara
Plaça Catalunya
Pelai

Plaça Urquinaona
Ⓜ Urquinaona
Fontanella
Trafalgar

13

MACBA
EL RAVAL
Museu d'Art Contemporani de Barcelona

CCCB
Tallers

ⓘ
Ⓜ Catalunya

Ciutat Vella & Waterfront

St. Marti

L'Eixample   Parc de la Ciutadella

Ciutat Vella   Map Area

Montjuïc

Universitat de Barcelona

L'EIXAMPLE

Plaça Gran Via Corts Catalanes
Universitat
Universitat Ⓜ

Ronda Universitat

Rambla Catalunya

Pg. de Gràcia

Casp

Rda. de St. Antoni

Plaça Castella

Pelai

Balmes

Bergara

Tallers

Pelai

Plaça Catalunya ⓘ

Urquinaona Ⓜ

Bruc

Ronda Sant Pere

Fontanella

Trafalgar

Casa de la Caritat

Catalunya Ⓜ

Santa Anna

Av. Porta de l'Angel

Comtal

Palau de la Música Catalana
St. Pere Més Alt

Museu d'Art Contemporani de Barcelona

Plaça Caramelles

Elisabets

Xucla

Canuda

Montsió

❷

Via Laietana

St. Pere Més Baix

LA RIBERA

Pintor Fortuny

Carme

Betlem

Palau de la Virreina

Palau Moja

Portaferrissa

La Rambla

Plaça Antoni Maura

Av. Francesc Cambó

Antic Hospital de la Sta. Creu

❸

Mercat de la Boqueria

St. Felip Neri

Sta. Maria del Pí ✝

Av. Catedral

Mercaders

Mercat Santa Caterina

Plaça Allada i Vermell

Hospital

Boqueria

❹

Catedral ✝

Bòria

Rec

La Rambla del Raval

Plaça Sant Agustí

❾

Liceu Ⓜ

❺

Generalitat

Jaume I Ⓜ

Museu Picasso

EL RAVAL

Gran Teatre del Liceu

Ferran

Call Plaça St. Jaume

BARRI GÒTIC

Argenteria

Banys Vells

Montcada

Marquès de Barberá

❻

Lleona

ⓘ

❶❶

Pg. Born

Nou de la Rambla

Plaça Reial

CIUTAT VELLA

Ataúlf

❶❷

Via Laietana

Santa Maria del Mar ✝

Palau Güell

Escudellers

❽

Avinyó

Gignàs

❶❸

Carbassa

Codols

❶❺ ❶❻

Arc del Teatre

Av. Drassanes

← ❿

Centre d'Art Sta. Monica

Palau March

Ample

Mercè Plaça Antonio López

Llotja de Mar

Plaça del Palau

Marquesa

La Mercè ✝

Portal de Sta. Madrona

Drassanes Ⓜ

Passeig de Colom

Cap de Barcelona

Barceloneta Ⓜ

Plaça Pau Vila

Reials Drassanes (Museu Marítim)

Plaça Portal de la Pau

Mirador de Colom

Moll de (Ronda Litoral)

Moll de Dipòsit

Palau de Mar (Museu d'Història de Catalunya)

Ginebra

Plaça Drassanes

Golondrinas

Moll de la Fusta

Moll d'Espanya

La Maquin

Moll de les Drassanes

Rambla da Mar

Port Vell

IMAX

BARCELONETA

Moll de Barcelona

Maremàgnum

L'Aquàrium de Barcelona

❶❽

❶❾

Plaça Poeta Boso

Moll dels Pescadors

Moll de la Barceloneta

Comte Sta. Clara

Passeig Joan de Borbó

Sant Car

Almirall Cerve

World Trade Center

Transbordador Aéri

Moll de Balears

Escar

Passeig de la Escollera

Almirall Aixada

Judici

❷⓪

Pg. de la Escollera Drasana
Plaça del Mar

Platja St. Sebastià

Plaça Palmeres

ⓘ Tourist Information

Ⓜ Metro Station

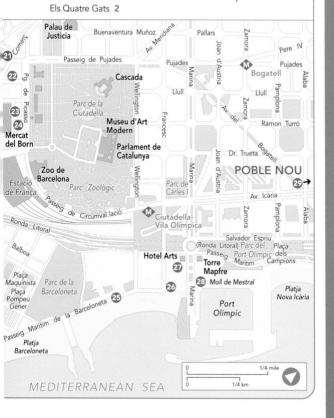

Barcelona Dining A to Z

Dining Hours Tip

Catalans generally have lunch between 2 and 4pm and dinner (sometimes well) after 9pm. Most kitchens stay open until 11:30pm, if not later.

★★★ **ABaC** ZONA ALTA *CATALAN/INTERNATIONAL* A longtime favorite with in-the-know foodies, ABaC is now part of a designer boutique hotel in new uptown digs, but the quiet confidence and creativity that garnered two Michelin stars continue under the watchful eye of chef Jordi Cruz. The (pricey) menu is innovative to the point of being experimental. *Av. Tibidabo, 1.* ☎ *93-319-66-00. www.abacbarcelona. com. Entrees 42€–72€; tasting menus 135€–155€. AE, DC, MC, V. Lunch & dinner Tues–Sat. Closed Aug. Map p 95.*

★ kids **Agua** WATERFRONT (VILA OLIMPICA) *MEDITERRANEAN* A casually cool spot with great beach views, Agua is popular for simply prepared fresh fish, rice dishes, and vegetarian items. It's a great spot for families with boisterous and picky young ones. *Pg. Marítim, 30.*

☎ *93-225-12-72. www.grupo tragaluz.com. Entrees 9€–22€. AE, DC, MC, V. Lunch & dinner daily. Metro: Ciutadella. Map p 96.*

★ **Agut d'Avignon** BARRI GÒTIC *CATALAN* A classic revered among locals for its consistently fine, traditional Catalan cooking, this rustic spot is a favorite of gourmands who want to sample the down-to-earth ingredients of *cuina catalana,* such as duck with figs and *langostino* (prawn) aioli. *c/ Trinitat, 3 (alley off Avinyó, 8).* ☎ *93-317-36-93. Entrees 30€–45€. MC, V. Lunch & dinner daily. Closed last 3 weeks in Aug. Metro: Jaume I or Liceu. Map p 96.*

★★ **Alta Taberna Paco Meralgo** L'EIXAMPLE *TAPAS* A casual, boisterous spot, popular with locals in the know, this amiable neighborhood restaurant is serious about its classic tapas; graze at the bar or grab a tall seat in one of the two dining rooms to work your way through a long list of tapas and original *montaditos* (gourmet sandwiches). Be prepared to wait if you don't have a reservation. The name, by the way, is a play on words, meaning roughly "to grab a bite." *c/ Muntaner, 117.* ☎ *93-430-90-27.*

Bestial's waterfront location is ideal for alfresco dining.

Arola, in the Hotel Arts.

www.pacomeralgo.com. Tapas 3.50€–18€. DC, MC, V. Lunch & dinner daily. Metro: Hospital Clínic. Map p 95.

★★ **Arola** WATERFRONT (VILA OLIMPICA) CATALAN/SPANISH Amid colorful, pop-art decor, chef Sergi Arola does a modern take on *pica-pica* ("nibbles") and adds bursts of flavor to Mediterranean standards, such as steamed mussels with citrus juice and saffron. The sleek, dark **Enoteca** within the hotel is another superb option. c/ Marina, 19–21 (Hotel Arts). ☎ 93-221-10-00. www.arola-arts. com. Entrees 18€–42€; tasting menu 75€. AE, DC, MC, V. Lunch & dinner Wed–Sun. Closed Jan. Metro: Ciutadella–Vila Olímpica. Map p 96.

kids Bestial WATERFRONT (VILA OLIMPICA) MEDITERRANEAN/ITALIAN This hip but relaxed spot has large picture windows framing a very attractive outdoor space and magnificent views of the beach. The Mediterranean menu has an Italian bent, offering pastas, risottos, and individual pizzas with fresh ingredients, and there's a good-value midday menu. c/ Ramón Trias Fargas, 2–4. ☎ 93-224-04-07. www.grupotragaluz. com. Entrees 15€–30€. AE, DC, MC, V.

Lunch & dinner daily. Metro: Ciutadella–Vila Olímpica. Map p 96.

★★ **Big Fish** LA RIBERA SEAFOOD A romantic place with high ceilings, funky chandeliers, and boho-chic style to burn, this contemporary spot, opened by a fifth-generation fishmonger, is very serious about market-fresh fish, with classic Mediterranean preparations and fun takes on sushi. c/ Comercial, 9. ☎ 93-268-17-28. www. bigfish.cat. Entrees 14€–32€. MC, V. Lunch & dinner daily. Metro: Arc de Triomf or Barceloneta. Map p 96.

★★★ **Botafumeiro** GRACIA SEAFOOD Among seafood restaurants, none has more pedigree than this perennial favorite, which has entertained Barcelona's elite as well as the king of Spain for years. Much of the incredibly fresh seafood is flown in daily from Galicia (read: it's not cheap). The long seafood bar has repeatedly been named the best in Spain. Gran de Gràcia, 81. ☎ 93-218-42-30. www.botafumeiro. es. Entrees 24€–70€. AE, DC, MC, V. Lunch & dinner daily. Closed last 3 weeks in Aug. Metro: Fontana or Diagonal. Map p 95.

★ **Café de L'Academia** BARRI GÒTIC *CATALAN* This dark, ancient-looking little restaurant on a lovely medieval square is a local favorite and is usually packed for lunch, when it offers a superb fixed-price menu. In warm weather, tables are set out on the terrace, a perfect place to drink in this quint-essential Barri Gòtic corner. *c/ Lledó, 1.* ☎ *93-319-82-53. Entrees 10€–14€. AE, MC, V. Lunch & dinner Mon–Fri. Closed last 3 weeks in Aug. Metro: Jaume I. Map p 96.*

★★ **Cal Pep** LA RIBERA/WATER-FRONT *SEAFOOD* This tiny place used to be a secret, but local food-ies and those from abroad now know that it serves some of the most succulent seafood in town. Cal Pep doesn't take reservations (except for groups of four or more), so wait until a seat at the counter opens up. There's no menu, either, but Pep and his boys will set you up with the works. *Pl. des les Olles, 8.* ☎ *93-310-79-61. www.calpep. com. Entrees 14€–28€. AE, DC, MC, V. Dinner Mon; lunch & dinner Tues–Fri; lunch only Sat. Closed Aug. Metro: Barceloneta or Jaume I. Map p 96.*

★ **Can Costa** WATERFRONT (BARCELONETA) *SEAFOOD* Since the 1930s, this has been one of the most dependable restaurants in Barcelona. Although there's no har-bor view, the freshly prepared seafood

makes up for it. Longtime admirers claim the sautéed baby squid is without equal. A good choice is *fideuà de peix,* similar to shellfish paella but made with thin, dark noodles rather than rice. *Pg. de Joan de Borbón, 70.* ☎ *93-221-59-03. www.cancosta.com. Entrees 12€–32€. AE, DC, MC, V. Lunch & dinner Mon–Tues & Thurs–Sat; lunch only Sun. Closed Wed. Metro: Barcelo-neta. Map p 96.*

★ **Can Culleretes** BARRI GÒTIC *CATALAN* Barcelona's oldest res-taurant has been serving traditional Catalan cooking since 1786. It's down-home and old-school, a good place to try such standards as *espinacas a la catalana* (spinach with pine nuts and raisins) and *buti-farra* (white sausage). *c/ Quintana, 5.* ☎ *93-317-64-85. www.culleretes. com. Entrees 8€–18€. MC, V. Lunch & dinner Tues–Sat; lunch only Sun. Closed late July to early Aug. Metro: Liceu. Map p 96.*

★★ **Can Majó** WATERFRONT (PORT VELL) *SEAFOOD* Insiders know that this tavern-style, harbor-front restaurant is one of the top places in Barcelona for superfresh seafood. Try the excellent *sopa de pescado y marisco* (fish and shell-fish soup), sautéed squid, or pael-las. *c/ Almirall Aixada, 23.* ☎ *93-221-54-55. www.canmajo.es. Entrees 12€–32€. AE, DC, MC, V. Lunch & dinner Tues–Sat; lunch only Sun. Metro: Barceloneta. Map p 96.*

★★ **Casa Calvet** L'EIXAMPLE *CATALAN/MEDITERRANEAN* Casa Calvet is housed within one of Antoni Gaudí's first *modernista* apartment buildings, with a gorgeous white-brick and stained-glass decor. The

An innovative dish at Cinc Sentits.

contemporary Catalan cuisine doesn't take a back seat to the surroundings. c/ Casp, 48. ☎ 93-412-40-12. www.casacalvet.es. Entrees 18€–28€; tasting menus 44€–68€. AE, DC, MC, V. Lunch & dinner Mon–Sat. Closed last 2 weeks in Aug. Metro: Pg. de Gràcia. Map p 95.

★ Cerveseria Catalana

L'EIXAMPLE TAPAS/CATALAN "Catalan beer tavern" certainly doesn't sound or look like much—it's primarily a beer tavern with finger foods—but Barcelonans know that some of the best tapas in town are served at this bustling institution. Knock back the montaditos (little sandwiches) and classic plates of shrimp and Spanish ham with one of the many international beers on hand. But be prepared to wait; this mainstay is as enduringly popular as they come. c/ Mallorca, 236. ☎ 93-216-03-68. Tapas 6€–15€. AE, DC, MC, V. Breakfast, lunch & dinner daily. Metro: Pg. de Gràcia. Map p 95.

★★★ Cinc Sentits L'EIXAMPLE

MEDITERRANEAN Haute cuisine, but also family-run, this relative newcomer is a unique synthesis of the Barcelona dining scene. The innovative fusion cuisine of Chef Jordi Artal, Catalan by way of Canada, is best sampled on the "Gastronòmic" menu offered to eight diners midday. Prepare yourself for monkfish sprinkled with bacon "dust" or a soft poached egg with tomato jam. c/ Aribau, 58. ☎ 93-323-94-90. www.cincsentits. com. Menus 65€, 79€, 109€. AE, DC, MC, V. Lunch Mon; lunch & dinner Tues–Sat. Closed Easter week & last 2 weeks in Aug. Metro: Pg. de Gràcia. Map p 95.

★★ Comerç 24 LA RIBERA (EL

BORN) CATALAN Chef-owner Carles Abellan reinvents classic Catalan dishes through the lens of world cuisine. Despite the innovation, this is vibrant, earthy food—not a speck of foam in sight. c/ Comerç, 24. ☎ 93-319-21-02. www.carles abellan.es. Entrees 18€–38€; tasting menus 92€, 116€. AE, DC, MC, V. Lunch & dinner Tues–Sat. Closed Christmas week & last 3 weeks in Aug. Metro: Jaume I. Map p 96.

★ Dolso L'EIXAMPLE MEDITER-

RANEAN Although best known for its heavenly desserts, this smart, slender cafe is a real find for a smoking lunch menú deal (around 12€) and creative tasting menus at night—with Asian touches and, of course, spectacular sweet endings. c/ València, 227. ☎ 93-487-59-64. Tasting menu 25€–50€. AE, DC, MC, V. Lunch & dinner Mon–Sat. Metro: Pg. de Gràcia. Map p 95.

★★★ Dos Palillos RAVAL CATA-

LAN/ASIAN FUSION The "in" spot in Barcelona, launched by a former chef de cuisine at famed elBulli, is both playful and deadly serious about fusing Catalan, Japanese, and Chinese ingredients and techniques. The creativity and execution are stunning—and a relative steal for this level of forward-looking dining. A sensual feast, in a wickedly cool sushi restaurant–like

The minimalist design at Comerç 24.

space reached through an amusing neighborhood bar. c/ Elisabets, 9. ☎ 93-304-05-13. www.dospalillos. com. Tapas 4€–15€. Tasting menus 75€–90€. AE, DC, MC, V. Lunch & dinner Thurs–Sat; dinner only Tues–Wed. Closed last week in Dec, 1st week in Jan & last 3 weeks in Aug. Metro: Catalunya or Universitat. Map p 96.

★★ **El Quim de la Boquería** LA RAMBLA *CATALAN* Tucked within the sumptuous La Boquería food market, this unsung kiosk with a tiny kitchen and a handful of stools around a bar is a gourmet secret, serving up spectacular Catalan comfort food, fresh seafood sourced from just a few feet away, and such specialties as scrambled eggs with *llanguetas* (tiny whitefish) or baby squid. La Rambla, 91. ☎ 93-301-98-10. www.elquimde laboqueria.com. Entrees 8€–20€. AE, DC, MC, V. Breakfast & lunch Tues–Sat. Metro: Liceu. Map p 96.

★★★ kids **Els Pescadors** WATERFRONT (POBLE NOU) SEA-FOOD Family-run, "the Fishermen" focuses, naturally, on providing superb fresh seafood, with just a hint of new-school preparations. The dining rooms include an atmospheric, old-world tavern with marble tables and ceiling beams, and a more modern room; in warm weather, though, you can't beat the outdoor terrace on the classic

A dish at Dos Palillos (p 101).

Barcelona square, dominated by an ombú tree. The kids' menu is a nice find at such an exalted fish house. Pl. Prim, 1. ☎ 93-225-20-18. www. elspescadors.com. Entrees 15€–37€. AE, DC, MC, V. Lunch & dinner daily. Closed Easter week. Metro: Poble Nou. Map p 96.

★ **Els Quatre Gats** BARRI GÒTIC *CATALAN* This legendary cafe was the turn-of-the-20th-century hangout of Picasso and other bohemian intellectuals. The "Four Cats" today is on the *modernista* tourist circuit, but it's a surprisingly good spot for simple, homey Catalan fare using fresh market ingredients. c/ Montsió, 3. ☎ 93-302-41-40. www.4gats.com. Entrees 12€–28€. AE, DC, MC, V. Breakfast, lunch & dinner daily. Metro: Catalunya. Map p 96.

★★ **Espai Sucre** LA RIBERA *DESSERT* Were Willy Wonka a restaurateur, this might be his temple. Yes, this tiny, minimalist restaurant ("Sugar Space") exclusively serves dessert, but the tasting menus of dessert courses actually work as (more or less) balanced dinner menus. Cheese and more varied tasting menus add savory dishes, such as lamb with endive or squid with rice. c/ de la Princesa, 53. ☎ 93-268-16-30. www.espaisucre. com. Entrees 10€–15€; tasting menus 28€–48€. MC, V. Dinner Tues–Sat. Closed mid-Aug & Christmas week. Metro: Arc de Triomf. Map p 96.

★★ **Hisop** GRACIA *CONTEMPORARY CATALAN* Less intimidating than some of Barcelona's superchic restaurants featuring *cocina de autor* (Catalan haute cuisine), Hisop is small, inviting, and dynamic. Although it's difficult to find, on a tiny side street edging toward Grà-cia, it's worth the hunt for subtly complex dishes, such as john dory with cockles steamed in

The very mod Moo.

vanilla-scented broth. *Pg. Marimón, 9.* ☎ *93-241-32-33. www.hisop.com. Entrees 24€–28€; tasting menu 67€. AE, DC, MC, V. Lunch & dinner Tues–Sat. Closed last 2 weeks in Aug. Metro: Hospital Clínic. Map p 95.*

★ **kids La Paradeta** LA RIBERA *SEAFOOD* You can pick your own seafood and *mariscos* (shellfish) from large plastic tubs; it's then weighed and served on a platter. Kids should love it, and parents can accompany dinner with a nice selection of wines. *c/ Comercial, 7.* ☎ *93-268-19-39. www.laparadeta. com. Entrees (cost is per kilo) 14€– 28€. No credit cards. Dinner Tues– Sat; lunch Sat–Sun. Closed Dec 22–Jan 22. Metro: Arc de Triomf. Map p 96.*

★ **L'Electricitat** WATERFRONT (BARCELONETA) *TAPAS* At mid-day, the atmosphere in this immensely popular neighborhood bar is, as the name says, electric. It's a great place to have steamed mussels or clams, maybe a bite of fried fish, some anchovies, a finger sandwich with smoked trout, and then perhaps a small crab salad. There's beer on tap and a lot of inexpensive Catalan wines. They also tap the big barrels of house vermouth that look more ornamental than they are. *c/ Sant Carles, 15.*

☎ *93-221-50-17. Tapas 1.50€–12€. MC, V. Breakfast, lunch & dinner Tues–Sat; lunch Sun. Metro: Barcelo-neta. Map p 96.*

kids Les Quinze Nits BARRI GÒTIC *MEDITERRANEAN* This smart, bargain-priced restaurant under the arches on Plaça Reial draws long lines of people looking for a solid meal and a great deal. Dishes are simple and straightfor-ward but surprisingly well prepared, and the lunch *menú* is a steal. *Pl. Reial, 6.* ☎ *93-317-30-75. www. lesquinzenits.com. Entrees 7€–14€. MC, V. Lunch & dinner daily. Metro: Liceu. Map p 96.*

★★ **Lolita Tapería** L'EIXAMPLE (ESQUERRA) *TAPAS* Like its prede-cessor in the space, Inopia, Lolita is a classic tapas bar (patatas bravas, cod-stuffed red peppers) where the decor and vibe are tongue in cheek. Co-founder Joan Martínez has preserved the original dining concept of only top-grade prod-ucts, but he's pushed the envelope on entertainment. At midnight, DJs cut loose, and Lolita becomes a cocktail bar with dance floor. *c/ Tamarit, 104.* ☎ *93-424-52-31. www. lolitataperia.com. Tapas 4€–15€. MC, V. Dinner Tues–Fri; lunch & dinner Sat. Closed in Aug. Metro: Poble Sec. Map p 95.*

The Best Dining

kids Lonja de Tapas WATER-
FRONT/LA RIBERA/BARRI GÒTIC
TAPAS A bright and casual tapas
restaurant in a good-looking space
with high ceilings, this place is solid,
especially if you're just in the mood
for grazing or don't quite know what
you want. Tapas cover the Spanish
standards, from Iberian ham and
steamed cockles to paellas and
monkfish with wild mushrooms.
Other locations are on carrer
Montcada and career Jaume I. *Pl.
del Palau, 7.* ☎ *93-268-72-58. www.
lonjadetapas.com. Tapas 4€–20€. AE,
DC, MC, V. Lunch & dinner daily.
Metro: Barceloneta. Map p 96.*

Los Caracoles BARRI GÒTIC
CATALAN Popular with tourists,
this old-school restaurant is one of
those only-in-Spain places. You're
first greeted by an open spit roasting chickens; inside is an ancient,
atmospheric labyrinth of cluttered
dining rooms. "The Snails" is all
about Catalan comfort food, such
as *arroz negre* (rice cooked in squid
ink), grilled squid, and roast
chicken. *c/ Escudellers, 14.*
☎ *93-302-31-85. www.los-caracoles.
es. Entrees 8€–27€. AE, DC, MC, V.
Lunch & dinner daily. Metro: Liceu.
Map p 96.*

★ **Orgánic** RAVAL *VEGETARIAN*
It took a while for vegetarian

restaurants to catch on, but this
cool, laid-back place with large
communal tables really filled a void.
There's a help-yourself soup and
salad bar, and organic-focused
main courses include vegetarian
pizza, pasta, and stir-fries. *c/ Junta
de Comerç, 11.* ☎ *93-301-09-02.
www.antoniaorganickitchen.com.
Main courses 6€–15€. AE, DC, MC, V.
Lunch & dinner daily. Metro: Liceu.
Map p 96.*

★ **kids Pla** BARRI GÒTIC *MEDI-
TERRANEAN* Popular with locals
and visitors alike for its well-pre-
pared dishes at exceedingly fair
prices, this attractive restaurant
serves excellent carpaccios, tasty
salads, and gently exotic main
courses, such as Thai curry or
Moroccan couscous. *c/ Bellafila, 5.*
☎ *93-412-65-52. www.restaurantpla.
cat. Entrees 15€–25€. DC, MC, V.
Dinner daily. Closed Dec 25–27.
Metro: Jaume I. Map p 96.*

★ **Pla de la Garsa** LA RIBERA
CATALAN House-made pâtés, ter-
rines, and charcuterie show the dark
and savory side of traditional Catalan cookery, while sturgeon and
duck are menu staples. *Priorats* top
the wine list. *c/ Assaonadors, 13.*
☎ *93-315-24-13. www.pladelagarsa.
com. Entrees 9€–14€. AE, MC, V. Dinner daily. Metro: Jaume I. Map p 96.*

For innovative Spanish tapas, try Tapas 24.

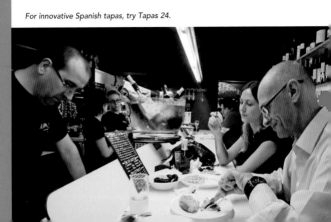

★★ Quimet i Quimet POBLE SEC *TAPAS* In the Poble Sec neighborhood, this incredible hole in the wall—with walls lined to the ceiling with liquor bottles and canned foods—is always jam-packed with hungry patrons and drinkers in the know, who come for the stunningly creative and delicious *montaditos* (little gourmet sandwiches). c/ Poeta Cabanyes, 25. ☎ 93-442-31-42. Tapas 4€–14€. MC, V. Lunch & dinner Mon–Fri; lunch Sat. Metro: Paral.lel. Map p 96.

★★ Restaurant Arrosseria Rosalert L'EIXAMPLE *SEAFOOD* In a hurry? The express menu gives you shellfish, a choice of finfish, and a pastry. More time? The arròs menu provides fish bites to nibble while the paella cooks. Order the *parrillada* of grilled fish and shellfish, and they don't stop until you say uncle. Av Diagonal, 301. ☎ 93-207-10-19. Entrees 22€–50€; express menu 15€; rice menu 27€. Lunch & dinner Tues–Sat; lunch only Sun. Metro: Verdaguer. Map p 95.

★★ Restaurant Embat L'EIXAMPLE *CONTEMPORARY CATALAN* This smart little restaurant, part of the "Bistronomic" wave in Barcelona, does clever Catalan cuisine at an extremely reasonable price. The dining room is relaxed, rustic chic, with rough-hewn tables and brown linens. Lunch is one of the best deals in the city. c/ Mallorca, 304. ☎ 93-458-08-55. www.restaurantembat.es. Entrees 18€–22€; tasting menu 42€. AE, DC, MC, V. Lunch Tues–Fri; dinner Thurs–Sat. Metro: Pg. de Gràcia. Map p 95.

★★★ Roca Moo L'EIXAMPLE *CATALAN* You can't get much more mod than Hotel Omm, home to this exquisite restaurant by the three Roca brothers who have assumed the mantle of Spain's avant-garde cuisine. The a la carte choices are few, but the menus let you choose Roca classics or Joan Roca's latest inventions. Wine pairings are terrific but cost extra. c/ Rosselló, 265. ☎ 93-445-40-00. www.hotelomm.es. Entrees 22€–45€; mid-day menu 37€; tasting menu 87€–110€. AE, DC, MC, V. Lunch & dinner Mon–Sat. Metro: Diagonal. Map p 95.

★ Senyor Parellada LA RIBERA *CATALAN/MEDITERRANEAN* One of the best values in Barcelona is this cheery, stylish restaurant carved out of a 19th-century mansion. The colorfully staged dining rooms are merely a prelude to dependably executed, fresh preparations of authentic Catalan fare, such as baked monkfish with mustard and garlic sauce, at welcome bargain prices. c/ L'Argenteria, 37. ☎ 93-310-50-94. www.senyor parellada.com. Entrees 9€–21€. AE, DC, MC, V. Lunch & dinner daily. Metro: Jaume I. Map p 96.

★★ 7 Portes WATERFRONT *CATALAN* A favorite of large dining parties since 1836, this elegant but unassuming place really does have seven doors under porticoes (hence the name). It's famous for its rice dishes, such as black rice with squid in its own ink; portions are enormous and reasonably priced. Pg. d'Isabel II, 14. ☎ 93-319-30-33. www.7portes.com. Entrees 23€–34€. AE, DC, MC, V. Lunch & dinner daily. Metro: Barceloneta or Drassanes. Map p 96.

★ Talaia Mar WATERFRONT (PORT OLIMPIC) *MEDITERRANEAN* The Olympic Port teems with restaurants, but none of them is as good as this one. The innovative chef has created a seafood-dominated menu, featuring grilled fresh fish and more audacious dishes that tempt the senses, including barnacles with a seawater

On the Menu

If you enjoy a Mediterranean-style diet, you'll feel right at home in Barcelona. *Catalunyan* cuisine depends heavily on fresh vegetables, such as tomatoes, eggplant, and artichokes, and because *Catalunyan* is one of Spain's major producers of pork products, you'll encounter a variety of sausages and the ubiquitous cured ham known as *jambon*. Barcelona is right beside the Mediterranean Sea, so you'll also find a wide variety of fish in restaurants, from fresh sardines and anchovies to tuna and cod.

Traditional *Catalunyan* cuisine is distinguished by stews and by dishes that mix sweet and savory flavors. Typical sauces and condiments include *allioli* (a thick sauce that literally translates as "garlic and oil"), *samfaina* (comparable to ratatouille), and *salvitxada* (a sauce based on nuts and red peppers). Chow down on escalivada (grilled vegetables), *ollada* (a meat and vegetable stew), pa amb tomàquet (bread smeared with tomato, oil, and garlic), or *esqueixada* (salted cod with tomato and onion), or combine the best of both worlds with mar I *muntanya* dishes combining meat and seafood.

Be sure to save room for dessert. *Crema catalana* is rightly the most famous of all *Catalunyan* desserts. A seemingly simple cream blending egg yolk, milk, and sugar, this *flanlike* concoction can appear as a stuffing for *xuixos* (fried pastries) or take center stage in its own right, served with fruit. Other mouth-watering offerings may include *mel i mató* (cheese and honey), *tortell* (a round pastry stuffed with *crema catalane* or a mixture of cacao, chocolate, and cream), and Barcelona's own version of *crema catalana, mató de monja*.

sorbet. *Marina, 16.* ☎ *93-221-90-90. www.barcelona-comercio.com/talaia. Entrees 18€–32€; fixed-price menu 51€. AE, DC, MC, V. Lunch & dinner Tues–Sun. Metro: Ciutadella–Vila Olímpica. Map p 96.*

kids **Taller de Tapas** BARRI GÒTIC *TAPAS* This pleasant "Tapas Workshop" simplifies the ordering of tapas. Although not innovative, the small dishes from across Spain—such as marinated anchovies, prawns with scrambled eggs, and sizzling chorizo cooked in cider—are prepared fresh in an open kitchen. Five other locations are scattered around the city. *Pl. Sant Josep Oriol, 9 (Pl. del Pi).*

☎ *93-301-80-20. www.tallerdetapas. com. Tapas 5€–26€. AE, DC, MC, V. Lunch & dinner daily. Metro: Liceu. Map p 96.*

★★ **Tapas 24** L'EIXAMPLE *CREATIVE TAPAS* Ultra-cool Comerç 24 does designer tapas, while this below-street-level bar is the more informal offshoot. But it shares an interest in fresh ingredients and just the right touch of creativity, and this location actually may be the more enjoyable of the two. *c/ Diputació, 269.* ☎ *93-488-09-77. www.carlesa-bellan.es.Tapas 4€–15€. MC, V. Breakfast, lunch & dinner Mon–Sat. Metro: Pg. de Gràcia. Map p 95.* ●

Nightlife Best Bets

Best **Old-World Atmosphere**
★★★ L'Ascensor, c/ Bellafila, 3
(p 113)

Best **Spot for Outlaw Liquor
(Absinthe)**
★★★ Marsella, c/ Sant Pau, 65 (p
113)

Best **Impersonation of a
French Port Bar**
★★★ Pastís, c/ Santa Mónica, 4
(p 113)

Best **People-Watching**
Café Zurich, Plaça de Catalunya, 1
(p 57)

Best **Wine Bar**
★★ La Vinya del Senyor, Plaça
Santa Maria, 5 (p 117)

Best **Pub for Soccer & Swearing in English**
The Black Horse, c/ Allada Vermell,
16 (p 112)

Best **Classic Cocktails**
★ Dry Martini Speakeasy, c/
Aribau, 162 (p 112)

Best **Xampanyeria (Cava Bar)**
★★★ El Xampanyet, c/ de la
Montcada, 22 (p 117)

Best **View**
★ Mirablau, Pl. Doctor Andreu, 2
(p 113)

Best **Beach Disco**
★★★ Opium, Pg. Marítim de la
Barceloneta, 34 (p 116)

Best **High-Design Bar/Lounge**
★★ Roca Bar/Ommsession Club,
c/ Rosselló, 265 (p 116)

Best **Latin Dance Club**
★★★ Antilla BCN Latin Club, c/
Aragó, 141 (p 114)

Best **Place to Lose Your Shirt**
Casino Barcelona, c/ Marina, 19–21
(p 114)

Best **Place to Dance Tango**
★★ Barcelona Pipa Club, c/ Pl.
Reial, 3. (p 114)

Best **Drag Show**
★★ Café Dietrich, c/ Consell de
Cent, 255 (p 115)

Best **Open-Air Dance Club**
★ La Terrazza, Av. Marquès de
Comillas, s/n (p 114)

Best **Lounge for Beautiful People & Paparazzi**
★ CDLC Barcelona, Pg. Marítim, 32
(p 116); and ★★ Roca Bar/
Ommsession Club, c/ Rosselló, 265
(p 116)

*Previous page: A performance at the
Apollo in Barcelona.*

Absinthe at Marsella.

L'Eixample

Ciutat Vella & Waterfront

L'EIXAMPLE

Universitat de Barcelona
Plaça Gran Via Corts Catalanes
Universitat
Universitat Ⓜ
Plaça Castella
Rda. de St. Antoni
Tallers
Balmes
Pelai
Ronda Universitat
Bergara
Plaça Catalunya ⓘ
Pg. de Gràcia
Casp
Rambla Catalunya
Plaça Urquinaona
Urquinaona Ⓜ
Fontanella
Ronda Sant Pere
Trafalgar
Girona

Casa de la Caritat
Museu d'Art Contemporani de Barcelona
Plaça ❶ Caramelles
❹ Pintor Fortuny
Carme
Elisabets
Xucla
Santa Anna
Canuda
Av. Portal de l'Angel
Comtal
Montsió
Via Laietana
St. Pere Més Alt
Palau de la Música Catalana
St. Pere Més Baix
LA RIBERA

Antic Hospital de la Sta. Creu
❺
Mercat de la Boqueria
Palau de la Virreina
✝ Betlem
Palau Moja
Portaferrissa
St. Felip Neri
Sta. María del Pi ✝
Av. Catedral Antoni Maura
Plaça Antoni Maura
✝ Catedral
Mercaders
Mercat Santa Caterina
Av. Francesc Cambó

EL RAVAL
La Rambla del Raval
Hospital
Plaça Salvador Segui
❻
Gran Teatre del Liceu
Liceu Ⓜ
Boqueria
Ferran
Cal
Plaça St. Jaume
BARRI GÒTIC
Bòria
Jaume I Ⓜ
Argenteria
Princesa
Plaça Allada Vermell ㉔
㉓
Museu Picasso ㉒
Montcada
Rec
Comerç

Marquès de Barberà
❼ ←
Nou de la Rambla
Palau Güell ❾
❿ ⓫
Escudellers
CIUTAT VELLA
Lleona
Plaça Reial
Ajuntament ⓘ
Plaça ⓭
Plaça Traginers
⓮
Gignàs
Ample
Correus (Post Office)
⓯
⓰⓱⓲
✝ Sta. María del Mar
Pg. Born

Arc del Teatre
Centre d'Art Sta. Monica
Palau March
❽ ⓬
Drassanes Ⓜ
Ample
Avinyó
Carabassa
Ataülf
Codols
Mercè
✝ La Mercè
Plaça Antonio López
Llotja de Mar
Plaça del Palau
Marquesa

Portal Sta. Madrona
Av. Drassanes
Reials Drassanes (Museu Marítim)
Plaça Drassanes
Portal de la Pau
Passeig de Colom
Cap de Barcelona
⓳
Barceloneta
Plaça Pau Vila Ⓜ

Mirador de Colom
Plaça Portal de la Pau
Golondrinas
Moll de la Fusta
Moll (Ronda Litoral)
Moll de Dipòsit
Palau de Mar (Museu d'Història de Catalunya) ⓴
㉑
Ginebra
La Maquinista

Moll de les Drassanes
Moll de Barcelona
Rambla da Mar
Port Vell
Moll d'Espanya
IMAX
L'Aquàrium de Barcelona
BARCELONETA
Plaça Poeta Boscà
Sant Carles

Maremàgnum
Moll dels Pescadors
Moll de la Barceloneta
Joan de Borbó
Passeig
Comte Sta. Clara
Almirall Cervera
Almirall Aixada

World Trade Center
Transbordador Aèri
Moll de Balears
Escar
de la Escollera
Pg.
Judici
Drassana
Plaça del Mar
Plaça Palmeres
Platja St. Sebastià

L'Eixample
St. Martí
Parc de la Ciutadella
Ciutat Vella
Map Area
Montjuïc

ⓘ Tourist Information
Ⓜ Metro Station

Barcelona Nightlife A to Z

Bars & Pubs

★★ Almirall RAVAL An old-school, dimly lit place with a bohemian bent and massive Art Nouveau mirror behind the bar. *c/ Joaquín Costa, 33.* ☎ *93-318-99-17. Metro: Sant Antoni or Universitat. Map p 110.*

★★ Bar Lobo RAVAL A chic, high-ceilinged tapas and cocktail joint, sleek, modern, and cool, with graffiti art and theater posters, and boasting a lovely outdoor terrace that's ideal for people-watching. *c/ Pinto Fortuny, 3.* ☎ *93-481-53-46. Metro: Sant Antoni or Universitat. Map p 110.*

★★ Bar Mut L'EIXAMPLE A smart, classic old Barcelona tapas joint and watering hole—its name is a play on the local pronunciation of vermouth—it has great snacks, all listed on a chalkboard, and plentiful wines tucked behind glass. *c/ Pau Claris, 192.* ☎ *93-217-43-38. Metro: Diagonal. Map p 109.*

★★ Bar Ocaña BARRI GÒTIC Inspired by the classic cocktail bars of Berlin, Ocaña focuses on high-end spirits and mixers for its menu of sophisticated traditional and innovative cocktails. Even the ice is always a perfect cube. *Pl. Reial, 13.* ☎ *93-676-48-14. Metro: Liceu. Map p 110.*

The Black Horse LA RIBERA With a host of British beers on tap, dartboards, and several TVs tuned to sports, this English free house with a worn pub feel is where expats come to watch soccer and put back a few pints. *c/ Allada Vermell, 16.* ☎ *93-315-20-53. Metro: Jaume I. Map p 110.*

★★ Boadas LA RAMBLA A classic cocktail bar from the 1930s, Boadas

A sign for Boadas cocktail bar.

is lined with old photos and has an intellectual, pre-revolutionary Havana vibe. A good place for a pre-dinner drink, such as a classic daiquiri. *c/ Tallers, 1.* ☎ *93-318-95-92. Metro: Catalunya. Map p 110.*

★ Dry Martini Speakeasy L'EIXAMPLE In this sober, narrow bar, popular with cocktail connoisseurs of a certain age, mixologist Javier de las Muelas serves up the classics in the stylish, dark-wood-and-banquettes ambience they deserve. *c/ Aribau, 162.* ☎ *93-217-50-80. Metro: Diagonal. Map p 109.*

El Bosc de las Fades BARRI GÒTIC A freaky and kitschy plunge into a fairy-tale forest, complete with gnomes, fairies, mermaids, waterfalls, and trees with leaves. Located in the Museu de Cera, it tries hard to be cinematic. *Pg. de la Banca, 7.* ☎ *93-317-26-49. Metro: Drassanes. Map p 110.*

★ El Jardí RAVAL Tucked into the Gothic courtyard of a historic hospital, this secretive little garden terrace is a terrific place to escape the Rambla crowds and grab a glass of wine or a cocktail and some tapas.

Occasionally a jazz or bossa nova combo will be on hand. *c/ de L'Hospital, 56.* ☎ *93-329-15-50. Metro: Liceu. Map p 110.*

The Fastnet Bar WATERFRONT This Irish pub with good grub has an outdoor terrace and location near the marina. Soccer and rugby fans gather around the large-screen TV. *Pg. Juan de Borbón, 22.* ☎ *93-295-30-05. Metro: Barceloneta. Map p 110.*

★★ **Ginger** BARRI GÒTIC This small, retro-styled cocktail bar is on a lovely little Gothic square. Its comfortable sofas and good selection of tapas make it a place to linger. One entrance leads to a wine bar, the other to a cocktail bar. *Palma de Sant Just, 1 (at c/ Lledó).* ☎ *93-310-53-09. Metro: Jaume I. Map p 110.*

★ **La Fianna** LA RIBERA This bar/ restaurant's ramshackle, vaguely North African ambience appeals to late-nighters and international sorts, who kick back on the cozy, cushion-topped platforms. All that's missing are the hookah pipes. *c/ Manresa, 4.* ☎ *93-315-18-10. Metro: Jaume I. Map p 110.*

★★★ **L'Ascensor** BARRI GÒTIC Named for its fantastic old-world elevator that serves as an entrance, this delightfully romantic spot on a tiny street has been around for 3 decades and is renowned for its rum-based caipirinhas and mojitos. It's a dependable late-night spot. *c/ Bellafila, 3.* ☎ *93-318-53-47. Metro: Jaume I. Map p 110.*

★★ **Marmalade** RAVAL In a gorgeous, dimly lit space that was once a cafe on the wrong side of the tracks, this sexy place has a terrific roster of well-priced cocktails, tasty tapas to go with them, and one swanky pool table. *c/ Riera Alta, 4–6.* ☎ *93-442-39-66. Metro: Liceu. Map p 110.*

★★★ **Marsella** RAVAL This dusty joint—around since 1820—is the place to try absinthe (absenta), the wickedly strong anise-flavored liqueur distilled from wormwood, said to be hallucinogenic and still banned in some countries. Picasso, Dalí, and Hemingway were allegedly regulars here. *c/ Sant Pau, 65.* ☎ *93-442-72-63. Metro: Liceu. Map p 110.*

★ **Mirablau** TIBIDABO The bar itself isn't anything special, really, but the view is stunning. Have an early evening cocktail and gaze from a picture window over all of Barcelona, laid out spectacularly beneath your feet. The bar is next to the funicular near the top of Mt. Tibidabo. *Pl. Doctor Andreu, 2 (top of Av. Tibidabo).* ☎ *93-434-00-35. Tramvia Blau from Metro: Tibidabo. Map p 109.*

★★★ **Pastís** LA RAMBLA/RAVAL This darkly romantic, midcentury spot, a shrine to Edith Piaf, reeks of an old seaside bar. The house special is pastis, the French anise-flavored elixir. The place isn't for everyone, but those with a sense of camp or an ascot will be in heaven here. *c/ Santa Mònica, 4.* ☎ *93-318-79-80. Metro: Drassanes. Map p 110.*

Picasso and Hemingway were regulars at Marsella.

Casino

Casino Barcelona WATERFRONT
Hugely popular, this casino also contains a disco, a restaurant, and all the gaming opportunities you could want. Don't forget to take your passport. *c/ Marina, 19–21.* ☎ *93-225-78-78. www.casino-barcelona.com. Admission 4.50€. Metro: Citutadella–Vila Olímpica. Map p 110.*

Dance Clubs

★★★ Antilla BCN Latin Club L'EIXAMPLE A fixture among Barcelona's large Latin American and Caribbean community, this happening salsateca is a great place to shake it if you know what you're doing (and if you don't, check out the club's dance school, Mon and Wed–Fri 9–11:30pm, free on Tues with cover). It also gets some big-name Latino performers. *c/ Aragó, 141.* ☎ *93-451-21-51. Cover 10€. Metro: Urgell. Map p 109.*

★★ Apolo POBLE SEC On Fridays and Saturdays, this wildly diverse nightclub, in a venerable turn-of-the-20th-century theater/ballroom, is a dance club called Nitsa. On other nights, it plays host to burlesque, rock shows, smaller music concerts, and DJ dance parties. *c/ Nou de la Rambla, 113.* ☎ *93-441-40-01. www.sala-apolo.com. Cover 10€–20€. Metro: Poble Sec. Map p 110.*

★★ Barcelona Pipa Club BARRI GÒTIC One of Barcelona's institutions, the "Pipe Club" hosts *le jazz hot* several nights a week and even holds a tertulia (intellectual discussion) on Wednesdays, but on Monday and Tuesday nights, Argentine tango music fills the hall, and a milonga (tango dance session) takes over the floor. *Pl. Reial, 3.* ☎ *93-302-47-32. Cover varies. Metro: Liceu. Map p 110.*

Check out the fantastic views from Mirablau.

★★ Bikini DIAGONAL/SANTS This cool, sprawling bar hosts live rock music but is also a great dance club. You'll find thumping Latin tunes in one salon, alternative rock in another. *c/ Deu i Mata, 105.* ☎ *93-322-08-00. www.bikinibcn.com. Cover 7€–15€. Metro: María Cristina–Hospital Clínic. Map p 109.*

★ City Hall Barcelona L'EIXAMPLE This popular, two-level club draws lots of rambunctious clubbers and their tourist counterparts, who come to party to techno and house music. The garden out back provides a nice respite from all the action. *Rambla de Catalunya, 2–4.* ☎ *93-238-07-22. www.cityhallbarcelona.com. Cover 12€. Metro: Catalunya. Map p 109.*

★ La Terrazza MONTJUIC This summer-only, open-air dance club is tucked inside Poble Espanyol, the faux Spanish village built for the 1929 World's Fair. La Terrazza rocks until dawn. An indoor dance option, Discotheque, is available by separate entrance and cover fee. *Poble Espanyol, Av. Marquès de Comillas, 13.* ☎ *93-272-49-80. Metro: Espanya. Map p 109.*

★ Le KasBah WATERFRONT With a Moroccan feel near the Olympic port—in the Palau del Mar building that houses the Museu de Catalunya—this bar's dance floor heats up as the evening wears on. Nice outdoor terrace. *Pl. Pau Vila, 1.* ☎ *93-238-07-02. Metro: Barceloneta. Map p 110.*

★ **New York** BARRI GÒTIC It still looks the part of erstwhile strip club and cathouse, and the young hipsters who hang out here make very late nights of it, dancing to indie, R&B, and vintage disco. *c/ Escudellers, 5.* ☎ *93-318-87-30. Cover (after 2am) 10€. Metro: Drassanes. Map p 110.*

★★★ **Otto Zutz** GRACIA The granddaddy of clubs in Barcelona, this multilevel favorite still draws trendsetters, the rich, the famous, and the wannabes. With eight bars and four main dance areas, spanning a variety of musical genres, you're bound to find something—or someone—you like. *c/ Lincoln, 15.* ☎ *93-238-07-22. www.ottozutz. com. Cover 15€–20€. Metro: Gràcia. Map p 109.*

★★★ **Razzmatazz** WATERFRONT (POBLE NOU) This five-in-one club, a monster multilevel warehouse, offers something for everyone, as long as you're young and overflowing with energy and hormones. From techno to Goth, pop to punk, and metal, a single admission to all five spaces can leave you dizzy. It's also a great live-music venue. *c/ Almogàvers, 122.* ☎ *93-320-82-00. Cover (except for special concerts) 12€–15€. Metro: Bogatell. Map p 110.*

Gay & Lesbian Bars/Clubs
★★ **Café Dietrich** L'EIXAMPLE For a great drag show, you can't beat this glam cafe, one of the city's most enduring popular gay hangouts. The bartenders wear little and seem to enjoy the attentions of their patrons. *c/ Consell de Cent, 255.* ☎ *93-451-77-07. Metro: Gràcia or Universitat. Map p 109.*

Kiut L'EIXAMPLE With few clubs catering to lesbians in Barcelona, this stylish spot—pronounced "cute"—with a mirrored dance floor draws a fashionable crowd of women (as well as a mix of straights on Thurs nights). *c/ Consell de Cent, 280.* ☎ *93-487-83-42. Metro: Pg. de Gràcia. Map p 109.*

★ **Metro Disco** LA RAMBLA/ RAVAL Cruisy, with two dance floors, Metro remains one of the most popular gay discos in Barcelona. The crowd ranges from pretty fashionistas to handlebar-moustache, macho types. One dance floor even spins traditional Spanish music and Spanish pop. The backroom isn't for the meek. *c/ Sepulveda, 185.* ☎ *93-323-52-27. Cover 10€. Metro: Universitat. Map p 109.*

New Chaps L'EIXAMPLE This bar is the place to find gay cowboys and bears. The downstairs darkroom is where the action is in the wee hours. *Av. Diagonal, 365.* ☎ *93-215-53-65. Metro: Diagonal. Map p 109.*

Punto BCN L'EIXAMPLE A 30-plus crowd, including a sprinkling of bears and daddies, keeps it moving to Spanish pop soundtrack. *c/ de Muntaner, 63.* ☎ *93-487-83-42. Metro: Universitat. Map p 109.*

A DJ spins records late into the Barcelona night.

Even the sign is glamorous at Café Dietrich.

Lounges & Beach Hangouts

★ **Bling Bling** L'EIXAMPLE This recent addition to L'Eixample nightlife scene attracts a lot of hetero couples for its dance floor but also has private areas if you want to go off in a small group to chill. Put on your party clothes, as wannabes in casual mode are turned away. c/ Tuset, 8–10. ☎ 93-414-63-62. Metro: Diagonal. Map p 109.

★ **CDLC Barcelona** WATERFRONT This trendy place is all attitude and *gente bella* (beautiful people). If you want to see and be seen, it's appropriately swanky, and right on the edge of the beach. To chill on the luxe white beds, you'll have to pony up for a pricey bottle of whiskey, but the outdoor terrace is just fine. Make sure you wear your best duds. Pg. Marítim, 32. ☎ 93-224-04-70. Metro: Ciutadella–Vila Olímpica. Map p 110.

★ **MIX** LA RIBERA Scenesters gather at this fashionable hangout in the trendy Born district to imbibe colorful cocktails and groove to nightly DJs spinning jazz, soul, funk, and freestyle mixes Tuesday through Saturday nights. The cocktail for four called "the orgy" might get things rolling. c/Comerç, 21. ☎ 93-319-46-96. Metro: Ciutadella–Vila Olímpica. Map p 110.

★ **Nick Havanna** L'EIXAMPLE Barcelona's original design bar began life in the 1980s. As other bars have caught the bug, Nick Havanna now revels in its retro glory. Its bathrooms are still conversation-worthy. c/ Rosselló, 208. ☎ 93-215-65-91. Metro: Diagonal. Map p 109.

★★★ **Opium Barcelona** WATERFRONT A huge dance floor, a killer sound system, and a roster of visiting international celebrity DJs make this beachfront disco one of Spain's best. Buy tickets ahead and show up early (midnight). The beach is right outside when you need a break. Pg. Marítim de la Barceloneta, 34. ☎ 90-226-74-86. Metro: Ciutadella–Vila Olímpica. Map p 110.

★★ **Roca Bar/Ommsession Club** L'EIXAMPLE Oozing mod style, this swanky lounge in the ultra-cool Hotel Omm is a favorite of design types, models, and others with beauty and euros to spare. After 1am, head to the dramatically lit, and oh-so-chic, sofa-laden nightclub. c/ Rosselló, 265. ☎ 93-445-40-00. Metro: Diagonal. Map p 109.

Shôko WATERFRONT A beachside lounge bar that's also an Asian-themed restaurant, this self-conscious place draws plenty of pretty and pouty fashionable sorts who don't have a problem with the

A glass of cava is sure to make your evening more bubbly.

On a cava crawl? A required stop is El Xampanyet.

cheesy decor, an odd backdrop for the amped-up weekend fiestas set to house, trance, and hip-hop. *Pg. Marítim, 36.* ☎ *93-225-92-00. Metro: Ciutadella–Vila Olímpica. Map p 110.*

Wine (& Cava) Bars

★★ **Can Paixano** WATERFRONT Usually jam-packed, this landmark bar with no sign out front serves the cheapest *cava* in Barcelona, plus an interminable list of sandwiches. In the evening, the rustic standing-room-only space gets pretty crazed (and you've got to fight for a bottle of *cava*, which will only set you back about 5€). *c/ Reina Cristina, 7.* ☎ *93-310-08-39. Metro: Barceloneta. Map p 110.*

★★★ **El Xampanyet** LA RIBERA This revered institution is as comfortable as an old tweed jacket. It's a great spot time to pop into for a fizzy *copa de cava* and some excellent snacks. Family-owned since the 1930s, this is as authentic as they come, with colored tiles, marble tables, an old zinc bar, and wine barrels. *c/ de la Montcada, 22.* ☎ *93-319-70-03. Closed Aug. Metro: Jaume I. Map p 110.*

★ **La Vinateria del Call** BARRI GÒTIC A dark and romantic wine haunt, right in the midst of the ancient Jewish Quarter, this is a good, non-touristy spot to sip *vino* with locals. *c/ de Sant Domènec del Call, 9.* ☎ *93-302-60-92. Metro: Jaume I. Map p 110.*

★★ **La Vinya del Senyor** LA RIBERA Across from Santa María del Mar, this tiny wine bar with an enviable terrace draws hordes of tourists and local wine connoisseurs for its spectacular list of Spanish wines and *cavas* and yummy selection of tapas. *Pl. Santa María, 5.* ☎ *93-310-33-79. Metro: Barceloneta or Jaume I. Map p 110.*

★★ **Mon Vínic** L'EIXAMPLE This sleek and sophisticated, even

The Best Nightlife

Getting to Know Cava

You may already know the sparkling wines that hail from Spain. But you're in for a real treat when you encounter cava in its native land.

Catalunya is home to most of the major producers of cava. The distinctive dry yet fruity taste of the wine is the result of blending three grapes: the lemony *macabeu*, the aromatic *xarel-lo*, and the zesty *paralleda*. Cava rosé is created by the addition of such grapes as *garnacha*, which adds a bit of a strawberry or raspberry aroma to the blend.

The word cava is the *Catalunyan* word for cave or cellar, appropriate because that is where early winemakers preserved or aged their wine. Although cava was once known as Spanish champagne, the European Union, which Spain joined in 1986, prohibits the use of the term "champagne" for any wine not produced in the Champagne region of France. In fact, *Catalunyan* wine growers have been using the word cava since 1970 to distinguish their wine from its French counterpart, but only wines produced in the traditional *champenoise* method—increasingly made with the French chardonnay grape—can be called cava. Wines produced under other processes are known simply as vinos *espumosos*, or sparkling wines.

Cava comes in a variety of *sweetnesses*, from the very dry brut nature to the very sweet *dolsec*. Although most people view cava as a light aperitif, winemakers are increasingly choosing to age their product, which produces a wine with a more substantial body and a nose that some describe as containing notes of apple and almond.

Catalunyans traditionally drink cava on important occasions, such as baptisms and weddings, but you will be able to find it easily during your stay in Barcelona—especially in one of the many *xampanyerías* or cava bars.

futuristic, design-and-wine temple offers a digital list 4,000 bottles strong, 30 wines by the glass (different each day), and a reference library for true wine geeks. Closed weekends. *c/ Diputació, 249.* ☎ 93-272-61-87. *Metro: Pg. de Grà-cia. Map p 109.*

★ **Va de Vi** BARRI GÒTIC This wine bar, owned by an artist and wine aficionado, inhabits a cinematic, stone-walled medieval house with Gothic arches. It has an extraordinary wine list, including some truly coveted bottles, such as

L'Ermita from Priorat. *c/ Banys Vells, 16.* ☎ 93-319-29-00. *Metro: Jaume I. Map p 110.*

★ **Xampú Xampany** L'EIXAMPLE Although the name may look impossible to pronounce for foreigners, this longtime *xampanyeria* (cava bar) is anything but intimidating. It serves up lots of excellent tapas alongside its house *cava* and wines and makes a good first stop. The tables outside are the place to be. *Gran Vía de les Corts Catalanes, 702 (corner Bailén).* ☎ 93-265-04-83. *Metro: Girona. Map p 109.* ●

Arts & Entertainment Best Bets

Best **Concert Acoustics**
★ L'Auditori, *c/ Lepant, 150 (p 124)*

Best **Jazz Club**
★★★ Harlem Jazz Club, *Comtessa de Sobradiel, 8 (p 127)*

Best **Flamenco, Flashy Dresses & All**
★★ Tablao Flamenco Cordobés, *La Rambla, 35 (p 126)*

Best **Opera House**
★★★ Gran Teatre del Liceu, *La Rambla, 51–59 (p 124)*

Best **Summer Arts Festival**
★★ Grec, *Montjuïc (p 128)*

Best **Sporting Event**
★★ Fútbol Club Barcelona, *Av. del Papa Joan XXIII (p 129)*

Best **Theater Performances**
★★★ Teatre Mercat de Les Flors, *c/ Lleida, 59 (p 130)*

Best **Impression Made by a Concert Hall**
★★★ El Palau de la Música Catalana, *c/ Sant Francesc de Paula, 2 (p 124)*

Best **All-Around Live Music Venue**
★★★ Luz de Gas, *c/ Muntaner, 246 (p 128)*

Best **Hipster Live Music Shows**
★★ Sala Razzmatazz, *c/ Pamplona, 88, (p 129)*

Best **Unexpected Theater/ Music**
★ La Casa dels Músics, *c/ Encarnació, 25 (p 124)*

Best **Hangout for Electronic Music Freaks**
Sonar and other venues *(p 128)*

Best **Movie House for V.O. (Subtitles)**
★★★ Verdi, *c/ Verdi, 32 (p 125)*

Best **Alternative Rock Festival**
Primavera Sound, *Parc del Fòrum (p 128)*

Most **Unusual Venue for Opera Arias**
★ Espai Barroc, *c/ de la Montcada, 20 (p 127)*

A performance at El Palau de la Música Catalana. Previous page: A scene from a Tchaikovsky opera at Gran Teatre del Liceu.

L'Eixample

Bikini 10
Camp Nou
(Fútbol Club Barcelona) 9
La Casa dels Músics 2
La Cova del Drac JazzRoom 6
La Pedrera 4
Luz de Gas 7
Palacio del Flamenco 5
Sala KGB 1
Tintitran 8
Verdi 3

i Tourist Information

M Metro Station

Ciutat Vella & Waterfront

Plaça Doctor Letamendi
Aragó
Passeig de Gràcia
Aragó

L'Eixample
St. Martí
Parc de la Ciutadella
Ciutat Vella
Map Area
Montjuïc

Consell de Cent
Balmes
Rambla
Catalunya
Passeig de Gràcia

L'EIXAMPLE
Consell de Cent
Girona
Diputació

Universitat de Barcelona
Plaça Universitat

Gran Via Corts Catalanes
Gran Via Corts Catalanes

Sepúlveda
St. Antoni
Universitat
Plaça Castella
Ronda Universitat
Pelai
Balmes
Bergara
Plaça Catalunya

Casp
Pau Clarís
Roger de Llúria
Bruc
Girona

Plaça Urquinaona
Urquinaona
Ronda Sant Pere

Floridablanca
Ronda
de
Casa de la Caritat
Tallers
Pelai

Fontanella

St. Pere Més Alt
Palau de la Música Catalana

Museu d'Art Contemporani de Barcelona
Catalunya
Elisabets
Santa Anna
Canuda
Comtal
Montsió
Trafalgar

LA RIBERA
St. Pere Més Baix

Plaça Pedro
Carme
Pintor Fortuny
Betlem
Palau Moja
Portaferrissa
Av. Portal de l'Àngel

Antic Hospital de la Sta. Creu
Mercat de la Boqueria
St. Felip Neri
Sta. María del Pi
Generalitat
La Rambla
Av. Francesc Cambó

EL RAVAL
Sant Pau
Catedral

Plaça Antoni Maura
Mercedes
Mercat Santa Caterina
Bòria
Plaça Allada i Vermell

Carretes
La Rambla del Raval

Gran Teatre del Liceu
Liceu
Plaça Ferran
St. Jaume
BARRI GÒTIC
Jaume I
Princesa
Montcada
Argenteria
Miralles
Museu Picasso

St. Pau del Camp
Rambla
Palau Güell
Arc del Teatre
Lleona
Ajuntament

Paral·lel
Nou de la Rambla

Av. Drassanes
Centre d'Art Sta. Monica
Palau March
La Mercè
CIUTAT VELLA
Avinyó
Arault
Gignàs
Plaça Traginers
Correus (Post Office)
Plaça Antonio López
Llotja de Mar
Santa Maria del Mar
Pg. Born
Comerç

Reials Drassanes (Museu Marítim)
Drassanes
Mirador de Colom
Passeig de Colom
Cap de Barcelona
Plaça del Palau
Marquesa

Plaça Portal de la Pau
Plaça Drassanes
Moll de les Drassanes
Moll de la Fusta
Golondrinas
Moll d'Espanya
Moll de Dipòsit
Palau de Mar (Museu d'Història de Catalunya)
Plaça Pau Vila
Barceloneta
Ginebra

Ronda Litoral
Moll de Barcelona
Rambla da Mar
Port Vell
IMAX
La Maquinista

Maremàgnum
L'Aquàrium de Barcelona
Moll de la Barceloneta
BARCELONETA
Joan de Borbó

World Trade Center
Transbordador Aeri
Moll de Balears
Moll dels Pescadors
Escar
Passeig
Judici
Drassana
Plaça del Mar
Plaça Palmeres
Platja St. Sebastià
Comte Sta. Clara
Almirall Cervera
Almirall Aixada
Sant Carles

(i) *Tourist Information*
(M) *Metro Station*

1
2
3
4
5
6
7
8
9
10
11
12
13
14
15
20

El Palau de la Música Catalana **3**
El Tablao del Carmen **20**
Espai Barroc **12**
Filmoteca **13**
Gran Teatre del Liceu **5**
Harlem Jazz Club **10**
Icária **19**
IMAX Port Vell **15**
Jamboree **7**
Jazz Sí Club (Taller de Músics) **2**
L'Antic Teatre **4**
L'Auditori **16**
Los Tarantos **8**
Palau Sant Jordi **20**

PocketClub **20**
Renoir Floridablanca **1**
Restaurante Nervión Flamenco **11**
Sala Apolo **14**
Sala Razzmatazz **18**
Sidecar Factory Club **9**
Tablao Flamenco Cordobés **6**
Teatre Mercat de les Flors **20**
Teatre Nacional de Catalunya **17**

Barcelona Arts & Entertainment A to Z

Classical Music & Concert Venues

★★★ El Palau de la Música Catalana

LA RIBERA This 1908 concert hall, designed by Domènech i Montaner, is a *modernista* masterpiece. Concerts are primarily classical, although the administration has sought to widen exposure to the hall by adding jazz, world, and alternative rock. For daily guided tours of the building, see p 15. A recent extension called Petit Palau includes a luxury restaurant and rehearsal space and occasionally hosts "Opera and Flamenco" programs (also held at Teatre Poliorama on La Rambla). *c/ Sant Francesc de Paula, 2.* ☎ *93-295-72-00. Tickets 10€–70€. www.palaumusica.org. Metro: Urquinaona. Map p 122.*

★★★ Gran Teatre del Liceu

LA RAMBLA Barcelona's great opera house, founded in 1874, is one of the grandest in the world. Although it was gutted by fire in 1994, it was quickly rebuilt with donations, preserving the look and feel of the original. The Liceu has long been the home turf of international opera stars José Carreras and Montserrat Caballé, both from Barcelona. In addition to opera, you'll find concerts as well as recitals and chamber music in the smaller El Petit Liceu. *La Rambla, 51–59.* ☎ *93-485-99-00. www.liceu barcelona.com. Tickets 12€–200€. Metro: Liceu. Map p 122.*

★ L'Auditori

POBLE NOU A modern concert hall for classical music designed by the preeminent Spanish architect Rafael Moneo, this is the permanent home for the Orfeó Catala choral society and the OBC (Barcelona's Symphony Orchestra). It also hosts renowned international musicians. Acoustics are superb. *c/ Lepant, 150.* ☎ *93-247-93-00. www.auditori.org. Tickets 10€–60€. Metro: Glòries. Map p 122.*

★ La Casa dels Músics

GRACIA Claiming to be the smallest opera house in the world, this tiny, atmospheric stage, in the 19th-century home of the pianist Luís de Arquer,

The lobby of the Gran Teatre del Liceu.

An orchestra plays at L'Auditori.

offers a unique opportunity for music lovers. Singers in the small-scale opera productions and bel canto are so close that you can see or even feel them sweat. Call ahead for reservations. *c/ Encarnació, 25.* ☎ *93-284-99-20. www.lacasadels musics.com. Tickets 20€–25€. Metro: Fontana. Map p 121.*

★ **Palau Sant Jordi** MONTJUIC This sleek indoor sports stadium, built for the '92 Olympics by the Japanese architect Arota Isozaki, hosts major rock and pop concerts by artists of such stature as Bruce Springsteen and the Cure. *Pg. Olímpic, 5–7.* ☎ *93-426-20-89. Tickets 20€–150€. Metro: Glòries. Map p 122.*

Film

★★ **Filmoteca** L'EIXAMPLE An art-house cinema funded by the Catalan government and a favorite of local and international cineastes. It shows classics and puts on such festivals as "Italian Neorealism." *Plaça de Salvador Seguí, 1.* ☎ *93-567-10-70. www.filmoteca.cat. Tickets 4€. Metro: Liceu-Drassanes. Map p 122.*

★ **Icária** WATERFRONT (VILA OLIMPICA) This multiplex of 15 screens is in a large mall in the Port Olimpic zone. Most films are mainstream releases, although a surprising number are small independent and European movies. Online booking all the time (general admission); numbered seats on weekends only. *Salvador Espriu, 61 (Vila Olimpica).* ☎ *90-222-09-22. www.yelmocines.es. Tickets 8.60€. Metro: Ciutadella–Vila Olímpica. Map p 122.*

★★ **IMAX Port Vell** WATERFRONT Barcelona's terrific IMAX theater shows all the latest large-format releases on three different types of projection systems (IMAX, OMNIMAX, and 3-D). *Moll de Espanya, s/n.* ☎ *93-225-11-11. www. imaxportvell.com. Tickets 8.75€–13€. Metro: Drassanes. Map p 122.*

★ **Renoir Floridablanca** L'EIXAMPLE A multitude of mainstream international releases (in their original language) are shown on seven screens (as many as 10 different films in a single day). *Floridablanca, 135.* ☎ *93-426-33-37. www.cinesrenoir.com. Tickets 7.50€ (6€ Mon). Metro: Universitat or Sant Antoni. Map p 122.*

★★★ **Verdi** GRACIA A legendary movie house for true film fans, and the first in Barcelona to show original-version movies, Verdi's five screens are usually devoted to the most artistic and challenging films. A nearby annex, Verdi Park, has four additional screens. *Verdi: c/ Verdi, 32; Verdi Park: c/ Torrijos 49 (Gràcia).* ☎ *93-238-79-90. www. cines-verdi.com. Tickets 9€ (6€ Mon). Late shows Fri–Sat. Metro: Fontana. Map p 121.*

Flamenco
El Tablao de Carmen MONTJUIC Within Poble Espanyol lies this tourist favorite, presenting

a pretty reliable flamenco show. Open Tuesday to Sunday 8pm to 1am; first show 9:30pm, second 11:30pm (midnight Fri–Sat). *Poble Espanyol de Montjuïc.* ☎ 93-325-68-95. *www.tablaodecarmen.com. Dinner & show 52€ (tapas), 70€ (dinner); drink & show 41€. Metro: Espanya. Map p 122.*

★★ Los Tarantos BARRI GÒTIC

The oldest flamenco club in Barcelona (1963) has hosted the likes of Antonio Gades and Rosario, and respected Andalusian flamenco artists regularly make the pilgrimage here. The attractive theater space is excellent for dance performances and music concerts. *Pl. Reial, 17.* ☎ 93-319-17-89. *www.masimas. com/tarantos. Cover 10€. Metro: Liceu. Map p 122.*

★★ Palacio del Flamenco

L'EIXAMPLE Barcelona's newest flamenco dinner show inhabits a handsome old theater, with a very nice ambience. Three shows daily with dinner at 6:40, 8:30, and 9:40pm. *c/ Balmes, 139.* ☎ 93-218-72-37. *www.palaciodelflamenco.com. Dinner & show 56€–100€; drink & show 40€. Discounted (5€ cheaper) tickets available at http://bcnshop.*

barcelonaturisme.com. Metro: Provença. Map p 121.

Restaurante Nervión Flamenco

LA RIBERA This small space near the Picasso Museum stages a more informal, and cheaper, version of the flamenco shows in town. It's intimate, and the restaurant serves all kinds of inexpensive tapas and paellas. Shows are Thursday at 8 and 10pm. *Princesa, 2.* ☎ 93-315-21-03. *www. restaurantenervion.com. Dinner & show 25€; drink & show 14€. Metro: Jaume I. Map p 122.*

★★ Tablao Flamenco Cordobés

LA RAMBLA Near the waterfront, this Andalusian-style club has been around since 1970. The upstairs room hosts traditional cuadro flamenco, performances by singers, dancers, and a guitarist. Although the shows don't approach the passionate displays seen in the deep south, they are perhaps the most authentic in Barcelona. Three shows nightly with dinner at 7, 8:30, and 10pm. *La Rambla, 35.* ☎ 93-317-57-11. *www.tablao cordobes.com. Dinner & show 78€; drink & show 42.50€. Metro: Drassanes. Map p 122.*

Flamenco dancers and a singer at El Tablao de Carmen.

★ **Tirititran** L'EIXAMPLE This col-mao flamenco—a neighborhood restaurant-bar with live flamenco performances near Avenida La Diagonal—is a good option for those uninterested in slick, costumed productions aimed primarily at tourists. Downstairs is a small stage for concerts, which are often informal. *c/ Buenos Aires, 28.* ☎ *93-405-38-71. Metro: Urgell. Map p 121.*

Jazz & Cabaret

★ **Espai Barroc** LA RIBERA This place is proudly over-the-top. Rooms in a medieval mansion, overflowing with objets d'art, busts, and baroque framed art, make a grand spot for a drink. But on Thursday nights, singers perform arias from opera's greatest hits. *c/ de la Montcada, 20.* ☎ *93-310-06-73. Cover varies. Metro: Jaume I. Map p 122.*

★★★ **Harlem Jazz Club** BARRI GÒTIC One of Barcelona's oldest and finest jazz clubs was remodeled, but the tiny spot remains intimate and the music wide-ranging, covering bebop, blues, bossa nova, and more. *Comtessa de Sobradiel, 8.* ☎ *93-310-07-55. www.harlem jazzclub.es. Tickets from 5€. 1-drink min. Closed Aug. Metro: Jaume I. Map p 122.*

★ **Jamboree** BARRI GÒTIC Tucked into a basement of Plaça Reial, this longtime standard-bearer for live blues and jazz—going strong for more than 5 decades— occasionally draws big names (back in the day, Chet Baker, Ella Fitzgerald, and Elvin Jones played here), although often the headlining acts are talented up-and-comers. Late in the evening, it gets rowdier and the space becomes a nightclub for a younger crowd, with hip-hop downstairs and world music upstairs. *Pl.*

The Harlem Jazz Club.

Reial, 17. ☎ *93-319-17-89. www. masimas.com/jamboree. Tickets 5€–10€. Metro: Liceu. Map p 122.*

Jazz Sí Club (Taller de Músics) RAVAL A free-flowing program of live music nightly is the *raison d'être* of this intimate music school, auditorium, and bar. Miguel Poveda and Enrique Morente, two current stars of flamenco, have played for students, teachers, and an enthusiastic public. Every night features a different musical genre, and programs go late. *c/ Reque-sens, 2.* ☎ *93-329-00-20. www. tallerdemusics.com. Admission 5€–8€. Metro: Sant Antoni. Map p 122.*

★★ **La Cova del Drac Jazz-Room** ZONA ALTA This sleek, modern, and posh new jazz club in the upper Barcelona neighborhood of Sant Gervasi—the uptown sister of Jamboree—offers live jazz from top international acts and DJ/dance music, but the tiny spot remains intimate and the music

Barcelona Music Festivals

A summer tradition in Barcelona is ★★ **Grec** (☎ 93-301-77-75; http://grec.bcn.cat), an annual festival of international theater, music, and dance. From the last week of June to the end of the first week in August, Grec showcases big names (such as Van Morrison) and everything from blues to Brazilian bossa nova and avant-garde dance at the Teatre Grec on Montjuïc and other venues. **Primavera Sound** (www.primaverasound.com), an alternative-rock festival held at the Parc del Forum in late May and early June, attracts major bands, such as Sonic Youth, Wilco, and Drive-By Truckers. **Sonar** (www.sonar.es), one of the biggest electronic-music festivals in the world (held in mid-June), showcases avant-garde dance music and multimedia art from across Europe. But its sheer size— on multiple stages both day and night—and such headlining artists as Björk and Massive Attack mean this is no marginal, niche festival. In Barcelona, it's pretty much mainstream.

wide-ranging, covering bebop, blues, bossa nova, and more. *Vallmajor, 33 (Pl. Adrià).* ☎ 93-319-17-89. www.masimas.com/la-cova-del-drac. *Free admission Mon–Thurs; 4€–10€ Fri–Sat, 1-drink min. Closed Aug. Metro: Jaume I. Map p 121.*

★ **La Pedrera** L'EIXAMPLE Live jazz concerts on the rooftop of Gaudí's emblematic *modernista* apartment building are offered from late June to early September, complete with a glass of *cava. Pg. de Gràcia, 92 (at Provença).* ☎ 90-220-21-38. www.lapedrera.com. *Admission 27€. Schedule varies. Metro: Diagonal or Provença. Map p 121.*

★★★ **Luz de Gas** L'EIXAMPLE For years, this glamorous turn-of-the-20th-century music hall has reigned supreme in Barcelona for its stylish looks (chandeliers and thick red curtains) and programming of live music, which is very often Latin jazz; past artists include Charlie Haden and Danilo Pérez. Several performance areas each

have their own bars. The lineup covers jazz, pop, folk, R&B, and salsa. Sala B is another space next door with a more modern, industrial look. *c/ Muntaner, 246.* ☎ 93-209-77-11. www.luzdegas.com. *Cover 12€–25€ (includes 1 drink). Metro: Diagonal. Map p 121.*

Pop & Rock

★ **Bikini** SANTS An out-of-the-way rock club near the L'illa shopping center, this space has a great dance floor and three separate performance areas. It has hosted some pretty big names in pop and rock, including Thievery Corporation and Marianne Faithfull. The club stays open late Wednesday through Sunday, spinning funk and hip-hop after shows. *c/ Déu i Mata, 105 (off Av. Diagonal).* ☎ 93-322-08-00. www.bikinibcn.com. *Cover 7€–15€. Metro: Les Corts or María Cristina. Map p 121.*

★★ **PocketClub** MONTJUIC Part of Teatre Mercat de les Flors, this cool little club schedules infrequent performances (just two Thurs a month), but they're the kind of alternative-rock shows that draw hipsters, such as Iron and Wine, Destroyer, the Clientele, and other indie bands. *c/ Lleida, 59 (Mercat de les Flors).* ☎ *93-285-26-26. www. pocketbcn.com. Admission 10€–25€. Metro: Espanya. Map p 122.*

★★ **Sala Apolo** POBLE SEC This 1940s dance hall covers the bases: besides "Nasty Mondays" and "Crappy Tuesdays," it programs alternative cinema, Latin music, funk nights, and gay nights, and on Fridays and Saturdays it becomes a happening dance club called Nitsa, with occasional big-name DJs. It fits in rock and jazz shows, too. *c/ Nou de la Rambla, 113 (Poble Sec).* ☎ *93-441-40-01. www.sala-apolo. com. Cover varies. Metro: Poble Sec. Map p 122.*

★ **Sala KGB** GRACIA Not exactly secretive, but a little out of the way, this club, a longtime hangout of young underground and garage rockers, programs independent rock, metal, and reggae bands as well as electronic house and dance music. *c/ Alegre de Dalt, 55.* ☎ *93-210-59-06. www.sala-kgb.es. Cover 10€–15€. Metro: Lesseps. Map p 121.*

★★ **Sala Razzmatazz** PORT OLIMPIC/POBLE NOU This sprawling, young-skewing club—with five separate music ambiences within—is also a rocking concert venue. Its "Pop Club" hosts Spanish and celebrated international pop, alternative, hip-hop, and rock acts, such as Arctic Monkeys, LCD Soundsystem, and Sonic Youth. *c/ Pamplona, 88.* ☎ *93-320-82-00. www.sala razzmatazz.com. Cover varies. Metro: Bogatell or Marina. Map p 122.*

★ **Sidecar Factory Club** BARRI GÒTIC Check out Barcelona's indigenous indie-rock scene at this basement club, which occasionally scores bands with international followings, such as Portastatic. *Pl. Reial, 7.* ☎ *93-302-15-86. www. sidecarfactoryclub.com. Shows 5€–20€. Metro: Liceu. Map p 122.*

Spectator Sports
★★ **Fútbol Club Barcelona** SANTS Barcelona's immensely popular football, or soccer, team—perennially one of the best in Europe—plays at Camp Nou, a 120,000-seat stadium. To see "Barça" (*bar-sa*), as the locals affectionately refer to the team, take on one of its chief rivals, such as Real Madrid, is a treat that transcends sport and approaches social anthropology. Although many games are sold out long in advance, individual tickets are frequently available. How popular is the team? The **Museu del Fútbol Club Barcelona (Soccer Museum)** is one of the most-visited museums

Teatre Mercat de Les Flors.

Advance Tickets & Listings

For the latest concert, theater, and event listings, pick up a copy of the weekly **Guía del Ocio** (www.guiadelocio.com/barcelona), a guide to all entertainment in Barcelona. It's available at newsstands and written in Spanish, but it's pretty comprehensible even to non-Spanish speakers, with a small English section at the back. Also worth a look are **Go-Mag** (www.go-mag.com), **What's On Barcelona** (www.whatsonbcn.com), and, in English, **Barcelona Metropolitan** (www.barcelona-metropolitan.com).

Other helpful services are **Tel-Entrada** (☎ 902-10-12-12; www.telentrada.com), **ServiCaixa** (☎ 902-33-22-11; www.servi caixa.com), and **Ticketmaster** (www.ticketmaster.es).

in Spain. *Av. del Papa Joan XXIII; ticket office c/ Aristides Maillol, 12–18.* ☎ *93-496-36-00. www.fc barcelona.com. Tickets start at 26€. Museum: c/ Aristides Maillol, 7–9.* ☎ *93-496-36-08. Admission 19€– 25€. Metro: María Cristina, Palau Reial, or Collblanc. Map p 121.*

Theater

★ **L'Antic Teatre** LA RIBERA This small, 18th-century theater is just steps from El Palau de la Música Catalana. It programs innovative and risky performances, which are likely to be all over the cultural map: dance, theater, multimedia, circus, music, and more, from both local and touring companies. The resident company is Semolina Tomic, headed by a Croatian residing in Barcelona. Tickets are inexpensive, so it's a good place for those looking for something new. *c/ Verdaguer i Callis, 12.* ☎ *93-315-23-54. www.anticteatre. com. Tickets 6€–15€. Metro: Urquina-ona. Map p 122.*

★★★ **Teatre Mercat de Les Flors** MONTJUIC Although the structure dates to the 1929 World's Fair, this Catalan theater's first performance was *Carmen* in 1983. The theater plays host to respected companies of drama, dance, and music and schedules occasional avant-garde art festivals. A restaurant overlooks the city's rooftops. *c/ Lleida, 59.* ☎ *93-426-18-75. www. mercatflors.org. Ticket prices vary. Metro: Pl. Espanya. Map p 122.*

★★ **Teatre Nacional de Catalunya** POBLE NOU A swanky, pseudo-Roman modern theater, the work of the architect Ricardo Bofill, is home to a major Catalan company that puts on both classic and contemporary plays, including those of such writers as Tom Stoppard, Oscar Wilde, and Harold Pinter, as well as modern dance. Productions are in Catalan except in rare instances. *Pl. de les Arts, 1.* ☎ *93-306-57-00. www.tnc.cat. Tickets 5€–35€. Metro: Glòries. Map p 122.* ●

9

The Best Lodging

Lodging **Best Bets**

Best **Old-City Location**
★★ Hotel Neri $$$ *c/ Sant Sever, 5 (p 142)*

Best **In-House Restaurants**
★★★ ABaC $$$$ *Av. Tibidabo, 1 (p 136)*; and ★★★ Hotel Omm $$$$ *c/ Rosselló, 265 (p 142)*

Best **for Would-Be Aristocrats**
★★ El Palace Barcelona $$$$ *Gran Vía de les Corts Catalanes, 668 (p 138)*

Best **Affordable Design**
★★ Praktik Rambla $$ *Rambla de Catalunya, 67 (p 143)*; and ★★★ The 5 Rooms $$ *c/ Pau Claris, 72 (p 144)*

Best **Cutting-Edge Design**
★★★ Hotel Omm $$$$ *c/ Rosselló, 265 (p 142)*

Best **Antidote to Minimalism**
★ Hostal L'Antic Espai $$ *Gran Vía de les Cortes Catalanes, 660 (p 139)*

Best **Business Hotel**
★★★ Hotel Arts $$$$ *c/ de la Marina, 19–21 (p 139)*

Best **In-House Museum**
★★★ Hotel Claris $$$$ *c/ Pau Claris, 150 (p 140)*

Best **Service**
★★★ Mandarin Oriental Barcelona $$$$ *Pg. de Gràcia, 28–30 (p 142)*

Best **Gay Hotel**
★ Hotel Axel $$$ *c/ Aribau, 33 (p 139)*

Best **Boutique Hotels**
★★★ ABaC $$$$ *Av. Tibidabo, 1 (p 136)*; and ★★ Duquesa de Cardona $$$ *Pg. Colom, 12 (p 137)*

Best **City Views**
★★★ Gran Hotel La Florida $$$$ *Ctra. de Vallvidrera, 83–93 (p 138)*

Best **Sea Views**
★★★ Hotel Arts $$$$ *c/ de la Marina, 19–21 (p 139)*; and ★ W Barcelona $$$ *Pl. de la Rosa dels Vents, 1 (p 144)*

Best **for Families**
★ Hispanos Siete Suiza $$ *c/ Sicilia, 255 (p 138)*

Best **Chic Bed & Breakfast**
★★★ The 5 Rooms $$ *c/ Pau Claris, 72 (p 144)*

Best **Swimming Pools**
★★ Grand Hotel Central $$$ *Vía Laietana, 30 (p 138)*; and ★★ Hotel 1898 $$$ *La Rambla, 109 (p 141)*

Best **Luxurious Hideaways**
★★★ ABaC $$$$ *Av. Tibidabo, 1 (p 136)*; and ★★★ Gran Hotel La Florida $$$$ *Ctra. de Vallvidrera, 83–93 (p 138)*

Best **Steps Up from a Hostel**
★ Raval Rooms $ *c/ Hospital, 155 (p 143)*; and ★ Hostemplo $ *c/ Sicilia, 276 (p 139)*

Best **Historic (*Modernista*) Hotel**
★★★ Hotel Casa Fuster $$$$ *Pg. de Gràcia, 132 (p 140)*

Best **Hipster Hotels**
★ Casa Camper $$$ *c/ Elisabets, 11 (p 136)*; and ★★ Chic & Basic Born $$ *c/ de la Princesa, 50 (p 136)*

Best **Spa Pampering**
★★★ Hotel Arts $$$$ *c/ de la Marina, 19–21 (p 139)*; and ★★★ Gran Hotel La Florida $$$$ *Ctra. de Vallvidrera, 83–93 (p 138)*

Previous page: A room at the Hotel 1898.

L'Eixample

ABaC Restaurant-Hotel 1
BCN Fashion House 23
Constanza 19
Diagonal 10
El Palace Barcelona 17
Gran Hotel La Florida 2
Hispanos Siete Suiza 20
Hostal Goya 21
Hostal L'Antic Espai 18
Hostemplo 6
Hotel Astoria 3
Hotel Axel 13
Hotel Casa Fuster 4
Hotel Claris 11
Hotel Condes
 de Barcelona 9
Hotel Jazz 16
Hotel Omm 5
Mandarin Oriental
 Barcelona 14
Murmuri Barcelona 7
Praktik Rambla 12
Pulitzer 15
Suites Avenue 8
The 5 Rooms 22

Ciutat Vella & Waterfront

Barcelona **Hotels A to Z**

★★★ kids **ABaC** ZONA ALTA
This new concept—gastrohotel—is a delight for sybarites and ideal for this design- and gastronomy-crazed city. A small, luxurious boutique hotel in a 19th-century villa on one of Barcelona's swankiest streets, it is built around a Michelin two-star restaurant that was formerly a centerpiece of the old quarter. This new, high-design place, which also offers seductive modern rooms and a small spa, is the perfect place for guests who come to take in the best of Barcelona with all their senses. *Av. Tibidabo, 1.* ☎ *93-319-66-00. www.abacbarcelona.com. 15 units. Doubles 220€–339€; suites 320€–504€. AE, DC, MC, V. Metro: Pl. Kennedy. Map p 133.*

kids **BCN Fashion House**
L'EIXAMPLE One of the few bed-and-breakfasts in Barcelona, this comfortable spot, in a nicely restored 19th-century town house with a leafy communal terrace, is a good-value, homey place to stay. Each pair of bedrooms shares one bathroom. Families should check out the suite, a self-catering apartment. *c/ Bruc, 13.* ☎ *93-790-40-44. www.bcn-fashionhouse.com. 35 units. Doubles 50€–104€; suites 75€–145€. Rates include breakfast. AE, MC, V. Metro: Urquinaona. Map p 133.*

★ **Casa Camper** RAVAL If you're a fan of funky Camper shoes, this idiosyncratic, design-trippy place, where all rooms have sitting rooms, is probably for you. The hotel's aesthetics are as playful as the company's shoe stores, although it's a little pricey for the transitional neighborhood and the young, design-obsessed crowd it courts. *c/ Elisabets, 11.* ☎ *93-342-62-80. www.casacamper.com/barcelona. 25*

Quirky touches can be found throughout Casa Camper.

units. Doubles 238€–293€. AE, DC, MC, V. Metro: Catalunya.

★★ kids **Chic & Basic Born** LA RIBERA The concept is simple: IKEA-designed, Euro-minimalist rooms that attract hordes of young and hip travelers in neighborhoods where they'll be partying as well as sleeping (more of the former). Rooms in the 100-year-old building are white-on-white and playfully urbane, with colored "light curtains." Rooms are M, L, and XL—some are quite compact, others very generous in size, with quiet balconies. It also offers apartments. *c/ de la Princesa, 50.* ☎ *93-295-46-52. www.chicandbasic.com. 78 units.*

Doubles 100€–175€. AE, DC, MC, V. Metro: Jaume I.

★ **Ciutat Barcelona Hotel** LA RIBERA A bargain hotel that offers a lot of cool design and comfort, this addition to the hip neighborhood, just steps from the Picasso Museum, is a winner. Rooms are crisply contemporary and clean, and there's a nice little rooftop pool and deck. *c/ de la Princesa, 35.* ☎ *93-269-74-75. www.ciutat barcelona.com. 78 units. Doubles 70€–135€. AE, DC, MC, V. Metro: Arc de Triomf or Jaume I.*

★★ **Constanza** L'EIXAMPLE Travelers looking for affordable Barcelona style will be pleased with this small boutique hotel. Although rooms aren't large, they are modern and comfortable, and the hotel is well located within walking distance of Plaça de Catalunya. A room with its own private terrace is a real bargain. *c/ Bruc, 33.* ☎ *93-270-19-10. www.hotel constanza.com. 20 units. Doubles 90€–146€. AE, MC, V. Metro: Urquinaona. Map p 133.*

★★ **Diagonal** L'EIXAMPLE/GRACIA Upping the ante of cutting-edge architecture is this massive Silken hotel. Mod and flashy, it may look playful, but the hotel is dead serious about hip design. Next to Torre Agbar, some rooms have straight-shot views of La Sagrada Família. *Av. Diagonal, 205.* ☎ *93-489-53-00. www.hoteles-silken.com. 240 units. Doubles 93€–180€; suites 186€–280€. AE, DC, MC, V. Metro: Catalunya or Liceu. Map p 133.*

★★ **Duquesa de Cardona** WATERFRONT A sedate boutique hotel across the street from the marina, this restored 19th-century palace is elegant and intimate. It also has something unique: a large rooftop solarium terrace with a pool and great views of the port. *Pg. Colom, 12.* ☎ *93-268-90-90. www.hduquesadecardona.com. 40 units. Doubles 165€–280€. AE, DC, MC, V. Metro: Jaume I or Drassanes.*

El Jardí Hotel BARRI GÒTIC Simple and easygoing, this small budget hotel has an extraordinary location overlooking two of the prettiest plazas in the heart of Ciutat Vella. Rooms are somewhat austere, with bright lighting, but five have private terraces. *Pl. Sant Josep Oriol, 1.* ☎ *93-301-59-00. www.eljardi-barcelona.com. 40 units. Doubles 45€–154€. MC, V. Metro: Liceu.*

A room at Duquesa de Cardona.

The luxurious lobby at El Palace Barcelona.

★★ El Palace Barcelona

L'EIXAMPLE Although this 1919 Art Deco hotel has changed names, many still refer to it as the Ritz, and the sense of grace and old-money elegance remain. It's white-glove treatment all the way here. Public rooms are grand and aristocratic; guest rooms are large and formal. *Gran Vía de les Corts Catalanes, 668.* ☎ *93-510-11-30. www.hotelpalace barcelona.com. 125 units. Doubles 262€–560€. AE, DC, MC, V. Metro: Pg. de Gràcia. Map p 133.*

★★ Grand Hotel Central LA

RIBERA In a palatial 1926 mansion owned by an old Catalan family, this property has been beautifully converted to a contemporary luxury hotel. Rooms are warmly decorated in rich creams and chocolates. The spectacular rooftop infinity pool, surrounded by wood decking and views of the Gothic Quarter and the sea, is a bonus and privilege to use. *Vía Laietana, 30.* ☎ *93-295-79-00. www.grandhotelcentral.com. 147 units. Doubles 162€–330€. AE, DC, MC, V. Metro: Jaume I.*

★★★ kids Gran Hotel La Flor-

ida MT. TIBIDABO/ENVIRONS High above Barcelona, this palatial hotel is a magnificent refuge if pampering, luxury, and relaxation are your primary concerns. Although the views

across Barcelona to the sea are astounding, the hotel's location is not convenient if you're set on seeing and doing lots of things. Yet the hotel, originally built in the 1920s, certainly earns the *gran* (great) in its name, with plush, soothing designer rooms, a spa, and an infinity pool. *Ctra. Vallvidrera (at Tibidabo), 83–93 (7km/4.3 miles from Barcelona).* ☎ *93-259-30-00. www.hotellaflorida.com. 74 units. Doubles 144€–393€. AE, DC, MC, V. Map p 133.*

★ kids Hispanos Siete Suiza

L'EIXAMPLE An aparthotel with the comforts of a top-flight hotel, the Suiza—with a lobby of vintage automobiles—is perfect for families and long-term stays. Apartments in the historic house are two-bedroom, two-bath, with a living room and kitchen, and guests have free access to a sports center with pool and yoga. But best of all, some of the hotel's profits go toward a cancer foundation established by the original owner of the house. *c/ Sicilia, 255.* ☎ *93-208-20-51. www.hispanos7suiza.com. 19 units. Doubles (2-bedroom apt) 129€–249€, including breakfast. AE, DC, MC, V. Metro: Sagrada Família. Map p 133.*

★ Hostal Goya L'EIXAMPLE A

refreshingly smart, centrally located hostal and a very good value, this small inn is clean and friendly. The best and quietest rooms are in the recently renovated Principal wing; others are small and dark. Most guests who stay here are young people in Barcelona looking to have a good time. *c/ Pau Claris, 74.* ☎ *93-302-25-65. www.hostalgoya. com. 19 units. Doubles 70€–112€. MC, V. Metro: Urquinaona. Map p 133.*

★ Hostal L'Antic Espai

L'EIXAMPLE If you've had it with generic contemporary minimalism, this is your place, a guesthouse stuffed to the gills with antiques of the (faux) Louis XV variety. Run by a Brazilian and a Cuban, it's also an antidote to impersonal and over-priced hotels. *c/ Gran Vía de les Cortes Catalanes, 660.* ☎ *93-304-19-45. www.anticespai.com. 10 units. Doubles 62€–120€. MC, V. Metro: Urquinaona. Map p 133.*

★ Hostemplo

L'EIXAMPLE Just above Avinguda Diagonal, just a couple blocks from Gaudí's Sagrada Família, this agreeable small hotel, inaugurated in 2009 in a *modernista* building, is clean, simple, and a very good value, even if rooms are a little tight. *c/ Sicília, 276.* ☎ *93-476-55-75. www. hostemplo.com. 10 units. Doubles 84€–135€. MC, V. Metro: Sagrada Família. Map p 133.*

★★★ Hotel Arts

WATERFRONT One of only three skyscrapers in Barcelona, this sleek, high-tech luxury hotel enjoys sweeping beach views. Service is personable and efficient, as you'd expect from a Ritz-Carlton property, making this a favorite spot for business travelers and celebs. The outdoor pool, swanky new spa overlooking the marina, and restaurant by star chef Sergi Arola only add to the allure. *c/ de la Marina, 19–21.* ☎ *800/241-3333 or 93-221-10-00. www.ritzcarlton.com/hotels/barcelona. 482 units. Doubles 199€–750€. AE, DC,* MC, V. Metro: Ciutadella–Vila Olímpica.

★ kids Hotel Astoria

L'EIXAMPLE A renovated 1950s hotel with enduring style, this winning member of the Derby chain (which owns the Claris) is elegant but relaxed. Its warmly decorated accommodations and rooftop pool and sauna make it a very good value, even if you have to walk a few blocks to restaurants and attractions near Passeig de Gràcia. *c/ París, 203.* ☎ *93-209-83-11. www. derbyhotels.com. 114 units. Doubles 87€–196€. AE, DC, MC, V. Metro: Diagonal. Map p 133.*

★ Hotel Axel

L'EIXAMPLE Filling a niche in Barcelona, this recently refurbished midsize hotel serves an international gay population and is confident enough to decorate rooms with erotic art (but declares itself "heterofriendly"). Rooms are stylish, with top-quality bedding, and the hip cocktail bar, rooftop

The Hotel Arts offers spectacular water views.

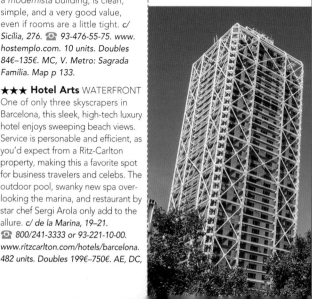

pool, and sun deck are prized. *c/ Aribau, 33.* ☎ 93-323-93-93. *www. hotelaxel.com. 105 units. Doubles 60€–188€; suites 211€–305€. AE, DC, MC, V. Metro: Universitat. Map p 133.*

★ **Hotel Banys Orientals** LA RIBERA A pioneer leading the way for stylish but inexpensive boutique hotels, this cool place is immensely popular, as much for its bargain rates and hip style as its terrific location near El Born. Rooms are small but chic, although noise-sensitive guests should seek one at the back; the area is full of late-night revelers. *c/ L'Argenteria, 37.* ☎ 93-268-84-60. *www.hotel banysorientals.com. 43 units. Doubles 96€–143€. AE, DC, MC, V. Metro: Jaume I.*

★ **kids Hotel Barcelona Cate-dral** BARRI GÒTIC Right across from the cathedral, this stylishly modern midsize hotel features unexpected bonuses, including a pool, terrace, cooking lessons, wine tastings, and guided tours around the old city. *c/ Capellans, 4.* ☎ 93-304-22-55. *www.barcelona catedral.com. 80 units. Doubles 144€–204€. AE, DC, MC, V. Metro: Jaume I.*

★★★ **Hotel Casa Fuster** GRA-CIA Occupying a lovely *modernista* building, Casa Fuster is one of the most emblematic places to stay in

the city. It has a feel of period indulgence yet offers every modern amenity, including a pool, a restaurant, a bar, lounges, illuminated night terrace, and cool jazz club. Rooms are luxe, with splashes of color and texture. *Pg. de Gràcia, 132.* ☎ 902-20-23-45 or 93-255-30-00. *www.hotelcasafuster.com. 105 units. Doubles 176€–347€. AE, DC, MC, V. Metro: Diagonal. Map p 133*

★★★ **Hotel Claris** L'EIXAMPLE This is one of the best-loved luxury hotels in Barcelona, where modern design commingles with a landmark 19th-century palace facade and a for-guests-only museum of Egyptian art. Rooms, many of which are split-level and even two-story, are a mix of cool chic and warm sophistication. The top-floor terrace includes a small pool and offers lovely views of the surrounding Eixample neighborhood. *c/ Pau Claris, 150.* ☎ 90-099-00-11 or 93-487-62-62. *www.hotelclaris.com. 120 units. Doubles 176€–440€. AE, DC, MC, V. Metro: Pg. de Gràcia. Map p 133.*

★ **Hotel Condes de Barcelona** L'EIXAMPLE With a prestigious corner location on Passeig de Gràcia, this late-19th-century mansion is elegant and sophisticated, although an annex across the street doesn't have quite the same style. The recent arrival of one of the

The Hotel Banys Orientals.

The underground pool at the Hotel 1898.

Basque Country's most celebrated chefs, Martín Berasategui, and his restaurant, Lasarte, have given the hotel new verve. *Pg. de Gràcia, 73–75.* ☎ *93-445-00-00. www. condesdebarcelona.com. 183 units. Doubles 148€–264€. AE, DC, MC, V. Metro: Pg. de Gràcia. Map p 133.*

★ **kids Hotel Curious** EL RAVAL In tune with the funky style of this emerging, artsy neighborhood, this value-oriented boutique hotel has a fun name and fun with its interiors, which have splashes of color and large-format, black-and-white landscape photographs above the beds. It's a good choice if you're looking for something different. *c/ Carme, 25.* ☎ *93-301-44-84. www.hotel curious.com. 25 units. Doubles 85€– 128€. MC, V. Metro: Liceu.*

★ **kids Hotel del Mar** BORN/ WATERFRONT This ultra-friendly Gargallo family hotel is a perfect choice for staying near the beach without busting your budget. Some of the newly refurbished rooms have port and sea views, and the beach is a mere 5-minute walk away. *c/ Pla de Palau, 19.* ☎ *93-319- 33-02. www.hoteldelmarbarcelona. com. 75 rooms. Doubles 56€–143€. AE, DC, MC, V. Metro: Barceloneta.*

★★ **kids Hotel 1898** LA RAM- BLA This large hotel, opened in 2002, occupies a late-19th-century building that was once the Philippine Tobacco Co. headquarters. It has been strikingly converted, with bold artwork, stripes, and colors; most spectacular is the underground pool beneath brick arches (although the rooftop bar and pool are a close second). *La Rambla, 109 (entrance on c/ Pintor Fortuny).* ☎ *93-552-95-52. www.hotel1898. com. 169 units. Doubles 181€–345€. AE, DC, MC, V. Metro: Catalunya.*

★ **Hotel Jazz** L'EIXAMPLE Around the corner from La Rambla, Hotel Jazz aims, by name and middle-of-the-road contemporary design, for a wide international clientele (many of whom appear to be young people on group junkets). The impressive lobby has plenty of glass and bleached-wood floors; soundproof rooms are attractive, if a bit generic. But the stars of the show are the rooftop pool and wood-deck terrace. *c/ Pelai, 3.* ☎ *93-552-96-96. www.nnhotels.es. 180 units. Doubles 105€–210€. AE, DC, MC, V. Metro: Catalunya or Universitat. Map p 133.*

★ **kids Hotel Miramar Barce- lona** MONTJUIC Tucked into the hillside, next to the Montjuïc Park gardens and with majestic views overlooking the city and the Mediterranean, this 1920s palace was restored and converted into a hotel. A bold, modern new addition by Oscar Tusquets envelops the original mansion. The result is a chic mix of period details and modern decor. Gardens and indoor and outdoor pools make this a relaxing option for families. *Pl. Carlos Ibáñez, 3. ☎ 93-281-16-00. www.hotel miramarbarcelona.com. 75 units. Doubles 140€–515€. AE, DC, MC, V. Metro: Paral.lel.*

★★ Hotel Neri BARRI GÒTIC A

sumptuous Gothic palace discreetly tucked away on charming Plaça Felip Neri, this small, upscale hotel is romance incarnate, all velvet drapes and soft-lit rooms. Rooms are luxurious and intimate, with fine linens, and the restaurant and cafe on the square are unexpected bonuses. A true find in the Old City, it's unlike any other hotel. *c/ Sant Sever, 5. ☎ 93-304-06-55. www.hotelneri.com. 22 units. Doubles 293€–375€. AE, DC, MC, V. Metro: Jaume I.*

★★★ Hotel Omm L'EIXAMPLE

The hotel with perhaps the most positive buzz in Barcelona is this sleek temple of hip, Zen-like design and an even cooler clientele. Its restaurant, Moo (p 105), is one of the city's best, and the lounges attract Barcelona's most stylish scenemakers. Design freaks will be in heaven; the place was created for them. The rooftop lap pool and deck offer views of La Pedrera. *c/ Rosselló, 265. ☎ 93-445-40-00. www.hotelomm.es. 59 units. Doubles 199€–355€. AE, DC, MC, V. Metro: Diagonal. Map p 133.*

H10 Racó Del Pi BARRI GÒTIC A

member of a small, Barcelona-based hotel chain, this attractive, small hotel is intimate and perfectly located in a historic building on one of the most atmospheric streets in the Gothic Quarter. Rooms aren't huge, but they do feature a clean, stylish aesthetic.

The Hotel Neri is well located on the delightful Plaça Felip Neri.

Plaça del Pi, 7. ☎ 93-342-61-90. www.hotelracodelpi.com. 37 units. Doubles 99€–178€. AE, DC, MC, V. Metro: Jaume I or Liceu.

★★★ Mandarin Oriental Barcelona L'EIXAMPLE In former bank

headquarters and a superb Passeig de Gràcia location, the Mandarin created a splash with its ultra-stylish, Zen-like rooms (light-filled, starkly modern, and largely white), stunning spa (in the old bank vault), jaw-dropping rooftop lap pool, and restaurant by a female chef with five Michelin stars. It has quickly become Barcelona's most prestigious hotel address and the place to be seen. *Pg. de Gràcia, 28–30. ☎ 93-151-88-88. www.mandarin oriental.com/barcelona. 98 units. Doubles 385€–585€. AE, DC, MC, V. Metro: Pg. de Gràcia. Map p 133.*

★★ Murmuri Barcelona

L'EIXAMPLE Barcelona's penchant for great design and the reinvigoration of classic buildings continue unabated, and this hotel is one of the newest and best examples. Noted British designer Kelly Hoppen's touch (most evident in public spaces) is warmer and more romantic, demonstrating more classic elegance than most of the new crop of hotels. *Rambla de Catalunya, 104. ☎ 93-492-22-44. www.murmuri.com.*

43 units. Doubles 149€–371€. AE, DC, MC, V. Metro: Diagonal. Map p 133.

★ **Park Hotel** LA RIBERA This sleek, recently updated hotel at the edge of El Born is a handsome example of midcentury architecture, notable for its spiral staircase and the lobby's mosaic-tiled bar. The crisply modern rooms are not huge, but they are a pretty fair value, and in a good location for someone who wants to be near, but not on top of, El Born. *Av. Marquès de l'Argentera, 11.* ☎ *93-319-60-00. www.parkhotelbarcelona.com. 91 units. Doubles 135€–147€. AE, DC, MC, V. Metro: Barceloneta or Jaume I.*

Petit Palace Opera Garden LA RAMBLA A member of a successful Spanish chain, this midsize hotel is near, but not on, La Rambla, and just seconds from La Boquería food market. Rooms have laptop computers with free Wi-Fi connections. *c/ La Boquería, 10.* ☎ *93-302-00-92. www.hthoteles.com. 69 units. Doubles 80€–187€. Metro: Liceu.*

★★ **Praktik Rambla** L'EIXAMPLE In a smartly converted, gorgeous 19th-century apartment building (by the original architect of La Sagrada Família!), on the quieter of the Ramblas, this midsize boutique hotel delivers chic design on a budget. It's the perfect blend of old and new Barcelona and has a coveted outdoor terrace. Its nearby sister property, Praktik Garden, is cheaper but not nearly as stylish. *Rambla de Catalunya, 67.* ☎ *93-343-66-90. www.hotelpraktikrambla.com. 43 units. Doubles 132€–237€. AE, DC, MC, V. Metro: Catalunya. Map p 133.*

★ **Pulitzer** L'EIXAMPLE Sleek and trendy, but pretty affordable for a hotel of its design and amenities, this relative newcomer to the scene has a stylish cocktail bar and alluring candlelit rooftop terrace, making it understandably popular. *c/ Bergara, 8.* ☎ *93-481-67-67. www.hotelpulitzer.es. 91 units. Doubles 104€–215€. AE, DC, MC, V. Metro: Catalunya. Map p 133.*

★ kids **Raval Rooms** RAVAL Just because you don't want to spend a lot of money doesn't mean you don't want some style. A major step up from hostels, this groovy place is popular with hipsters, design sorts, young families, and travelers with more style than cash. Now under new management and name (it used to be Gat Raval), its rooms are still small and spare, with a bright green, white, and black aesthetic, and it has a cool rooftop terrace. *c/ Hospital, 155.* ☎ *93-324-88-17. www.ravalrooms.com. 35*

The hip lobby of Hotel Omm.

units. Doubles 89€–151€, including breakfast. AE, MC, V. Metro: Liceu.

★★★ kids Suites Avenue

L'EIXAMPLE Behind a curvy stainless steel facade by noted Japanese architect Toyo Ito, these swank luxury apartments with full kitchens ooze sleek style. It's great for longer stays, business trips, or the style-conscious family. Some apartments overlooking Passeig de Gràcia have privileged direct views of Gaudí's La Pedrera. Pg. de Gràcia, 83. ☎ 93-487-41-59. www.suitesavenue.com. 43 units. Doubles 141€–368€. AE, DC, MC, V. Metro: Pl. Provença. Map p 133.

★★★ kids The 5 Rooms

L'EIXAMPLE Much more like staying in a friend's cool Eixample apartment than anything resembling a hotel, this intimate and urbane, well-decorated B&B on two floors is great for both Bs and perfectly located within walking distance of the old quarter and major modernista sights. It actually has 12 rooms as well as a handful of apartments, making it great for families. c/ Pau Claris, 72. ☎ 93-342-78-80. www.thefiverooms.com. 7 units. Doubles 135€–185€, including breakfast. DC, MC, V. Metro: Urquinaona. Map p 133.

★ Vincci Marítimo Hotel

WATERFRONT (POBLE NOU) In a recently developed waterfront district near Mar Bella beach, this forward-looking hotel pushes the envelope of sleek design, with miles of glass, warm wood, and brushed steel. It's perfect if you're mostly interested in hanging out at less-populated beaches, and a fair deal, too. c/ Llull, 340. ☎ 93-356-26-00. www.vinccihoteles.com. 144 units. Doubles 75€–150€. AE, DC, MC, V. Metro: Poble Nou.

★ W Barcelona WATERFRONT

(BARCELONETA) One of Barcelona's newest hotels, this huge, gleaming, sail-shaped building rising high over the old port is not without controversy. But it was designed by Ricardo Bofill, a Barcelona native, and offers stunning panoramic sea views from rooms, the sleek bar, and the terrace pool. Rooms are crisp and modern, in that chic, contemporary W style, and there's a Bliss spa—but it's way out past Barceloneta, requiring taxis or a lot of walking. Pl. de la Rosa dels Vents, 1 (Pg. Joan de Borbó). ☎ 93-295-28-00. www.w-barcelona.com. 473 units. Doubles 225€–765€. AE, DC, MC, V. Metro: Barceloneta. ●

A room at The 5 Rooms.

Montserrat

① Aéri de Montserrat/
Rack Railway
② Monestir de Montserrat/
La Moreneta
③ Escolania de Montserrat
④ Museu de Montserrat
⑤ Funicular Railways

A very popular half-day inland trip, this spectacularly jagged peak (the "saw-tooth mountain"), 50km (31 miles) northwest of Barcelona, is home to a Benedictine monastery founded in A.D. 1025 and La Moreneta (the Black Madonna), the patron saint of Catalunya. A sacred place of pilgrimage, Montserrat is overrun on the holy days April 27 and September 8. It's also a popular place for hiking and hard-core cycling.

① ★★ **Aéri de Montserrat/ Rack Railway.** The most scenic way to Montserrat is by 1930 cable car. The FGC train leaves from Barcelona and connects to it both ways. However, the more comfortable, panoramic **Montserrat rack railway** is also a spectacular way to get there, and it leaves you right in the middle of the monastery. ☎ 93-205-15-15. www.aeridemontserrat.com or

Previous page: Montserrat Monastery.

www.fgc.net/eng/bitllets_oci_turisme. asp. Cable car 10€ roundtrip; rack railway 9.80€ roundtrip.

② ★ **Monestir de Montserrat/ La Moreneta.** The Benedictine monastery, tucked into the 1,219m (4,000-ft.) ridges of Montserrat, holds a shrine to the famous Black Madonna icon, which according to legend was discovered in the 12th century (and said to have been carved by St. Luke in A.D. 50). The library holds some 300,000 volumes, though many were lost during raids by Napoleon's forces in 1811 (they also razed the 16th-c. Basilica). About 100 Benedictine monks continue in residence at Montserrat. ☎ 93-877-77-01. www.montserratvisita.com. Free admission. Daily 7:30am–8pm.

❸ ★★ Escolanía de Montserrat. One of the oldest boys' choirs in Europe (dating to the 14th c.) performs Monday to Friday at 1pm (Salve) and Monday to Thursday at 6:45pm (Vespers). On Sundays and holidays, you can hear them at 11am and again at 6:45pm. ☎ 93-877-77-67. For more information about the choir (including an amusing FAQ) & the current calendar, visit www.escolania.cat.

❹ ★ Museu de Montserrat. The museum next door to the Basilica contains minor paintings by such artists as Caravaggio, Degas, Monet, and El Greco, as well as early works by Picasso, Miró, and Dalí. Pl. de Santa María, s/n. ☎ 93-877-77-77. www.abadia montserrat.net. Admission 7€. Mon–Fri 10am–5:30pm, Sat-Sun 10am-5:45pm (until 6:45pm summer).

❺ ★★ Funicular Railways. A funicular climbs to the peak of **Sant Joan,** where there's a small hermitage and panoramic views, but the only way up to the **Sant Jeroni** hermitage and summit beyond is by foot (about a 45-min. walk). A separate funicular goes to **Santa Cova,** a 17th-century chapel built in the shape of a cross, where La Moreneta was allegedly discovered. www.cremallerademontserrat.com. Combined funicular ticket 8.10€ round-trip; included in Tot Montserrat & TransMontserrat tickets.

The Montserrat monastery nestled into the mountain.

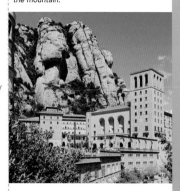

Practical Matters: Montserrat

The convenient Tot Montserrat ticket (44€) includes the Barcelona Metro, a round-trip train to Montserrat, entry into the museum, funiculars, and lunch at the Montserrat restaurant; the TransMontserrat ticket (28€), is for the Metro, train, and funiculars only. Trains depart from Barcelona's **Plaça d'Espanya station** (☎ 93-205-15-15; www.fgc.net/eng/bitllets_oci_turisme.asp; Metro: Espanya). By car, take the A-2 out of Barcelona toward Tarragona and Martorell, or the Barcelona–Terrassa highway via the Túneles de Vallvidrera. The **Tourist Information Office** is on Plaça de la Creu, s/n; ☎ 93-877-77-01. Additional information on Montserrat and transport, including funiculars and hiking in the area, can be found at www.cremallerademontserrat.com or by calling ☎ 902-31-20-20.

Sitges

1. Museu Cau Ferrat
2. Museu Maricel del Mar
3. Cafe-Bar Roy
4. Beaches
   - Aiguadolç
   - Sant Sebastià
   - La Fragata
   - La Ribera
5. Sitges nightlife:
   Carrer St. Bonaventura

An excellent day or overnight trip is to the pretty beach town of Sitges, 37km (23 miles) southwest of Barcelona along the Costa Daurada (Golden Coast). Long a cultural and intellectual center, with a wealth of *modernista* architecture, Sitges was a favorite of the painters Santiago Rusiñol and Salvador Dalí, as well as the poet Federico García Lorca. This quiet beach town is also one of Spain's most prominent gay resorts (especially during Carnaval).

1 ★★ **Museu Cau Ferrat.** The former home of Rusiñol is packed to the rafters with artwork by El Greco, Ramón Casas, Ignacio Zuloaga, and others; ceramics and wrought iron; and a collection of the artist's personal effects. The museum is expected to open in late 2014 after extensive renovation. *c/ del Fonollar, s/n.* ☎ *93-894-03-64. www.museusdesitges.com. Admission 3.50€. mid-June–Sept Tues–Sat*

9:30am–2pm & 4–7pm; Sun 10am–3pm; Oct–mid-June Tues–Sat 9:30am–2pm & 3:30–6:30pm; Sun 10am–3pm

2 ★ **Museu Maricel del Mar.** This early-20th-century mansion houses a collection of Gothic and Romantic artworks, as well as modern Catalan pieces. The museum is expected to open in late 2014 after renovations. *c/ del Fonollar, s/n. For details, see Museu Cau Ferrat (above).*

Practical Matters: Sitges

Trains (40 min.; ☎ 902-32-03-20; www.renfe.com) make departures (every 15–30 min.) from Barcelona's Sants station. A simple round-trip is 8.20€. By car, take C-246 or toll highway A-7 (40km/25 miles south of Barcelona; allow 45 min. to an hour). The **Tourist Information Office** (☎ 93-894-42-51; www.sitgestour.cat) is at Pl. Eduard Maristany, 2. (The website has good hotel links). Gay travelers should consult http://gaysitgesguide.com for information on Carnaval and gay-friendly hotels, restaurants, and bars.

Lodging: El Xalet, c/ Isla de Cuba, 33–35 (☎ 93-811-00-70; www.elxalet.com; doubles 63€–110€), is a quirky *modernista* house within walking distance of the beach; **Estela Barcelona Hotel** del Arte (Av. Port d'Aiguadolç, 8; ☎ 93-811-45-45; www.hotelestela.com; doubles 160€–190€ but big discounts online) is an art-filled place overlooking the marina and beach, with a full spa and good restaurant.

Dining: The finest restaurant in Sitges is the sleek, elegant **Fragata** ($$$; Pg. de la Ribera, 1; ☎ 93-894-10-86), serving innovative Mediterranean fare and seafood. With its terrace facing the sea, it's a place to splurge. Less exalted but still very dependable restaurants on Passeig de la Ribera include **El Velero de Sitges** at no. 38 ($$$; ☎ 93-894-20-51) and **Mare Nostrum** at no. 60 ($$; ☎ 93-894-33-93).

3 **Cafe-Bar Roy.** A good stop for a coffee or a glass of cava and snacks, this classic, old-fashioned coffeehouse has marble tables, hand-painted tiles, and Art Nouveau touches (and free Wi-Fi). *c/ de les Parellades, 9.* ☎ 93-811-02-69. *$.*

4 **★★ Beaches.** Sitges's biggest draw is its 17 beaches. Those in the town center and along the eastern end are the most laid-back. The most popular are **Aiguadolç** and **Balmins. Sant Sebastià** and **La Fragata** are known as family beaches, something that would probably not be said for those to the west. A young crowd heads to **La Ribera,** and farthest west are the beaches, such as **Platges del Mort,** that are the haunts of the least inhibited beachgoers, including nudists and large groups of gays.

5 **★ Nightlife.** In the town center, Carrer Sant Bonaventura, a 5-minute walk from the beach, teems with gay bars and party spots. **Mediterráneo**, c/ Sant Bonaventura, 6 (no phone), is the largest gay disco. One of Spain's most flamboyant parties is **Carnaval in Sitges**, celebrated the week before Lent.

La Ribera Beach.

Girona

**Map labels:**

Information

St. Feliu
Pont de Sant Feliu
Plaça Sant Feliu
Catedral
Museu d'Art
Jardins dels Alemanys
Plaça Catedral
Plaça Llendoners
Museu d'Història
Plaça de Sant Domènec
Sant Domènec
Força
EL CALL
Pont d'en Gomèz
Ballesteries
Jardins Maristes
Sant Martí Sacosta
Berenguer Carnicer
Passeig
Real de Fontclara
Canalejas
Plaça de la Independència
Pont de Sant Agustí
BARRI VELL
Lola Café
Portal Nou
B. Carreras P. Ciutadans
Fontana d'Or
Argenteria
Santa Clara
Plaça Mercaders
Llebre
Torre dels Socors
Pont de Ferro
Riu Onyar
Llibertat
Plaça del Vi
Sèquia Obra
Pont de Pedra

1. El Call
2. Banys Àrabs
3. Catedral
4. Roman Walls
5. Museu d'Art
6. Monestir de St. Pere de Galligants (city archaeology museum)
7. Lola Café
8. Cases de l'Onyar/Pont de Ferro
9. Museu del Cinema

ANDORRA FRANCE
Girona
CATALUNYA
Aragón
BARCELONA
MEDITERRANEAN SEA

An hour north of Barcelona is Girona, one of Spain's most historic cities. Its pristine Old Quarter is among the most beautiful in Spain. Built on an old Roman settlement and steeped in the layered histories of the Romans, Moors, and Jews, the town center is a compact jumble of narrow stone streets, dark alleyways, and the medieval arches of El Call—the ancient Jewish neighborhood. Bustling by day, the cobblestone streets of the Old Quarter turn quiet as night falls. Though one of Spain's wealthiest cities, Girona has a reputation as a provincial and emphatically Catalan city.

1 ★★★ **El Call.** Girona was home to a prosperous Jewish community for more than 6 centuries, until its members were expelled in 1492. The Jewish district ("El Call" in Catalan) is a tangle of narrow, dark, atmospheric streets tucked within the Old Quarter and said to be the best-preserved ghetto in western Europe. Carrer de la Força is the principal street, where buildings date from the 13th to 15th centuries. The Museu d'Historia dels Jueus is a well-designed history center that documents the Jewish population of Girona; the last known synagogue in the city, built in the 15th century, is part of the center. *c/ de la Força, 8.* ☎ *972-21-67-61. www.ajuntament.*

Practical Matters: Girona

By car from Barcelona, take the ronda (beltway) in the direction of France and then the A-7 to Girona; the trip is 97km (60 miles). Frequent (40–90-min.) trains leave from Barcelona's Estació Sants and arrive at Girona's Plaça de Espanya (☎ 902-24-02-02; www.renfe.com); if you're only traveling to Girona (city), the train is the way to go. The main Oficina de Turisme is on the pedestrian-only main drag, Rambla de la Llibertat, 1 (☎ 97-201-00-01; www.girona.cat/turisme). A trip to Girona can (and really should, if you have the time) easily be combined with visits to L'Empordà and the Costa Brava (see p 154).

Lodging: The swankest hotel in town is **AC Palau de Bellavista**, just outside the Old Quarter and near Plaça de Catalunya, with a glass-box exterior and elegant rooms (Pujada Polvorins, 1; ☎ 97-208-06-70; www.marriott.com; doubles 70€–135€). **Hotel Citutat de Girona** (c/ Nord, 2; ☎ 972-48-30-38; www.hotel-ciutat-degirona.com; doubles 88€–135€) is a stylishly modern midsize hotel at the edge of the Old Quarter. **Bellmirall** is a charming guesthouse in the heart of the Old Quarter, with just seven rooms in a restored 14th-century stone mansion (c/ Bellmirall, 3; ☎ 972-20-40-09; www.bellmirall.eu; doubles 65€–85€; closed Jan–Feb).

Dining: **Le Bistrot** ($), a terrific little place that spills out onto the steep steps of an Old Quarter alleyway with candlelit tables, is a great place for gourmet pizzas, salads, and crepes (Pujada Sant Domènec, 4; ☎ 972-21-88-03). **Blanc** ($), connected to the Hotel Ciutat de Girona, is a chic, excellent-value restaurant that serves Catalan and Mediterranean dishes (c/ Nord, 2; ☎ 972-41-56-37). **El Celler de Can Roca** ($$$$), in sleek new surroundings, is one of the top upscale restaurants in Catalunya, if not in all of Spain—by itself it may be worth a trip to Girona (Can Sunyer, 48, in Taialà, northeast of Girona; ☎ 972-22-21-57; www.cellercanroca.com).

gi/call. Admission to museum 2€, 1.50€ students & seniors (audio guide including admission 4€). May–Oct Mon–Sat 10am–8pm, Sun 10am–3pm; Nov–Apr Mon–Sat 10am–6pm & Sun 10am–2pm.

② ★ **Banys Àrabs.** The 12th-century Arab baths are one of the few reminders of Girona's Moorish community. Restored in the 1920s, the Romanesque baths are among the best preserved in Spain. c/ Ferran el Catòlic, s/n. ☎ 972-21-32-62.

www.banysarabs.org. Admission 2€ adults, 1€ seniors & students. Apr–Sept Mon–Sat 10am–7pm & Sun 10am–2pm; Oct–Mar Mon–Sat 10am–2pm.

③ ★ **Catedral.** Steep Baroque stairs climb to Girona's imposing cathedral overlooking the city. The cloister and tower are the only surviving elements of the original, early-11th-century Romanesque building. The single nave is the widest Gothic nave in the world

A street in Girona's El Call neighborhood.

(and the second-widest of any style, after St. Peter's in the Vatican). In the treasury is a magnificent collection of religious art. Perhaps the most important piece is the 11th– or 12th–century *Tapestry of the Creation*, an embroidered depiction of humans and animals in the Garden of Eden. *Pl. de la Catedral.* ☎ *972-21-58-14. www.catedralde girona.org. Admission (nave, cloister & treasury) 7€ adults, 5€ seniors & students (audio guide included); free admission on Sun. Apr–Oct daily*

10am–8pm; Nov–Mar daily 10am–7pm.

❹ ★ **Roman Walls.** For great views of the old town, walk along a 5km (3.1-mile) portion of the original Roman wall, which dates to the 1st century A.D. Afterward, don't miss the pretty, serene gardens tucked behind the cathedral and just below the city wall: Jardins de la Francesa (French Woman's Gardens) and Jardins de les Alemans (German Gardens).

❺ ★★ **Museu d'Art.** Girona's Art Museum, in a former Episcopal palace, covers almost 1,000 years of history and art. It features excellent Catalan Romanesque and Gothic paintings, as well as a significant collection of contemporary art. Among the highlights is a 15th-century altarpiece, Sant Miquel de Cruïlles, one of the finest works of Catalan Gothic art anywhere. The museum also boasts its altarstone of Sant Pere de Roda, from the 10th and 11th centuries; this work in wood and stone, depicting figures and legends, was once embossed in silver. *Pujada de la Catedral, 12.* ☎ *972-20-38-34. www. museuart.com. Admission 2€ adults, 1.50€ students & seniors, free for children 15 & under. May–Sept*

Houses on the Onyar River.

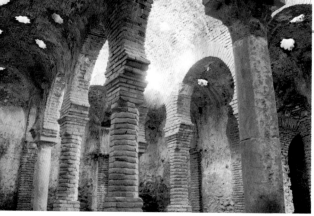

Banys Àrabs.

Mon–Sat 10am–7pm, Sun 10am–2pm; Oct–Apr Mon–Sat 10am–6pm & Sun 10am–2pm.

6 ★ Monestir de Sant Pere de Galligants. This 12th-century Catalan Gothic Benedictine monastery houses the city archaeology museum, with several items culled from the Roman ruins at nearby Empúries. *Pl. de Santa Llúcia, s/n.* ☎ *972-20-26-32. www.mac.cat. Admission 2.30€ adults, 1.60€ students, free for seniors & children 15 & under. Oct–May Tues–Sat 10am–2pm & 4–6pm, Sun 10am–2pm; June–Sept Tues–Sat 10:30am–1:30pm & 4–7pm; Sun 10am–2pm.*

7 Lola Café. On the most atmospheric street in the old Jewish Quarter, this hip, dark cafe frequently features live music on weekend nights. *c/ de la Força, 7.* ☎ *972-22-88-24. $$.*

8 ★ Cases de l'Onyar. The picturesque, multicolored houses (cases) along the Onyar River shimmer in the water's reflection, with drying laundry fluttering in the breeze. Many of the houses date to the Middle Ages, when they were outside the original walls of the Old City. Leading to the modern city is the **Pont de Ferro,** an iron bridge built by the Eiffel Company in 1877, 12 years before the Eiffel Tower.

9 ★ Museu del Cinema. Spain's only cinema museum is the extensive private collection of one man, Tomàs Mallol. The museum houses his collection of some 25,000 cinema artifacts, including photographs, posters, engravings, and interactive exhibits, as well as the original camera of the Luimière brothers. *c/ Sèquia, 1.* ☎ *972-41-27-77. www.girona.cat/cinema. Admission 5€ adults, 2.50€ students. Oct–Apr Tues–Fri 10am–6pm, Sat 10am–8pm, Sun 11am–3pm; May–June & Sept Tues–Sat 10am–8pm, Sun 11am–3pm; July–Aug daily 10am–8pm.*

The Tapestry of the Creation *in the Girona cathedral (p 151).*

L'Empordà & Costa Brava

ANDORRA **FRANCE**
Map Area
CATALUNYA
BARCELONA
Aragón
MEDITERRANEAN SEA

FRANCE
SPAIN

0 ____ 6 miles
0 ____ 6 kms

Portbou
Colera
GULF OF LIONS
Port de Llança
Llança
El Port de la Selva
N260
Pau
Parc Natural de Cap de Creus
Cap de Creus
Peralada
Pau-saverdera
Port Lligat
Cadaqués
Figueres
N2
Castelló d'Empúries
C260
Roses
Lladó
Empuriabrava
Cap de Norfeu
N260
See the "Dalí Triangle" map ❺
Golf de Roses
Esponellà
Parc Natural dels Aiguamolls de l'Empordà
AP7
Orriols
Cornellà de Terri
EMPÚRIES ❻
L'Escala
Punta Grossa
Torroella de Montgrí
L'Estartit
Cap de la Barra
Illes Medes
C66
AP7
Ullastret
C31
Púbol
C252
Peratallada
Girona
Monells ❶
Pals
❷
❸
Begur
❹ Cap de Begur
Cruïlles
La Bisbal d'Empordà
C66
Aigua Blava
Fornells
Palafrugell
Cassà de la Selva
❼ Cap de St. Sebastià
Llafranc
C65
Les Gavarres
❾ Calella de Palafrugell
Cap Roig
Romanyà de la Selva
Palamós
Llagostera
❽
C65
Platja d'Aro
C35
Castell d'Aro
S'Agaró
❿ **Sant Feliu de Guíxols**
Costa Brava
Rosamar
Tossa de Mar
Lloret de Mar
Blanes
MEDITERRANEAN SEA

❶ Cruïlles & Monells
❷ Peratallada
❸ Pals
❹ Begur
❺ Dalí Triangle
❻ Empúries
❼ Palafrugell beach coves
❽ Palamós
❾ Cap Roig
❿ Sant Feliu de Guíxols

L'Empordà, the plains and rolling green hills surrounding Girona, is Spain's Tuscany. Inland from the coast are small and mostly unassuming medieval villages, clusters of ancient stone houses—many converted into weekend and summer homes by affluent Barcelonans. The Costa Brava, the "untamed coast," is a stretch of rocky coves and sandy beaches, with deep cobalt-blue Mediterranean waters, pine trees, and whitewashed fishing villages. Sadly, the natural beauty of the coastline's southern end, nearest Barcelona, has been marred by sand-and-sun mass-market tourism.

① ★★ Cruïlles & Monells.

These two quiet villages are attractive enclaves of medieval stonework. Monells's main claim to fame is a magnificent porticoed main square, while at the center of Cruïlles, once enclosed by walls, is a Romanesque 11th-century monastery.

② ★★★ Peratallada.

Less slick than Pals (see below), this picturesque town grew up around an unusual castle. You'll also find a 14th-century palace, a porticoed main square, and houses rich with Gothic details, several of which house inns and antiques shops.

③ ★★★ Pals.

Almost too pretty and perfect, this medieval town rising above the plains is hugely popular with tourists. Pals's alleyways and stone walls look as though they might be part of a movie set.

④ ★★ Begur.

This attractive hilltop town is topped by the ruins of a 13th-century castle, with commanding 360-degree views of the whole of L'Empordà and the Costa Brava, all the way up the coast to Cadaqués. Many houses below are colonial in style, built by returning locals who set out for Cuba in the early 19th century. On the outskirts of Begur are excellent beaches, including Aiguablava, Sa Riera, and Sa Tuna.

⑤ ★★★ Dalí Triangle.

The Empordà region is marked by the trail of Spain's famous oddball, the surrealist painter Salvador Dalí, who hailed from northern Catalunya and lived much of his life on the Costa Brava. Three points, including a museum and two curious homes, form the Dalí Triangle. Together they are a must-see for anyone with an appreciation for Dalí and the absurd.

Pals, a picturesque town.

The Best Day Trips & Excursions

Dalí Triangle

Pau

Port Lligat

Cadaqués 5B

5A

Figueres

Castelló
d'Empúries

Roses

*Parc Natural
de Cap de Creus*

Fortià

Empuriabrava

Puig
Rom

*Cap de
Norfeu*

C31

Riumors

Golf de Roses

Garrigàs

Sant Pere
Pescador

*Parc Natural
dels Aiguamolls
de l'Empordà*

St. Miquel
de Fluvià

Torroella
de Fluvià

MEDITERRANEAN
SEA

Ventalló

C31

Saus

Viladamat

EMPÚRIES

Camallera

L'Escala

Colomers

Albons

FRANCE

Map
Area

CATALUNYA

BARCELONA

MEDITERRANEAN
SEA

Verges C31

Montgri

Flaçà

C252

Torroella
de Montgrí

Serra de
Daró

C66

Parlavà

0   4 miles
0   4 kms

Púbol 5C

5A ★★★ Figueres: Teatre Museu Dalí. Dalí's Museum-Theater, which he designed as his legacy in his birthplace of Figueres, is part theater, part amusement park—fittingly idiosyncratic and witty. Dalí is buried in a crypt here. The red building is topped by giant white eggs and decorated with glazed ceramic loaves of bread; inside is a salon with furniture re-creating Mae West's face. In the courtyard sits a black Cadillac with sprinklers inside. *Pl. de Gala–Salvador Dalí, 5.* ☎ *972-67-75-00. www.salvador-dali.org.*

5B ★★ Cadaqués/Port Lligat: Casa-Museu Salvador Dalí. Next to the seaside village of Cadaqués, Dalí built his first home with Gala, his eccentric Russian-born wife. They cobbled together several fishers' residences and decorated them in Dalíesque fashion: with stuffed swans, a lip sofa, and Dalí-designed chimneys. ☎ *972-25-10-15. www.salvador-dali.org.*

5C ★ Púbol: Castell Gala Dalí de Púbol. Dalí bought a medieval castle in an isolated L'Empordà village for his beloved princess in the late 1960s, but Gala allowed Dalí to visit only when she invited him. Even into her late 60s, she entertained a coterie of much younger men here. There are odd Dalíesque touches throughout, though the castle is less nutty than the other two points in the Triangle. ☎ *972-48-86-55. www.salvador-dali.org.*

Calella de Palafrugell.

6 ★★ Empúries. The extensive ruins of a Greco-Roman city, one of the most fascinating archaeological finds in Spain, are on view at the **Museu d'Empúries.** Three different civilizations settled on the coast here between the 7th and 3rd centuries B.C.: Empúries is the only place in Spain with incarnations as a Greek village, an Iberian settlement, and a Roman town. ☎ 972-77-02-08. www.mac.es. Admission 3€adults, free under 16 & over 60. June–Sept daily 10am–8pm; Oct–May daily 10am–6pm.

7 ★★ Palafrugell Beach coves. Several of the most beautiful coves and sandy beach spots along the Costa Brava are near Palafrugell. Calella de Palafrugell, Llafranc, and Tamariu are gentle, protected spots with good swimming and walking paths through pine-forested hills.

8 Palamós. The tensions of a Costa Brava town caught between tradition and modern development focused on tourism are apparent in this old fishing village.

9 ★ Cap Roig. On a cliff-top peninsula is a magnificent estate that once belonged to a Russian army general and is now home to beautiful Mediterranean botanical gardens (Jardí Botànic) with extraordinary views of the coast. In summer months, the **Festival**

The bizarre meets the absurd at the Dalí Museum in Figueres.

Practical Matters: L'Empordà & Costa Brava

Car is by far the best way to travel around the region. Figueres is 150km (93 miles) north of Barcelona on A-7 and 50km (31 miles) north of Girona. To get to Cadaqués, take C-260 from Figueres and then a long, twisting, maddening road (GI-614). Púbol is 40km (25 miles) south of Figueres along highway C-252 or 16km (10 miles) east of Girona along C-255. From Girona, trains travel to the Costa Brava towns of Llançà, Blanes, and Colera, as well as Figueres. For additional information, see **http://en.costabrava.org**.

Lodging & Dining: The following hotels all have very good, and in some cases, superb, restaurants: **El Far Hotel-Restaurant** is a cliff-top property formed by a 17th-century hermitage and a 15th-century lighthouse, with drop-dead views of the bay and Mediterranean and nine elegant, cheery rooms (Platja de Llafranc, near Palafrugell; ☎ 972-30-16-39; www.elfar.net; doubles 135€–250€). In L'Empordà, near the coast, is **Castell de'Empordà**, a 700-year-old castle converted to an outstanding luxurious small hotel. It's 3km (2 miles) from La Bisbal (☎ 972-64-62-54; www.castelldemporda.com; doubles 170€–310€; closed Nov–Mar). **La Plaça de Madremanya**, in a small Catalan village halfway between Girona and the coast, is a gorgeous country hotel, with one of the region's finest restaurants, and a comparatively great value (c/ Sant Esteve 17, Madremanya; ☎ 972-49-04-87; www.laplacamadremanya.com; doubles 75€–145€, suites 120€–185€). In Begur, **AiguaClara Hotel-Restaurant** is an exquisite, excellent-value boutique hotel in a small colonial-style palace, with charmingly shabby-chic decor (c/Sant Miquel, 2; ☎ 972-62-29-05; www.aiguaclara.com; doubles 85€–155€, suites 125€–175€). A terrific little restaurant in Begur is **Can Climent i Sa Cuina** ($$), with an elegantly rustic dining room like the kitchen of an old farmhouse and fresh and creative market Catalan cuisine by a young chef; the set menu at lunch is a steal (Av. Onze de Setembre; ☎ 972-62-20-31).

Jardins de Cap Roig features live jazz, rock, flamenco, world music, theater, and opera (including big names like Bob Dylan). ☎ 972-61-45-82. www.caproigfestival.com. Admission 3€. The gardens are open daily, Apr–Sept 9am–8pm & Oct–Mar 9am–6pm. On concert days (July–Aug) they close at 2pm.

🔟 **Sant Feliu de Guixols.** The beginning of the "good" Costa Brava after miles of overdevelopment, this easygoing town has a 10th-century church and chapel, Sant Martí, high on a hill overlooking the coastline. ●

Before You Go

Government Tourist Offices

In the U.S.: 60 E. 40th St., 53rd Floor, New York, NY 10165 (☎ 212/265-8822); 8383 Wilshire Blvd., Ste. 956, Beverly Hills, CA 90211 (☎ 323/658-7188); 845 N. Michigan Ave., Ste. 915E, Chicago, IL 60611 (☎ 312/642-1992); and 1221 Brickell Ave., Ste. 1850, Miami, FL 33131 (☎ 305/358-1992). **In Canada:** 2 Bloor St. W., Ste. 3402, Toronto, ON M4W 3E2 (☎ 416/961-3131). **In the U.K.:** 79 New Cavendish St., 2nd Floor; W1W 6XB, London (☎ 207/317-2010; www.spain.info/uk/Tour-Spain). A full list of Spanish tourist offices worldwide can be found at www.spain.info.

The Best Times to Go

March to May and **September to late October** are perhaps the best times to visit Barcelona, with fewer crowds than in summer. Weather-wise, however, almost any time of year is the right time to go. Although humid, Barcelona is as hot in summer as Madrid and the south. In **August,** much of the city shuts down as residents head for the beaches. August is the major vacation month in Europe, and traffic from England, France, the Netherlands, and Germany to Spain becomes a stampede. **November** to **February** can be pleasantly temperate, crowds are nonexistent, and prices drop for hotels and airfares. But some coastal resorts, especially on the Costa Brava, shut down during this slow season. The **Christmas** season in Barcelona, beginning in early **December** and extending through the first week of **January,** is especially festive.

Previous page: The Metro stop near Torre Agbar.

Barcelona is officially Spain's most popular destination, and tourism is now year-round; it is also a major international trade fair and conference destination throughout the year, so mid- to high-range hotels should be booked well in advance.

Festivals & Special Events

SPRING. One of the high points is **Semana Santa** (Holy Week). On Palm Sunday, palm leaves are blessed in La Sagrada Família, while in the city cathedral's cloister, the curious *L'ou com balla*—a hollowed-out eggshell—is placed on top of a fountain to bob around and "dance." **La Diada de Sant Jordi,** on April 23, is the colorful celebration of Saint George (*Sant Jordi* in Catalan), the patron saint of Catalunya; the tradition is for men to give a single red rose to the significant women in their lives (mother, girlfriend, sister, and so on), and for women to give a book in return (although many forward-thinking men now also give women books). Rose sellers are everywhere, and bookshops set up open-air stalls along Passeig de Gràcia. May 1 is **May Day,** or Labor Day, and the streets are full of marching trade-union members. During **Corpus Christi,** which usually falls in June (but can fall in May in years when Easter is early), the streets of Sitges are carpeted in flowers.

SUMMER. During the *Verbena de Sant Juan* (June 23), Catalunya celebrates Midsummer Eve with fireworks ablaze in streets and squares, bonfires lit along the beach, and liters of *cava* consumed. It's

Useful Websites

- **www.spain.info**: The Tourist Office of Spain's official U.S. site has loads of practical advice and tips on driving, destinations, travel routes, recipes, wines, bringing pets, and even learning Spanish.
- **www.tourspain.es**: Turespaña's website offers helpful primers on leisure travel, adventure travel, and business travel as well as Spanish news features from around the world.
- **www.renfe.com**: The official site of Spanish rail is easy to use for routes, schedules, and booking.
- **www.barcelonaturisme.com**: The city's official tourism site offers excellent information in English as well as in Catalan and Spanish. Attraction tickets and transport passes are available here at a discount.
- **http://en.costabrava.org**: This site provides information about Costa Brava, the city of Girona, and other parts of Catalunya, including L'Empordà.

traditional to have the first dip of the year in the sea at dawn, the unofficial first day of summer. **El Grec,** at the beginning of July, is a culture festival that brings marquee names in all genres of music and theater to perform in various open-air venues. **Festa Major de Gràcia** (early to mid-Aug) is a weeklong *festa* held in the Gràcia neighborhood, which is elaborately decorated; by day, long tables are set up for communal lunches and board games, and at night thousands invade the narrow streets for outdoor concerts and revelry.

FALL. La Diada de Catalunya (Sept 11), the National Day of Catalunya, is the most politically and historically significant holiday in the region, celebrating the region's autonomy and the date the city was besieged by Spanish and French troops in 1714 during the War of Succession. Demonstrations calling for independence are everywhere, and the *senyera,* the flag of

Catalunya, is hung from balconies. **La Mercè** (Sept 24) honors Our Lady of Mercy, the city's patron saint (who, according to legend, rid Barcelona of a plague of locusts). Free concerts are held in squares, and such folkloric figures as the *gigants* (giants) and *cap grosses* (big heads) take to the streets. People come out to perform the *sardana* (traditional Catalan dance) and to watch the forming of *castellers* (human towers). Fireworks displays light up the night, and the hair-raising *correfocs,* parades of fireworks-brandishing "devils" and dragons, are the grand finale. This is one of the best times to be in Barcelona, especially for children.

WINTER. All Saints' Day (Nov 1), a public holiday, is reverently celebrated: Relatives and friends lay flowers on the graves (or *nichos*—in Spain, people are often buried one on top of another in tiny compartments) of the dead. The night before, some of the bars in the city hold Halloween parties. The weeks leading to **Nadal,** or Christmas, are marked by **Fira de Santa Llúcia,** a huge open-air market near the cathedral selling handicrafts, Christmas decorations, trees, and figurines (including *caganers;* see p 62) for *pessebres* (nativity dioramas). A life-size nativity is constructed in Plaça Sant Jaume. **Día de los Reyes** (Three Kings Day), January 6, remains the traditional Catholic celebration of Christmas gift-giving (even though Santa Claus has made inroads and many families now exchange gifts on Dec 25). The evening prior, public celebrations take place in cities and towns across Spain; in Barcelona, three costumed Magi arrive by boat at the port to dispense candy to children. **Carnaval** (just prior to Lent) in Barcelona is low-key, with only groups of children or stall owners in the local markets dressing up for it. Not so in Sitges, the seaside town south of Barcelona, where locals, especially the gay community, go all out with hedonistic costumes, parades, and other forms of revelry.

The Weather

Barcelona is blessed with a Mediterranean climate, and spring and fall are unfailingly pleasant, with sunny skies and moderate temperatures. Even in the winter, days are crisp but not exceedingly cold and often sunny. Snow is rare and never lasts more than a day or two. Most rainfall occurs in April. July and August are hot and humid, even at night, as the temperature often only drops minimally. The surrounding sea is warm enough to swim in from the end of June to early October. Inland, the temperatures drop slightly, as does the humidity. North on the Costa Brava, a strong wind known as the *tramontana* often blows.

Cellphones (Móviles)

World phones—or GSM (Global System for Mobiles)—work in Spain (and most of the world). If your cellphone is on a GSM system, and you have a world-capable multiband phone, you can make and receive calls from Spain. Just call your wireless operator and ask for "international roaming" to be activated, but note that it is typically quite expensive. If you cell is unlocked, you can put a local carrier's SIM card into it. Many travelers opt to simply buy a pre-paid cell phone on location. Department store **FNAC** (main branch at Pl. Catalunya, 4; Metro: Catalunya; ☎ 93-344-18-00; www.fnac.es) provides several pay-as-you-go mobile phone packages. **Vodafone** (www.vodafone.com), **Movistar** (aka Telefónica; www.movistar.com), **Orange** (www.orange.es), and **Yoigo** (www.yoigo.com) are the four largest and most reliable mobile phone service providers in Spain.

Car Rentals

Driving in Barcelona isn't advised, especially with the preponderance of inexpensive taxis and metro services. Exploring L'Empordà and Costa Brava is much easier by car, however. North America's biggest car-rental companies, including **Avis, Budget,** and **Hertz,** maintain offices in Barcelona and Catalunya, including at El Prat airport and the Girona rail station. Avis, Hertz, and Budget also have offices at Sants railway station and other spots in Barcelona. Two other agencies of note are **Kemwel Holiday Auto** and **Auto Europe.**

Getting There

By Plane

From Barcelona's newly expanded **El Prat de Llobregat** airport (www. barcelona-airport.com)—its new Terminal 1 is absolutely stunning— 12km (7 miles) from the city center, there are several ways to get into town. A train runs between the airport and Barcelona's Estació Central de Barcelona-Sants every 15 to 30 minutes daily from 5:40am to 11:10pm (from Sants) or 11:40pm (to Sants). The 20-minute trip costs 4.20€. You can take the Metro from Sants to anywhere in Barcelona. If your hotel is near Plaça d'Espanya or Plaça de Catalunya, it might be worth the slight extra expense to take an **Aerobús** (☎ 93-415-60-20; www.aerobusbcn.com). It runs every 5 to 10 minutes between 5:30am and 1am from the airport, and until 12:30am from Plaça de Catalunya. The fare is 5.90€ single trip, 10€ round-trip. A **TMB bus** (1.40€ one-way; www.tmb.cat) travels from the airport to Plaça de Espanya from 5:30am to 12:45am. The last but most convenient method of getting to the city from the airport is by **taxi** (about 30€) from ranks outside all terminals.

Travelers arriving from within the European Union on budget airlines, such as Ryanair, may land at **Girona** (103km/64 miles northeast of Barcelona) or **Reus** (110 km/68 miles west of the city). **Barcelona Bus** (☎ 93-232-04-59) travels to Barcelona from the airport in Girona (12€ one-way, 21€ round-trip; 70 min.) and Reus (11€; 90 min.). The train from either city is cheaper, but you'd have to catch a bus to each town's rail station. A taxi to Barcelona from Girona or Reus will cost upwards of 140€.

By Car

Highway **A-7** leads to Barcelona from France and northern Catalunya (Costa Brava and Girona). The **A-2** leads to Barcelona from Madrid, Zaragoza, and Bilbao. From Valencia or the Costa del Sol, take the **E-15** north. Close to the city, look for one of two signs into downtown Barcelona: CENTRE CIUTAT takes you downtown into the Eixample district, while RONDA LITORAL is a beltway that takes you quickly to the port area.

By Train

Most national (**Renfe;** ☎ 902-32-03-20; www.renfe.com) and international trains arrive at **Estació Sants,** Plaça dels Països Catalans, s/n (☎ 93-495-62-15; Metro: Sants). High-speed AVE rail service from Madrid to Barcelona takes 2½ hours.

Getting Around

By Metro

The **Metro** (☎ 010 or 93-318-70-74; www.tmb.net) is Barcelona's excellent, modern, and clean subway. Its five lines are by far the fastest and easiest way to navigate the city. Red diamond symbols mark stations. Single-ticket fares (senzill, or sencillo) are 2€. You can also get free rides on all public transport by purchasing the Barcelona Card discount pass (www.barcelonacard. com) or the Hola BCN! card sold at TMB terminals. The Metro runs

Monday to Thursday 5am to 11pm, Friday and Saturday 5am to 2am, and Sunday 6am to midnight.

The Metro shares some terminals with **FGC Trains** (☎ 93-205-15-15; www.fgc.net), run by the provincial government (they cost the same as the Metro, and you can use the same Metro multi-trip tickets) and connecting the city center to upper neighborhoods, including Sarrià, Vallvidrera, Tibidabo, and Gràcia. The only problem you may encounter is when you need to switch between an FGC train and a regular Metro train: You have to exit the first and reenter the second, paying separately for each line.

Transportation Tip

TMB (Transports Metropolitans de Barcelona) has a nice online feature that allows you to plug in your destination, address, and mode of transport to get from one point to another (both within and beyond the city): www.tmb.cat/vullanar/en_US/vullanar.jsp.

By Taxi

Black-and-yellow taxis are plentiful and reasonably priced; few journeys cost more than 8€ to 10€. You can either hail a cab in the street (the green light on the roof means it's available) or grab one where they're lined up (usually outside hotels). There's no negotiating over fares; you pay what the meter reads (it starts at 2€). Most locals round up the fare to the next half- or full euro, if they tip at all. Fares include special surcharges for airport trips as well as luggage. Night fares are also higher. Reliable taxi companies include **Servi Taxi** (☎ 93-330-03-00) and **ZBarna Taxi** (☎ 93-358-11-11). For more information, visit www.taxibarcelona.cat.

By Bus

Buses (☎ 010 or 93-223-51-51; www.emt-amb.com; same tickets and price as Metro) are plentiful but much less convenient than the Metro. Most bus routes stop at the Plaça de Catalunya. Routes are clearly marked on each stop, as are timetables—but most buses stop running well before the Metro closes. The **Nitbus** (☎ 010 or 93-223-51-51), which runs from 11pm to 4am and is often the only alternative to the dearth of taxis in the wee hours, is bright yellow and clearly marked with an N; most leave from Plaça Catalunya. Travel Cards and other TMB passes are not valid on Nitbuses. Tickets (2€) are bought directly from the driver.

By Car

Trying to negotiate Barcelona's unfamiliar, traffic-clogged streets can be nerve-racking, and parking is an expensive nightmare. However, a car is useful if you plan to head out on day trips to Sitges, Montserrat, or the Penedès wine country or to travel to the Costa Brava or L'Empordà. See p 162 for a list of rental-car companies.

On Foot

Strolling in Barcelona is a pastime and an art, and the compact city is ideal for walking, especially along La Rambla, Passeig de Gràcia, Rambla de Catalunya, and in the labyrinthine quarters Barri Gòtic and La Ribera (Ciutat Vella).

Fast Facts

AMERICAN EXPRESS TRAVEL OFFICES
Passeig de Gràcia, 101 (☎ **93-255-00-29**) and c/ Llull, 321
(☎ **93-217-10-04**).

APARTMENT RENTALS The city's tourism bureau, **Barcelona Turisme** (www.barcelonaturisme.com), maintains a long list of tourist apartments rented either by the day or week, and private online brokers, including www.friendlyrentals.com, offer stylish properties at a surprisingly good value; check out www.oh-barcelona.com, which lists more than 300 apartments for rent. Two buildings with 13 chic, modern apartments for rent in the old city (Born and waterfront) can be found at **La Casa de les Lletres** (☎ **93-226-37-30**; www.cru2001.com). Based mainly in Barri Gòtic and Born, **apartmentsinbarcelona.net** (c/ Jaume I, 30; ☎ **93-439-56-64**) has a wide variety of choices, mostly studio or one-bedroom units.

ATMS/CASHPOINTS Maestro, Cirrus, and Visa cards are readily accepted at all ATMs, which are plentiful throughout the city. Exchange currency either at banks or *casas de cambio* (exchange houses). You can also find currency-exchange offices at the Sants rail station and El Prat airport. Spanish banks include **La Caixa, Caixa de Catalunya, BBV,** and **Central Hispano.** Branches are located near Plaça Catalunya. Most banks offer 24-hour ATMs. Currency-exchange houses include **BCN World** and **BCN Change & Transfer.** Spain's ATMs use four-digit PINs; if you have a six-digit number, change it at your bank before you leave.

BUSINESS HOURS Banks are open Monday through Friday from 8:30am to 2pm. Most offices are open Monday through Friday from 9am to 6 or 7pm (in July, 8am–3pm). In August, businesses maintain only skeleton staff or are closed altogether. At restaurants, lunch is usually served from 1:30 or 2 to 4pm, and dinner is served from 9 to 11:30pm or midnight. Major stores are open Monday through Saturday from 9:30 or 10am to 8pm; staffers at smaller establishments, however, often still close for siesta in the midafternoon, doing business from 9:30am to 2pm and 4:30pm to 8 or 8:30pm.

CONSULATES & EMBASSIES U.S. Consulate, Pg. Reina Elisenda de Montcada, 23 (☎ **93-280-22-27**; http://barcelona.usconsulate.gov); **Canadian Consulate,** Plaça de Catalunya, 9, 1st floor, 2nd office (☎ **93-412-72-36**; www.canadainternational.gc.ca); **U.K. Consulate,** Av. Diagonal, 477, 13a planta (☎ **93-366-62-00**; http://ukinspain.fco.gov.uk/en). Australia and New Zealand have only honorary consuls in Barcelona.

DOCTORS, DENTISTS & HOSPITALS Dial ☎ **061** to find a doctor. For hospitals, the **Centre d'Urgències Perecamps** (☎ **93-441-06-00**), located near Les Ramblas at Avinguda de las Drassanes, 13–15, is a good, centrally located choice. For a dentist, try **Dental Clinic Center,** Passeig de Gràcia, 8, (☎ **93-412-16-95**).

ELECTRICITY Most hotels operate on 220 volts AC (50 cycles). Some older places have 110 or 125 volts AC.

EMERGENCIES For an ambulance or medical emergencies, dial ☎ **061**; for fire, dial ☎ **080**. For other emergencies, call ☎ **112**.

GAY & LESBIAN TRAVELERS In 1978, Spain legalized homosexuality among consenting adults, and in 1995, Spain banned discrimination based on sexual orientation. Marriage between same-sex couples became legal in 2005. Catalunya has helped pave the way in rights for gay couples, preempting national laws by granting same-sex couples the same official status and conjugal rights as heterosexual ones. Barcelona is one of the major centers of gay life in Spain, and Sitges, one of Europe's most popular resorts for gay travelers (see www.gaysitgesguide.com), lies just south of Barcelona. The website www.gayinspain.com provides very complete and destination-specific listings for gay travelers.

HOLIDAYS Holidays observed include January 1 (New Year's Day), January 6 (Feast of the Epiphany), March/April (Good Friday and Easter Monday), May 1 (May Day), May/June (Whitmonday), June 24 (Feast of St. John), August 15 (Feast of the Assumption), September 11 (National Day of Catalunya), September 24 (Feast of Our Lady of Mercy), October 12 (Spain's National Day), November 1 (All Saints' Day), December 8 (Feast of the Immaculate Conception), December 25 (Christmas), and December 26 (Feast of St. Stephen).

INSURANCE Check your existing insurance policies before you buy travel insurance to cover trip cancellation, lost luggage, medical expenses, or car-rental insurance. For more information, contact one of the following recommended insurers: **Access America** (☎ 866/807-3982; www.access america.com); **Travel Guard International** (☎ 800/826-4919; www.travelguard.com); **Travel Insured International** (☎ 800/243-3174; www.travelinsured.com); and **Travelex Insurance Services** (☎ 888/457-4602; www.travelex-insurance.com). For travel overseas, most U.S. health plans (including Medicare and Medicaid) do not provide coverage, and the ones that do often require payment for services upfront. If you require additional medical insurance, try **MEDEX Assistance** (☎ 410/453-6300; www.medexassist.com) or **Travel Assistance International** (☎ 800/821-2828; www.travelassistance.com; for general information on services, call the company's **Worldwide Assistance Services, Inc.** (☎ 800/777-8710).

INTERNET Most lodgings offer free Wi-Fi access, at least in public areas, if you have your own device. Bandwidth on free hotel Wi-Fi is usually good enough to surf the web, use email, look up maps, and sometimes even make VOIP phone calls. It is not adequate for streaming video or music. Some hotels give away basic Wi-Fi but charge for faster access. Somewhat slower free Wi-Fi access is usually available in cafes and some stores. The city government also provides free Wi-Fi at 109 hotspots in L'Eixample and 61 spots in the old city. You will have to sign up for a free account to use it, and it is limited to minimal service to "respect the marketplace." Buses and some Metro lines also have free Wi-Fi. If you are planning to use a phone or tablet, download the GOWEX Free Wi-Fi app (iOs or Android). With the proliferation of free hotspots, Internet cafes are vanishing—usually they are coupled with long-distance phone services in immigrant neighborhoods. Expect to pay 2€ to 4€ per hour.

LOST PROPERTY Call credit card companies the minute you discover your wallet has been lost or stolen and file a report at the nearest police precinct. Your credit card company or insurer may require a police report number or record. **Visa**'s U.S. emergency number is ☎ **800/847-2911,** or 90-099-11-24 in Spain. **American Express** card-holders and traveler's check holders should call ☎ **800/221-7282** in the U.S., or 90-237-56-37 in Spain. **MasterCard** holders should call ☎ **800/307-7309** in the U.S., or 90-097-12-31 in Spain.

MAIL & POSTAGE Spanish post offices are called *correos* (koh-ray-os), identified by yellow-and-white signs with a crown and the words CORREOS Y TELÉGRAFOS. Main offices are generally open from 9am to 8pm Monday through Friday and Saturday 9am to 7pm. The **Central Post Office** is at Plaça de Antoni López, s/n, at the end of Vía Laietana (☎ **902-19-71-97**). Other branches are at Aragó, 282, and Ronda Universitat, 23.

MONEY The single European currency in Spain is the euro. For up-to-the-minute exchange rates between the euro and the dollar, check the currency converter website www.xe.com/ucc.

PASSPORTS Visas are not required for U.S., U.K., New Zealand, and Canadian visitors to Spain, provided your stay does not exceed 90 days. Australian visitors do need a visa. If your passport is lost or stolen, contact your country's embassy or consulate immediately. See "Consulates & Embassies," above. Make a copy of your passport's critical pages and keep it separate from your passport.

PHARMACIES Pharmacies (*farmàcies*) operate during normal business hours, and one in every district remains open all night and on holidays. The location and phone number of this *farmàcia de guàrdia* are posted on the door of all the other pharmacies. A central pharmacy open 24/7 is **Farmàcia** Álvarez, Pg. de Gràcia, 26 (☎ **93-302-11-24**). You can also call ☎ **010** or 93-481-00-60 to contact all-night pharmacies.

POLICE The national police emergency number is ☎ **091.** For local police, call ☎ **088.**

SAFETY Violent crime in Barcelona is a rarity, but criminals frequent tourist areas and major attractions, such as museums, restaurants, hotels, beach resorts, trains, train stations, airports, subways, and ATMs. Exercise care around major tourist sights, especially La Rambla (in particular, the section closest to the waterfront), Barri Gòtic, Raval, and La Sagrada Família. You shouldn't walk alone at night in either the Gothic Quarter or Raval. *Turisme Atenció* (Tourist Attention Service), La Rambla, 43 (☎ **93-256-24-30**), has English-speaking attendants who can aid crime victims in reporting losses and obtaining new documents. The office is open 24/7.

SMOKING Spain has joined the rest of the European Union in banning indoor smoking in public places, including on public transportation and in offices, hospitals, and bars and restaurants. Of course, you may have to pass through a blue cloud to get in some doorways.

TAXES The value-added (VAT) tax (known in Spain as IVA) ranges from 7% to 33%, depending on the commodity being sold. Food, wine, and basic necessities are taxed at 7%; most goods and services (including car rentals) at 13%; luxury items (jewelry, all tobacco, imported liquors) at 33%; and hotels at 7%. Non-E.U. residents are entitled to a reimbursement of the 16% IVA tax on most purchases worth more than 90€ made at shops offering

The Savvy Traveler

"Tax-Free" or "Global-Refund" shopping. Forms, obtained from the store where you made your purchase, must be stamped at Customs upon departure. For more information, see www.agencia tributaria.es.

TELEPHONES For national telephone information, dial ☎ **1003**. For international telephone information, call ☎ **025**. You can make international calls from booths identified with the word INTERNACIONAL. To make an international call, dial ☎ **00**, wait for the tone, and then dial the country code, area code, and number. If you're making a local call, dial the two-digit city code first (93 in Barcelona) and then the seven-digit number. To make a long-distance call within Spain, the procedure is the same; dial the city prefix no matter where you're calling.

TIPPING More expensive restaurants add a 7% tax to the bill and cheaper ones incorporate it into their prices. This is not a service charge, and a tip of 5% to 10% is expected in these establishments. For coffees and snacks, most people just leave a few coins or round up to the nearest euro. Taxis do not expect tips. Tip hotel porters and doormen 1€ and maids about the same amount per day.

TOILETS In Catalunya, they're called *aseos*, *servicios*, or *lavabos*, and are labeled CABALLEROS for men and DAMAS or SEÑORAS for women.

TOURIST INFORMATION **Turisme de Barcelona,** Plaça de Catalunya, 17 (underground; ☎ **93-285-38-34**), is open daily 9am to 9pm; it offers a hotel-booking service, sells tickets for tours and performances, and has a well-stocked gift shop.

Informació Turística de Catalunya has information on Barcelona and the entire region; it's located in Palau Robert, Pg. de Gràcia, 107 (☎ **93-238-40-03**). City tourism information offices are also at **Plaça Sant Jaume** (c/ Ciutat, 2; Mon–Fri 9am–10pm, Sat 10am–8pm, and Sun 10am–2pm), **Estació de Sants** (Pl. dels Països Catalans, s/n), **Mirador de Colom** (Pl. Portal de la Pau, s/n), and **El Prat** airport (terminals 1 and 2). There are also smaller tourism information kiosks (*cabines*) in several places, including **La Sagrada Família, Plaça de Espanya,** and aboveground on **Plaça de Catalunya.** Call ☎ **010** for general visitor information.

TRAVELERS WITH DISABILITIES Many buildings in Barcelona have stairs, making it difficult for visitors with disabilities to get around, although conditions are slowly improving. Newer hotels are more sensitive to the needs of persons with disabilities, and more expensive restaurants are generally wheelchair-accessible. However, because most places have few, if any, facilities for people with disabilities, you might consider an organized tour specifically designed to accommodate such travelers. **Flying Wheels Travel** (☎ **507/451-5005;** www.flying wheelstravel.com) offers escorted tours to Spain ("Spanish Symphony"), and **Access-Able Travel Source** (☎ **303/232-2979;** www. access-able.com) has access information for people traveling to Barcelona. **TMB** (the public transportation system for both bus and Metro) has a help line for travelers with disabilities (☎ **93-486-07-52**), and **ECOM** is a federation of private organizations for people with disabilities (☎ **93-451-55-50**).

A Brief **History**

550 B.C. Greeks settle at Empúries in northern Catalunya.

212 B.C. Romans, using Empúries as an entry point, subjugate Spain.

206 B.C. Romans defeat Carthaginians.

1ST C. A.D. Christians spread throughout Catalunya.

15 Barcino is founded by Romans.

70 First Jewish settlements appear in Barcino.

415 Barcelona is occupied by the Visigoths; capital until 554.

719 Moorish invasion of Iberian Peninsula reaches Barcelona.

878 Guifré el Pilós (Wilfred the Hairy) defeats Moors and founds dynasty of Counts of Barcelona (5-centuries-long autonomous rule).

1064 The *Usatges*, the first Catalan Bill of Rights, is drafted.

1137 A royal marriage unites Catalunya and the neighboring region of Aragón.

1213–35 Jaume I consolidates empire and conquers Mallorca, Ibiza, and Valencia.

1249 Barcelona forms the *Consell de Cent* (Council of 100) municipal government.

1283 Corts (Parliament) to govern Catalunya is created.

1347–59 The Black Plague halves the city's population; the Generalitat (autonomous government) is founded.

1469 Fernando II, monarch of Catalunya-Aragón, marries Isabel, queen of Castile, uniting all of Spain.

1492 Columbus discovers America; the "Catholic Monarchs" expel all remaining Jews and Muslims.

1494 Catalunya falls under Castilian rule.

1522 Under the rule of Charles V, Catalans are refused permission to trade in the New World.

1640–50 Catalan revolt known as the *Guerra dels Segadors* (Harvesters' War) occurs; Catalunya declares itself a republic, allied with France.

1701–13 Spanish War of Succession.

1759 Barcelona falls to the Franco-Spanish army; the Catalan language is banned.

1808–14 French occupy Catalunya in Peninsular War with England.

1832 Industrial Revolution begins in Barcelona with the first steam-driven factory.

1854–1865 Old City walls are torn down; work begins on the "new city," an expansion called *L'Eixample*.

1873 First Spanish Republic is established.

1888 First Universal Exposition in Barcelona is held at *Parc de la Ciutadella*.

1892–93 Collectives demand Catalan autonomy; anarchist throws bombs in the Gran Teatre Liceu Opera House.

1909 *Setmana Tràgica* (Tragic Week): Anarchists go on anticlerical rampage in Barcelona.

1924 Dictatorship is established by General Primo de Rivera; Catalan language is banned.

1929 Second International Exhibition is held, on Montjuïc.

1931 Francesc Macià negotiates autonomy for Catalunya during the Second Republic and declares himself president.

1936–1939 Spanish Civil War is fought; it ends with anarchist-occupied Barcelona being taken by Franco's army.

1960S Package tourism boom takes off on Catalunya's Costa Brava.

1975 Franco dies; Juan Carlos becomes king.

1978 King Juan Carlos grants Catalunya autonomous rule; Catalan language is restored.

1981 Coup attempt by right-wing officers fails; democracy prevails.

1982 Socialists gain power after 43 years of right-wing rule.

1986 Spain joins the European Community (now the European Union).

1992 Barcelona hosts 25th Summer Olympic Games.

1994 Gran Teatre del Liceu opera house is destroyed by fire for second time.

2004 Spanish Prime Minister José Luis Zapatero officially requests that Catalan, along with Basque and Galician, be recognized as a working language of the E.U.

2006 A statute granting Catalunya additional autonomous powers is passed by the Spanish Socialist government.

2009 Barcelona wins the European Champions League football championship.

2010 Spain wins the FIFA World Cup (football/soccer) in South Africa to claim the first championship in the nation's history; seven key members of the team represent the local club FC Barcelona. Pope Benedict XVI consecrates La Sagrada Familia for religious use. In December, high-speed AVE service cuts train travel time between Madrid and Barcelona to 2½ hours.

2014 Juan Carlos I abdicates the throne in favor of his son, Felipe VI. Spain continues a slow recovery as unemployment hovers at more than double the European average.

Barcelona's Architecture

Roman (2nd C. B.C.–4th c. A.D.)
The early conquerors of Spain were extraordinary engineers. Relics of the Roman colony of Barcino can be seen in the surviving columns of the **Temple d'Augustus,** originally part of the Roman forum, and gates and sections of the 3rd- and 4th-century walls that encircled the city. The finest Roman ruins are beneath **Plaça del Rei,** in the **Museu d'Història de Barcelona** (see p 31).

Medieval (Romanesque, 9th–12th c.; & Gothic, 12th–16th c.)
Beautiful in its simplicity and austerity, Romanesque architecture featured wide aisles, round arches, and heavy walls (mostly in churches). Examples abound in the La Ribera and Barri Gòtic districts of the Ciutat Vella. The finest example in Barcelona is **Sant Pau del Camp** (9th–12th C.).

Catedral de Barcelona.

Catalan Gothic emerged in Catalunya in the 12th century, with harsher lines and more austere ornamentation than traditional Gothic architecture. Employed in both civic and religious buildings, it featured pointed arches, soaring buttresses and spires, airy naves, and massive columns. The purest example anywhere is **Santa María del Mar,** the basilica in La Ribera. Other fine examples include **Esglé-sia de Santa María del Pi** and the **Saló del Tinell** (on the stunning Plaça del Rei). Although the entire

Barri Gòtic is named for the style, the neighborhood reflects an evolution and mix of styles, of which the **Catedral** is the best example. See the special-interest tour (p 30) and walking tour (p 60) focusing on the Ciutat Vella's ancient architecture.

Modernisme (late 19th to early 20th c.)

The distinctive modernisme style of architecture that dominates much of modern Barcelona is not "modernism," or what is usually defined as 20th-century functionality, but Catalan Art Nouveau, a derivative of the European movement in the arts of the late 19th century. In Barcelona, modernista architecture—marked by curved rather than straight lines, ample ornamentation, organic forms, and wrought iron and stained glass, among other elements—was spearheaded by **Antoni Gaudí** (La Sagrada Família, La Pedrera), but many other celebrated modernista architects, including **Lluís Domènech i Montaner** and **Josep Puig i Cadafalch,** transformed the city with elegant mansions, concert halls, and churches perfectly suited to the enlightened prosperity of the Catalan bourgeoisie. Perhaps the greatest examples are Gaudí's La

La Pedrera.

Pedrera (Casa Milà), Domènech i Montaner's Palau de la Música Catalana and Hospital de Sant Pau, and Puig i Cadafalch's Casa Amatller. Although excellent examples can be found outside Barcelona—in Girona, Valencia, Sitges, Reus, and even the Basque Country—the Catalan capital boasts the highest concentration of modernista architecture in the world. The mid-19th-century L'Eixample district, the new city expansion grid by **Ildefons Cerdà**, is the style's finest showcase (it's not called the **Quadrat d'Or**, or Golden Square, for nothing). See the special-interest tour (p 24) and walking tour (p 68) focusing on L'Eixample and modernisme.

Modern & Contemporary (1929–present)

The stark pavilion built by **Mies Van der Rohe** for the 1929 International Exposition in Barcelona is a landmark of modern architecture.

Barcelona took advantage of the 1992 Olympic Games to reorient the city to the sea and create urban beaches, residential neighborhoods, a port and marina, and ring roads and to introduce daring public sculptures, promenades, and squares weaving through the Old City. In 1999, the Royal Institute of British Architects presented Barcelona's City Council with its Gold Medal, the first time a city (rather than an architect) had received the accolade. Spanish (**Rafael Moneo** and **Santiago Calatrava**) and international (**Arata Isozaki** and **Norman Foster**) architects have also made their mark on the city, as have a number of young, daring Catalans. The French architect **Jean Nouvel**'s audacious Torre Agbar is the newest symbol—at night it's illuminated with the colors of none other than Barça, the beloved local fútbol team—along with the stunning new El Prat airport terminal, by native son **Ricardo Bofill,** of a city embracing the future with bravado.

Mies Van der Rohe pavilion.

Useful Phrases

Useful Words & Phrases

ENGLISH	SPANISH/CATALAN	PRONUNCIATION
Good day	Buenos días/ Bon dia	*bweh*-nohs *dee*-ahs/ bohn *dee*-ah
How are you?	¿Cómo está?/ Com està?	koh-moh es-*tah*/ com ehs-*tah*
Very well	Muy bien/Molt bé	mwee byehn/mohl beh
Thank you	Gracias/ Gràcies	*grah*-thee-ahs/ *grah*-see-uhs
You're welcome	De nada/De res	*deh nah*-dah/duh ress
Goodbye	Adiós/Adéu	ah-dyos/ah-*deh*-yoo
Please	Por favor/ Si us plau	por fah-*vohr*/ see yoos plow
Yes	Sí	See
No	No	Noh
Excuse me	Perdóneme/ Perdoni'm	pehr-*doh*-neh-meh/ per-*don*-eem
Where is . . . ?	¿Dónde está . . . ?/ On és . . . ?	dohn-deh es-*tah*/ ohn ehs
To the right	A la derecha/ A la dreta	ah lah deh-*reh*-chah/ ah lah *dreh*-tah
To the left	A la izquierda/ A l'esquerra	ah lah ees-*kyehr*-dah/ ahl ehs-keh-*ra*
I would like . . .	Quisiera/ Voldría	kee-*syeh*-rah/ vohl-*dree*-ah
I want . . .	Quiero/Vull	*kyeh*-roh/*boo*-wee
Do you have . . . ?	¿Tiene usted?/Té?	tyeh-neh oo-*sted*/teh
How much is it?	¿Cuánto cuesta?/ Quant és?	*kwahn*-toh *kwehs*-tah/ kwahnt ehs?
When?	¿Cuándo?/Quan?	*kwahn*-doh/kwahn
What?	¿Qué?/Com?	Keh/Cohm
There is	¿Hay (. . . ?)/Hi ha?	aye/ee ah/
(Is there . . . ?)	or Hi han?	ee ahn
What is there?	¿Qué hay?/Que hi ha?	keh aye/keh ee ah
Yesterday	Ayer/Ahir	ah-*yehr*/ah-*yeer*
Today	Hoy/Avui	oy/ah-*wee*
Tomorrow	Mañana/ Demá	mah-*nyah*-nah/ deh-*mah*
Good	Bueno/Bon	*bweh*-noh/bohn
Bad	Malo	Mah-*loh*
Better (Best)	(Lo) Mejor/ Millor	(loh) meh-*hohr*/ mee-*yohr*
More	Más	Mahs
Less	Menos	Meh-*nohs*

ENGLISH	SPANISH/CATALAN	PRONUNCIATION
Do you speak English?	¿Habla inglés?/ Parla anglès?	*ah*-blah een-*glehs*/ *pahr*-lah ahn-*glehs*
I speak a little Spanish/Catalan	Hablo un poco de español/ Parlo una mica de Catalá	*ah*-bloh oon *poh*-koh deh es-pah-*nyol*/ *pahr*-loh *oo*-nah *mee*-kah deh kah-tah-*lah*
I don't understand	No entiendo/ No comprenc	noh ehn-*tyehn*-doh/ noh cohm-*prehnk*
What time is it?	¿Qué hora es?/ Quina hora és?	keh *oh*-rah ehss/ *kee*-nah *oh*-rah ehss
The check, please	La cuenta, por favor/ El compte, si us plau	lah *kwehn*-tah pohr fah-*vohr*/ehl *cohmp*-tah see yoos plow
the station	`la estación/ la estació	lah es-tah-*syohn*/ la esta-*cyo*
a hotel	un hotel/l'hotel	oon oh-*tehl*/ehl ho-*tehl*
the market	el mercado/ el mercat	ehl mehr-*kah*-doh/ ehl mehr-*kaht*
a restaurant	un restaurante/ un restaurant	oon rehs-tow-*rahn*-teh/ oon rehs-tow-*rahn*
the toilet	el baño/ el lavabo	ehl *bah*-nyoh/ ehl lah-*vah*-boh
a doctor	un médico/ un metge	oon *meh*-dee-koh/ oon meht-*jah*
the road to . . .	el camino a/ al cami per	ehl kah-*mee*-noh ah/ ahl kah-*mee* pehr
to eat	comer/menjar	ko-*mehr*/mehn-*jahr*
a room	una habitación/ un habitació	*oo*-nah ah-bee-tah-*syohn*/ oon ah-bee-tah-*syohn*
a book	un libro/ un llibre	oon *lee*-broh/ oon *yee*-breh
a dictionary	un diccionario/ un diccionari	oon deek-syoh-*nah*-ryoh/oon deek-syoh-*nah* ree

Numbers

NUMBER	SPANISH	CATALAN
1	uno (*oo*-noh)	un (oon)
2	dos (dohs)	dos (dohs)
3	tres (trehs)	tres (trehs)
4	cuatro (*kwah*-troh)	quatre (*kwah*-trah)
5	cinco (*theen*-koh)	cinc (sink)
6	seis (says)	sis (sees)
7	siete (*syeh*-teh)	set (seht)
8	ocho (*oh*-choh)	vuit (vweet)
9	nueve (*nweh*-beh)	nou (noo)
10	diez (dyehth)	deu (*deh*-yoo)
11	once (*ohn*-theh)	onze (*ohn*-zah)
12	doce (*doh*-theh)	dotze (*doh*-tzah)

NUMBER	SPANISH	CATALAN
13	trece (*treh*-theh)	tretze (*treh*-tzah)
14	catorce (kah-*tohr*-theh)	catorza (kah-*tohr*-zah)
15	quince (*keen*-seh)	quinza (*keen*-zah)
16	dieciséis (dyeh-thee-*says*)	setze (*seh*-tzah)
17	diecisiete (dyeh-thee-*syeh*-teh)	disset (dee-*seht*)
18	dieciocho (dyeh-thee-*oh*-choh)	divuit (dee-*vweet*)
19	diecinueve (dyeh-thee-*nweh*-beh)	dinou (dee-*noo*)
20	veinte (*bayn*-teh)	vint (vehnt)
30	treinta (*trayn*-tah)	trenta (*trehn*-tah)
40	cuarenta (kwah-*rehn*-tah)	quaranta (kwah-*rahn*-tah)
50	cincuenta (theen-*kwehn*-tah)	cinquanta (theen-*kwahn*-tah)
60	sesenta (seh-*sehn*-tah)	seixanta (see-*shahn*-tah)
70	setenta (seh-*tehn*-tah)	setanta (seh-*tahn*-tah)
80	ochenta (oh-*chehn*-tah)	vuitanta (vwee-*tahn*-tah)
90	noventa (noh-*behn*-tah)	noranta (noh-*rahn*-tah)
100	cien (*thyehn*)	cent (sent)

Recommended Spanish Wines

Spain has taken the wine world by storm in the last decade. While touring Spain, seek out the wines listed below. Catalunya also produces some excellent wines: If you want to drink local, stick to wines from Penedès, Priorat, and Montsant.

Reds (Tintos)
Rioja Artadi, Bodegas Lan, Castillo de Ygay, Contador, CVNE, El Puntido, Finca Allende, Imperial, La Rioja Alta, López de Heredia, Marqués de Riscal, Muga, Remírez Ganuza, Roda, San Vicente, Sierra Cantabria, Viña Ardanza, Viña Izadi
Ribera del Duero Reds Aalto, Alión, Atauta, Condado de Haza, Emilio Moro, Flor de Pingus, Hacienda Monasterio, Leda, Mauro, Pago de los Capellanes, Pesquera, Vega Sicilia
Toro Dos Victorias (Gran Elias Mora), Numanthia, Pintia, Quinta Quietud, San Román
Priorat Àlvaro Palacios Les Terrasses Cims de Porrera, Clos Martinet, Clos Mogador, L'Ermita, Mas Alta, Mas Doix, Mas d'En Compte, Vall Llach
Jumilla Casa Castillo, Clio/El Nido, Finca Sandoval
Monsant Acústic, Can Blau, Capçanes, Joan d'Anguera, La Universal Venus
Others Gran Claustro/Castillo de Perelada (Penedès), Artazu, Chivite and Faustino (Navarra), Dominio de Tares, Dominio de Valdepusa/Marqués de Griñón (Toledo), Paixar (Bierzo), Torres (Penedès)
Whites (Blancos)
Albariño (from Galicia) Lagar de Cervera, Laxas, Martín Codax, Pazo de Señorans, Terras Gaudia
Penedès Castillo de Perelada, René Barbier
Rioja Allende, López de Heredia, Marqués de Riscal, Muga

Rueda   Belondrade y Lurton, Dos Victorias José Pariente, Martinsancho, Viñedo de Nieva Pie Franco
Other
Cava (sparkling wine from Catalunya)   Agustí Torelló, Avinyó, Gramona, Juvé y Camps, Raventós i Blanc, Segura Viudas
Sherry   San León, La Guita (manzanilla), Tío Pepe (fino), Alvear (Pedro Ximénez)

For more on Spanish wines, visit www.winesfromspainusa.com.

Recommended Vintages for Rioja, Ribera del Duero & Priorat

YEAR	RIOJA	RIBERA DEL DUERO	PRIORAT
2000	Excellent	Excellent	Good
2001	Outstanding	Outstanding	Outstanding
2002	Average	Average	Good
2003	Good	Good	Very good
2004	Outstanding	Outstanding	Outstanding
2005	Excellent	Very good	Excellent
2006	Good	Very good	Very good
2007	Very good	Excellent	Very good
2008	Very good	Very good	Very good
2009	Very good	Excellent	Excellent
2010	Excellent	Excellent	Very good
2011	Excellent	Excellent	Excellent

Index

See also Accommodations and Restaurant indexes, below.

Carrer dels Banys Nous, 63
Carrer dels Sombrerers, 67
Carrer de Montcada, 31, 67
Carrer Montcada, 16
Carrer Petritxol, 48
Carrer Sant Bonaventura
  (Sitges), 149
Carretera de les Aigües, 92
Car travel, 163, 164
Casa Amatller, 10–11, 27
Casa Batlló, 9–10, 27
Casa Calvet, 29, 69
Casa de la Caritat, 45
Casa de la Ciutat, 33
Casa de les Punxes, 70
Casa del Llibre, 76
Casa dels Músics, 125
Casa Lleó Morera, 11, 27
Casa Milà (La Pedrera), 6, 9,
  26
    musical performances,
    128
Casa-Museu Castell Gala
  Dalí (Púbol), 156
Casa Museu Gaudí, 21
Casa-Museu Salvador Dalí
  (Cadaqués), 156
Casas, 82
Casa Thomas, 70
Cascada Fountain, 87
Cases de l'Onyar (Girona),
  153
Cases dels Canonges, 63
Cashpoints, 165
Casino Barcelona, 114
Castell dels Tres Dragons,
  86
Castell de Montjuïc, 84
Catalunya, 16, 34
Catedral de Barcelona, 13,
  31, 61
Catedral (Girona), 151
Cathedrals and churches
    Catedral (Girona), 151
    Catedral de Barcelona,
      13, 31, 61
    Església dels Sants Just
      i Pastor, 62
    La Sagrada Família, 9,
      25
    Santa María del Mar, 6,
      15–16, 31, 65, 171
    Santa María del Pi, 63
    Sant Pau del Camp, 35
Cava, 5
Cava bars, 117–118
CDLC Barcelona, 116
Cellphones (móviles), 162
Centre d'Art Santa Mònica,
  59

Centre de Cultura Contem-
  porània de Barcelona
  (CCCB), 45
Centre d'Urgències Pere-
  camps, 165
Ceramics and pottery, 76
Cereria Subira, 82
The Cha Cha Original Shop,
  80
Chic & Basic, 165
Chillida, Eduardo, 39, 62
Christmas, 62, 160
Churches and cathedrals
    Catedral (Girona), 151
    Catedral de Barcelona,
      13, 31, 61
    Església dels Sants Just
      i Pastor, 62
    La Sagrada Família, 9,
      25
    Santa María del Mar, 6,
      15–16, 31, 65, 171
    Santa María del Pi, 63
    Sant Pau del Camp, 35
CicloBus Barcelona, 92
Cinemas, 125–126
City Hall Barcelona, 114
Ciutat Vella, 12, 30–35. See
  also Barri Gòtic (Gothic
  Quarter); La Ribera
    galleries, 39
    shopping, 77
Classical music and concert
  venues, 124–125
Classic Bikes Barcelona, 92
Climate, 160, 162
Colmado Quílez, 47
Columbus, Christopher, 19
Conjunt Monumental de la
  Plaça del Rei, 31–32
Consulates and embassies,
  165
Cor Caliu, 70
Corpus Christi, 160
Cosmetics, 77
CosmoCaixa (Museu de la
  Ciència), 54
Costa Brava, 154–158
Cruïlles, 155
Crustó, 47
Cuisine, 5, 47–49
Currency and currency
  exchange, 167
Custo-Barcelona, 79

D
Dalí, Salvador, 155
    Casa-Museu Salvador
      Dalí (Cadaqués), 156
Dalí Triangle, 155
Dance clubs, 114–115

Demasié, 80–81
De Moda, 79
Dental Clinic Center, 165
Dentists, 165
Department stores, 77
Desigual, 78–79
Día de los Reyes, 162
Diana Cristó, 81
1748 Artesana i Coses, 76
Dining. See also Restaurants
  Index
    best, 94
    Girona, 153
    L'Empordà & Costa
      Brava, 158
    Sitges, 149
Disabilities, travelers with,
  168
Discos Castelló, 82
Discounts and passes, 10
Montserrat, 147
Doctors, 165
Domènech i Montaner,
  Lluís, 26
    Casa Amatller, 10
    El Palau de la Música
      Catalana, 4–5, 15, 28,
      67, 124
Drassanes Reials, 59
Dry Martini Speakeasy, 112

E
E&A Gispert, 49, 67
El Bosc de las Fades, 112
El Call, 63, 150
El Corte Inglés, 78
Electricity, 165
El Jardí, 112–113
El Llac, 87
El Palau de la Música Cata-
  lana, 4–5, 15, 28, 67, 124
El Poble Espanyol, 54
El Prat de Llobregat airport,
  163
Els Quatre Gats, 28
El Tablao de Carmen,
  125–126
El Triangle, 78
El Xampanyet, 38, 117
Emergencies, 165
Empúries, 157
Escolanía de Montserrat,
  147
Escribà, 58
Església dels Sants Just i
  Pastor, 62
Espai Barroc, 127
Estació de Sants, tourism
  information office, 168
Estació Sants, 163
Estadi Olímpic, 20
Etxart & Panno, 79

Photo Credits